Favorite Recipes from The Microwave Times

Volume I

AF711313

Recipes Unlimited Inc.

The recipes in this book were tested in 600 to 650-watt countertop microwave ovens. Some recipes include timings in parenthesis or in the Tips for the Combination Microwave Range that operates at about 400 watts of power. For other powered ovens, some adjustment in cooking time may be necessary to achieve the doneness described.

ISBN: 0-918620-20-1

Second Printing 1983

Printed in the United States of America

Pictured on Cover: Colorful Fisherman's Kabobs, page 16, Taco Salads, page 45, and Grasshopper Tarts, page 111.

Favorite Recipes from

The Microwave Times

Contents

Dear Reader,

It is rewarding to see the readership of "The Microwave Times" continually expand as we reach more and more microwave oven owners. It is especially gratifying to receive many letters from readers expressing how much the publication has helped them to better use and understand their microwave oven. Now, it is with great enthusiasm that we present this selection of our favorite recipes from the first five years of "The Microwave Times" issues.

Selecting and organizing the recipes into easy-to-use chapter categories has brought back many memories. (We have even rediscovered a few choice recipes we had forgotten about.) We think you will appreciate the convenience of having the food categories together. And, in this new format, you may discover some recipes and ideas that were overlooked when reading the individual issues.

In this book, we have focused primarily on the recipes and included only excerpts from the wealth of information contained in the original features. If you find topics of interest or would like to have a complete set of the back issues, we will be happy to send you order information.

All of the recipes have been thoroughly tested in our test kitchen. The majority are ones that we developed, but you can also enjoy a few from some of our readers. Most of these were part of our popular section on microwave adapting. Here, readers submit favorite recipes and upon request, we adapt them to microwave use. We thank the readers who submitted those recipes that were selected to be included with other favorites in this book.

We continue to enjoy developing and presenting a variety of features about microwave cooking—adapting recipes, using simmer pots, combining the microwave and food processor, saving energy, cooking for two, reducing calories, cooking for special diets, microwaving for kids, and more. And so, with great pleasure, we present this collection of microwave favorites.

Sincerely,

Janet L. Sadlack
Recipes Unlimited, Inc.
Box 1271
Burnsville, Minnesota 55337

P.S. If you are interested in other Recipes Unlimited cook books or in a subscription to "The Microwave Times", you will find a convenient order blank on the last page.

Chapter 1

Appetizers & Beverages

Fresh Vegetable Dippers, page 9.

Vegetables always make favorite hors d'oeuvres and these breaded cauliflower snacks are no exception. This recipe has been a favorite in classes and seminars, and can also be used with broccoli or zucchini pieces.

CAULIFLOWER PICK-UPS

1 small head cauliflower
1/3 cup butter or margarine
1/4 cup dry bread crumbs
1/4 cup grated Parmesan cheese
1 teaspoon tarragon leaves, crushed
1 teaspoon paprika
1/2 teaspoon salt
Dash pepper

1. Wash cauliflower and pat dry. Separate into flowerettes; cut larger flowerettes into bite-sized pieces.

2. MICROWAVE (high) butter in small glass dish 1 to 1½ minutes or until melted. Combine remaining ingredients in plastic bag.

3. Dip several pieces cauliflower at a time in butter. Add to crumbs and shake to coat evenly. Repeat with remaining cauliflower. Arrange in single layer in 12 x 8-inch glass baking dish. Cover with paper towel.

4. MICROWAVE (high) 4½ to 5½ minutes or until tender. Serve warm on toothpicks.

About 40 Snacks

This recipe utilizes a browner grill to toast the bread while the microwaves heat the filling.

QUICK CHEESE APPETIZERS

1 cup (4 ozs.) shredded Cheddar cheese
2 tablespoons mayonnaise or salad dressing
1 tablespoon chopped green or ripe olives
3 drops Tabasco sauce
1 tablespoon butter or margarine, softened
3 slices bread

1. Combine cheese, mayonnaise, olives and Tabasco sauce. Spread one side of each bread slice with butter. Spoon cheese mixture onto other side of bread, spreading to cover. Cut each slice into quarters.

2. MICROWAVE (high) browner grill or skillet 3 to 4 minutes. Place bread on hot browner, buttered-side-down.

3. MICROWAVE (high) 1 to 1½ minutes or until cheese is melted and bread toasted.

12 Appetizers

TIP • For crisper appetizers, toast the bread before spreading with butter.

Soy Soy Drummies, page 7, and Cauliflower Pick-Ups, this page.

Meatballs are easily prepared in the microwave. These are teamed with golden pineapple chunks and served in a tasty sweet-sour sauce.

ORIENTAL MEATBALLS

1 lb. ground beef
½ lb. ground pork
⅓ cup finely chopped canned water chestnuts (half of 8-oz. can)
¼ cup finely chopped green pepper
3 to 4 green onions, chopped
½ teaspoon salt
2 tablespoons soy sauce
2 tablespoons juice from pineapple

Sauce:
1 tablespoon instant beef bouillon
¼ cup packed brown sugar
2 tablespoons cornstarch
1 tablespoon soy sauce
2 tablespoons vinegar
½ cup water
1 can (20 oz.) chunk pineapple in natural juice

1. Combine meatball ingredients in large mixing bowl; mix well. Shape into 1-inch meatballs. Arrange in 12 x 8-inch glass baking dish, stacking any extra meatballs along outer edge. Cover with paper towel.

2. MICROWAVE (high) 6 minutes (11). Carefully rearrange meatballs. Cover.

3. MICROWAVE (high) 2 to 3 minutes (6 to 7) or until no longer pink.

4. Combine beef bouillon, brown sugar, cornstarch, soy sauce, vinegar and water in 4-cup glass measure. Stir in juice from pineapple.

5. MICROWAVE (high), uncovered, 3 to 4 minutes (6 to 7) or until mixture boils and thickens. Stir in pineapple. Drain meatballs; pour sauce over meatballs.

6. MICROWAVE (high), uncovered, 2 to 3 minutes (4 to 5) or until heated through. Serve with toothpicks.

45 to 50 Meatballs

TIPS • Meatballs can be prepared ahead through step 5. Increase time in step 6 to 3 to 4 minutes if at room temperature and 5 to 6 minutes if mixture has been refrigerated.

• For ease in shaping meatballs, occasionally wet hands with cold water.

These smoky, glazed chicken wings make interesting nibblers.

SOY SOY DRUMMIES

3 lbs. chicken wings (about 12 wings)
½ cup soy sauce
¼ cup water
1 tablespoon lemon juice
1 teaspoon liquid smoke
¼ cup water
2 teaspoons cornstarch

1. Cut wings at joints into 3 pieces each; discard tips. Wash wing pieces and pat dry. Place in plastic bag.

2. Combine soy sauce, ¼ cup water, lemon juice and liquid smoke. Set aside ⅓ cup of mixture. Pour remaining over wings. Close bag tightly and rotate to coat all pieces. Marinate 4 hours or overnight.

3. Before cooking, add ¼ cup water and the cornstarch to reserved soy mixture. Stir until smooth.

4. MICROWAVE (high), uncovered, 2 to 3 minutes or until mixture boils and thickens, stirring once or twice.

5. Arrange half of wing pieces, skin-side-up and spoke fashion, on glass plate with thicker ends toward edge of plate. Brush with thickened glaze. Cover with waxed paper.

6. MICROWAVE (high) 5 minutes. Brush with additional glaze.

7. MICROWAVE (high), uncovered, 3 to 4 minutes or until done. Repeat with remaining wing pieces.

About 24 Pieces

TIPS • For additional browning and crispness, place cooked wings under broiler for a few minutes.

• If "drummies" are cooked ahead of time, reheat a plate of about 12 pieces for 2½ to 3 minutes.

• With Combination Oven, microwave in step 4 for 4 to 5 minutes and place both plates in oven together and microwave 16 to 18 minutes for cooking in steps 6 and 7.

Potato cubes make easy and economical appetizers or snacks.

PARMESAN POTATO NUGGETS

1/3 cup dry bread crumbs
1/4 cup Parmesan cheese
1 1/4 teaspoons onion salt
1 teaspoon paprika
1/4 cup butter or margarine
2 medium potatoes, peeled and cubed (1/2 inch)
3 tablespoons flour

1. Combine bread crumbs, cheese, onion salt and paprika in plastic bag.

2. MICROWAVE (high) butter in small dish about 1 minute (2 to 3) or until melted. Coat potatoes with flour, shaking off excess. Dip into butter and then shake in bag with crumbs to coat evenly. Arrange on lightly-buttered glass plate. Cover with paper towel.

3. MICROWAVE (high) 10 to 12 minutes (10 to 12) or until tender, rotating plate twice. Serve warm or cold on toothpicks.

About 6 Servings

TIP • To make ahead, prepare through step 2. Allow to stand 2 to 3 hours at room temperature before cooking as directed in step 3.

Parmesan Potato Nuggets, this page, and Chilled Vegetable Tray, page 9.

This variation of our popular vegetable trays is an ideal addition to any hors d'oeuvres table. We've included a recipe for a vegetable dip, but you can also use a favorite salad dressing.

CHILLED VEGETABLE TRAY

4 to 5 medium carrots, peeled
¼ cup water
1 pint (8 oz.) fresh mushrooms
1 small head cauliflower
2 medium zucchini

Vegetable Dip:
1 clove garlic, minced
3 green onions, sliced
½ cup mayonnaise or salad dressing
¼ cup sour cream
2 tablespoons tarragon wine vinegar
1 teaspoon parsley flakes
¼ teaspoon salt

1. Cut carrots into ½-inch thick slices. Place in 4-cup glass measure; add water. Cover with plastic wrap.

2. MICROWAVE (high) 5 to 6 minutes (8 to 10) or until steaming hot, stirring once. Let stand 3 to 4 minutes.

3. Wash and trim mushrooms; cut cauliflower into bite-sized pieces. Cut zucchini into quarters lengthwise and then into 1-inch slices.

4. Place a small dish (about 1-cup size) in center of a 12-inch glass plate. Arrange cauliflower and mushrooms on opposite sides of dish. Between these vegetables arrange the zucchini on one side and the drained, partially-cooked carrots on the other. Cover tightly with plastic wrap.

5. MICROWAVE (high) 8 to 10 minutes (10 to 12) or until vegetables are tender-crisp. Lift wrap from one side and drain liquid from vegetables. Uncover; cool.

6. Prepare Dip by combining all ingredients; spoon into dish in center of tray. Cover tray completely and refrigerate 1 to 2 hours or until served.

8 to 10 Servings

TIPS • Other favorite vegetable combinations can be used. Just select vegetables with similar cooking times and contrasting colors and shapes.

• ¼ teaspoon tarragon leaves and 2 tablespoons lemon juice can be substituted for tarragon vinegar.

• If desired, 2 cups frozen crinkle-cut carrots can be substituted for fresh. Microwave in step 2 for about 5 minutes.

Serve this attractive vegetable combination with toothpicks for dipping as hors d'oeuvres or with a serving spoon at mealtime. The artichoke requires longer cooking so is partially cooked before arranging with the other items.

FRESH VEGETABLE DIPPERS

Medium artichoke
Fresh mushrooms (about 8 ozs.)
Fresh broccoli (about 1 lb.)
Fresh cauliflower (about 1 lb.)

Sauce:
⅓ cup butter or margarine
½ teaspoon garlic salt
½ teaspoon seasoned salt
½ tablespoon lemon juice

1. Cut 1 inch straight across top of artichoke. Remove any loose or damaged leaves around bottom; trim off stem so artichoke can stand upright. With kitchen shears, snip off tip of each outer leaf. If desired, separate center and remove prickly portion of artichoke with grapefruit spoon or knife. Place stem-side-down in 4-cup glass measure. Drizzle with a mixture of ¼ cup water and 1 tablespoon lemon juice. Cover with plastic warp.

2. MICROWAVE (high) 3 to 3½ minutes (5 to 6) or until just about tender. Drain and place on 12-inch glass serving plate. Wash mushrooms and trim as needed. Trim broccoli and cauliflower; cut into pieces about the same size as mushrooms. Arrange equal quantities of mushrooms, broccoli and cauliflower on plate, leaving a space in center for sauce. Combine sauce ingredients in 6-oz. glass custard cup or dish. Place in center of plate. Cover plate tightly with plastic wrap. (Can stand several hours at room temperature.)

3. MICROWAVE (high) 8 to 9 minutes (10 to 12) or until vegetables are tender. Drain excess liquid. Remove plastic wrap and serve.

6 to 8 Servings

This warm dip combines shrimp and cream cheese. Delicious served with crackers!

HOT SHRIMP DIP

1 package (8 oz.) cream cheese
2 tablespoons milk
2 green onions, thinly sliced (tops included)
1 tablespoon chopped pimiento
1 teaspoon prepared horseradish
1 teaspoon lemon juice
¼ teaspoon salt
Dash pepper
Dash Tabasco sauce
1 can (4½ oz.) small shrimp, drained
Assorted crackers or vegetables

1. MICROWAVE (high) cream cheese in glass bowl ½ to 1 minute or until softened. Blend in milk until smooth. Stir in remaining ingredients except crackers.

2. MICROWAVE (high), uncovered, 1½ to 2½ minutes or until hot, stirring once. Serve warm with favorite crackers or raw vegetables.

About 1¾ Cups

Seafarer Zucchini Hors d'Oeuvres.

Zucchini makes the interesting and colorful base for these seafood hors d'oeuvres. This recipe was part of a low calorie feature in "The Times".

SEAFARER ZUCCHINI HORS D'OEUVRES

½ package (8-oz. size) Neufchatel cheese
1 teaspoon Ranch-flavor dry salad dressing mix
2 teaspoons lemon juice
1 package (6 oz.) frozen crabmeat, thawed and well drained
3 to 4 medium zucchini
Paprika or fresh parsley

1. MICROWAVE (high) cheese in glass bowl ½ to 1 minute (1 to 2) or until softened. Stir in salad dressing mix and lemon juice until smooth. Mix in crabmeat with fork.

2. Cut zucchini into ¼-inch thick slices. Arrange about 20 slices on a glass serving plate. Spoon a scant teaspoonful of crab mixture onto each slice. Sprinkle with paprika or garnish with parsley sprigs.

3. MICROWAVE (high), uncovered, 1½ to 2 minutes (2 to 3) or until hot. Repeat with remaining zucchini and topping. Serve warm or cold.

60 Hors d'oeuvres, about 10 calories each.

TIPS • A 6-oz. can canned crabmeat can be substituted for frozen. Or, substitute a 6-oz. can water packed light tuna for the crabmeat.

• To thaw crabmeat, microwave (low — 30%) 2 minutes. Rearrange crabmeat. Microwave (low — 30%) 1 to 2 minutes longer.

Frozen packaged spinach soufflé makes the flavorful, attractive stuffing for these mushrooms caps. The combination has a pleasantly mild flavor that is sure to be a favorite.

SOUFFLE-STUFFED MUSHROOMS

1 package (12 oz.) frozen spinach soufflé
½ teaspoon lemon pepper
½ teaspoon salt
¼ teaspoon garlic powder
1½ lbs. (24 ozs.) large fresh mushrooms
1 tablespoon butter or margarine
1 tablespoon finely chopped onion
Parmesan cheese

1. Remove frozen soufflé from metal container and place in 1-quart glass casserole. Cover with casserole lid.

2. MICROWAVE (high) 4 minutes (5½ to 6) or until just about thawed. Stir in lemon pepper, salt and garlic powder. Cover.

3. MICROWAVE (high) 3 to 4 minutes (4½ to 5) or until thickened, stirring once. Set aside.

4. Remove stems from mushrooms by twisting. Chop about half of stems finely to make 1½ cups. (Save remaining stems for another use.) Place chopped stems, butter and onion in 2-cup glass measure.

5. MICROWAVE (high), uncovered, 4 to 5 minutes (8 to 9) or until onion is tender, stirring once.

6. Stir onion mixture and 2 tablespoons Parmesan cheese into thawed soufflé. Place mushroom caps, stem-side-up, on 2 large glass serving plates. Cover with paper towel.

7. MICROWAVE (high), one plate at a time, 2½ to 3 minutes (4 to 4½) or until steaming hot. Drain or use paper towel to remove excess liquid. Spoon soufflé mixture into each cap, mounding up mixture. Sprinkle each with additional Parmesan cheese.

8. MICROWAVE (high), uncovered, 2 to 2½ minutes (4 to 4½) or until filling is hot and mushrooms are tender.

35 to 40 Mushrooms

TIP • Mushrooms can be prepared through step 7 and allowed to stand for several hours before heating in step 8.

Fresh pineapple wrapped in ham slices makes a quick and easy appetizer or snack.

HAM AND PINEAPPLE SNACKS

1 package (6 oz.) sliced cooked ham (5 slices)
20 pieces fresh pineapple
¼ cup orange marmalade

1. Cut each slice of ham into 4 strips, each about 1 inch wide. Place a piece of pineapple on end of each strip; roll up with pineapple inside. Fasten with toothpick.

2. MICROWAVE (high) marmalade in glass dish or cup ¼ to ½ minute or until hot. Dip each snack in marmalade; arrange on glass serving plate.

3. MICROWAVE (high), uncovered, 2 to 2½ minutes or until hot.

20 Snacks

TIP • You can prepare these a few hours ahead through step 2. Do not prepare more than 4 or 5 hours ahead as the fresh pineapple contains an enzyme used in tenderizing meat which causes the ham to become mushy.

Although these directions are for bread sticks, you can also use holiday shapes or squares, rounds or diamonds.

SEASONED TOAST NIBBLERS

¼ cup butter or margarine
2 tablespoons grated Parmesan cheese
½ teaspoon parsley flakes
⅛ teaspoon garlic powder
⅛ teaspoon onion powder
⅛ teaspoon celery salt
4 slices bread

1. MICROWAVE (high) butter in 12 x 8-inch glass baking dish 1 to 1½ minutes (2 to 3) or until melted. Stir in remaining ingredients except bread.

2. Cut each slice bread into six ½-inch strips. Add to butter mixture, turning to coat with butter.

3. MICROWAVE, uncovered, 5 to 5½ minutes (9 to 11) or until lightly browned and toasted, rearranging once. Serve warm or cold.

24 Nibblers

TIP • For uniform-sized strips, use sandwich bread slices. Crusts can be trimmed, if desired.

Cheese-topped crackers are popular hors d'oeuvres for heating in the microwave. This variation combines spicy Mexican flavors.

MEXICALI CRACKERS

1 cup (4 ozs.) shredded Cheddar cheese
¼ cup chopped black olives
2 tablespoons chopped green chilies
2 tablespoons mayonnaise or salad dressing
¼ teaspoon chili powder
⅛ teaspoon onion salt
4 drops Tabasco sauce
40 to 48 favorite crackers

1. Combine all ingredients except crackers in bowl. Arrange crackers on two glass serving plates. Spoon about ½ teaspoonful of mixture onto each cracker.

2. MICROWAVE (high) one plate at a time, uncovered, ¾ to 1 minute (1½ to 2) or until cheese starts to melt, rotating once.

40 to 48 Crackers

TIP • If heating all the crackers at one time, increase time in step 2 to 1 to 1½ minutes.

Hot beverages are popular during chilly winter days. Just heat the amount needed right in the serving cups.

SPICY WINE WARMER

4 whole cardamoms
8 whole cloves
2 slices orange, halved
2 sticks cinnamon
4 tablespoons sugar
4 tablespoons raisins
4 whole almonds
1 bottle (4/5 quart) dry red wine

1. Remove cardamom seeds and discard pods. Divide seeds among 4 glass mugs or cups. Insert 2 cloves into each orange slice. Divide slices and remaining ingredients among mugs. Stir to mix in sugar.

2. MICROWAVE (high), uncovered, about 4 minutes or until heated. Stir until sugar is dissolved. Remove seeds with slotted spoon.

4 Servings

TIP • To avoid the need to remove spices, add cardamom seeds, cloves and cinnamon to wine early in day. Then, to retain the spices, fasten cheese cloth over bottle before pouring.

Favorite Recipes from

The Microwave Times

Chapter 2

Fish & Poultry

Chicken Fricassee with Dumplings, page 21, and Sour Cream-Raisin Pie, page 115.

This recipe for torsk in a flavorful shrimp sauce can be served in a shallow casserole or individual shells.

TORSK-SHRIMP THERMADOR

1½ lbs. torsk fillets
1 small onion, sliced
1 lemon slice
1 can (10¾ oz.) condensed cream of shrimp soup
3 tablespoons flour
¼ cup milk
¼ cup dry white wine
½ cup (2 ozs.) shredded Mozzarella cheese
2 tablespoons snipped parsley
1 can (4½ oz.) shrimp, drained
2 tablespoons butter or margarine
⅓ cup dry bread crumbs
2 tablespoons Parmesan cheese
½ teaspoon paprika

1. Cut fillets into 1-inch pieces. Combine with onion and lemon in shallow 1 to 1½-quart glass casserole. Cover with casserole lid.

2. MICROWAVE (high) 5½ to 6 minutes or until fish flakes apart easily; set aside.

3. Combine soup, flour and milk in 4-cup glass measure.

4. MICROWAVE (high), uncovered, 3 to 4 minutes or until mixture boils, stirring once or twice. Stir in wine, cheese, parsley and shrimp. Pour over torsk in baking dish.

5. MICROWAVE (high) butter in small glass dish ½ to 1 minute or until melted. Stir in crumbs, cheese and paprika. Sprinkle over fish.

6. MICROWAVE (high), uncovered, 3 minutes while preheating broiler. Place under broiler for 3 to 5 minutes or until lightly toasted.

5 to 6 Servings

TIPS • If desired, omit broiling; increase microwave time to 4 to 5 minutes in step 6.

• Mixture can be spooned into 5 or 6 individual-serving dishes or shells. Top with crumb mixture and heat as directed.

• To prepare ahead, prepare through step 5. Complete step 6 when ready to serve.

Fish cooks beautifully in the microwave and combined with colorful stuffing is sure to be a favorite. If you don't have a food processor, crumble bread and finely chop vegetables before mixing with other ingredients.

FILLETS FLORENTINE

1 lb. fish fillets (pike, sole or red snapper)
3 slices bread
1 small onion
2 cups (3 ozs.) fresh spinach leaves
1 cup (4 ozs.) fresh or drained canned mushrooms
1 egg
3 tablespoons Parmesan cheese
¾ teaspoon salt
⅛ teaspoon seasoned pepper

1. Cut fish into 4 or 5 long strips. Curl each piece loosely inside 4 or 5 buttered custard cups leaving space in center; set aside.

2. Insert metal blade into food processor bowl. Break slices of bread in half; add to bowl along with quartered onion. Process with on-off motion until in fine crumbs. Add remaining ingredients. Process with on-off motion until thoroughly mixed and spinach is finely chopped. Spoon mixture evenly into fish cups. Arrange evenly on glass plate. Cover with paper towel.

3. MICROWAVE (high) 4 to 5 minutes (6 to 7) or until fish flakes easily with fork, rotating plate once. Cool a few minutes. Slide out of cups onto serving plate.

4 to 5 Servings

This combination of fish is uniquely flavorful and attractive. Seasoned salmon is rolled inside sole fillets. We preferred the fresh salmon (see Tips), but the canned also is very good.

SALMON-SOLE ROLLS

1 pint (8 ozs.) fresh mushrooms, chopped or sliced
1 small onion, chopped
¼ cup butter or margarine
1 can (8 oz.) salmon, drained
2 tablespoons mayonnaise or salad dressing
1 teaspoon parsley flakes
2 lbs. sole fillets
2 tablespoons flour
½ teaspoon instant chicken bouillon
½ teaspoon dill weed
¼ teaspoon salt
¾ cup water
2 tablespoons white wine, if desired

1. Combine mushrooms, onion and butter in 4-cup glass measure.

2. MICROWAVE (high), uncovered, 3½ to 4 minutes (6½ to 7) or until just about tender, stirring once.

3. Combine salmon, mayonnaise and parsley. Add mushrooms and onion to salmon mixture, leaving butter in cup; mix well. Divide salmon mixture among sole strips; spread to within 1 inch of ends. Roll up strips with filling inside. Fasten with toothpicks. Place in shallow glass serving dish. Cover with waxed paper. Set aside.

4. Add flour, bouillon, dill weed and salt to remaining butter mixture; blend well. Stir in water.

5. MICROWAVE (high), uncovered, 1½ to 2 minutes (3 to 4) or until mixture boils, stirring twice. Stir in wine. Set aside.

6. MICROWAVE (high) fish rolls 7½ to 8½ minutes (12 to 13) or until fish flakes easily with fork, rotating dish once.

7. MICROWAVE (high) sauce, uncovered, 1 to 2 minutes (2 to 3) to reheat. Spoon sauce over fish rolls.

About 8 Servings

TIPS • Cooked fresh salmon can be substituted for canned. Use 8 ozs. or 1 cup flaked and boned salmon. Add 1 teaspoon salt with mayonnaise. If salmon is uncooked, microwave, covered, about 2 minutes (3½) or until it flakes easily.

• The sauce can be omitted if desired.

• To prepare ahead, complete through step 5 and allow to stand several hours at room temperature or in refrigerator. To serve, continue with steps 6 and 7.

Salmon-Sole Rolls.

Fish usually requires 4 minutes microwave time per pound. We have increased the time in this recipe because of the vegetables in the kabob. The broccoli and onions are precooked since they require longer cooking time than the fish. Pictured on cover.

COLORFUL FISHERMAN'S KABOBS

16 small pearl onions
8 ozs. untrimmed fresh broccoli
1 tablespoon water
1 lb. boneless fish (halibut, torsk or pike)
1 medium cucumber
8 cherry tomatoes

Marinade:
⅔ cup soy sauce
¼ cup cooking oil
2 tablespoons honey
2 tablespoons vinegar
½ teaspoon ginger
⅛ teaspoon garlic powder
8 wooden skewers (8-inch)

1. Place unpeeled onions in 4-cup glass measure; add water to cover. Cover with plastic wrap.

2. MICROWAVE (high) 2 to 2½ minutes (5 to 6) or until water boils. Drain; cool.

3. Trim broccoli; cut flowerettes into pieces 2 inches long and ¼ inch thick. Place in glass dish; add water. Cover with plastic wrap.

4. MICROWAVE (high) 2 to 2½ minutes (4 to 5) or until steaming hot; drain.

5. Cut fish into about 16 pieces. Cut cucumber into 1-inch slices; quarter each slice. Peel onions.

6. Place fish and vegetables in plastic bag. Combine ingredients for Marinade, stirring until honey is dissolved. Pour over fish and vegetables. Turn to coat all pieces with marinade. Let stand at room temperature 1 hour or in refrigerator 6 to 8 hours, turning bag so all pieces are evenly coated.

7. Drain marinade. Thread fish and vegetables alternately on wooden skewers. Arrange on bacon-meat rack or in large shallow baking dish. Cover with waxed paper.

8. MICROWAVE (high) 5½ to 6½ minutes (6 to 7) or until fish flakes easily with fork.

4 to 6 Servings

Sole or other favorite fish fillets steam nicely in the microwave. Here is a lower calorie version where we have enhanced the color and flavor with a few canned shrimp.

SOLE AND SHRIMP TURBANS

1½ lbs. sole fillets
1 can (4½ oz.) large shrimp, drained and rinsed
1 tablespoon lemon juice
¼ teaspoon salt
1 green onion, sliced
1 can (4 oz.) mushroom pieces, undrained
1 tablespoon cornstarch

1. Cut sole fillets lengthwise into strips about 1½ inches wide. Roll up each strip; fasten with an uncolored toothpick. Arrange cut-side-down in 8-inch glass baking dish. Divide shrimp among rolls, filling centers. Drizzle with lemon juice; sprinkle with salt and onion. Spoon undrained mushrooms over fish. Cover with plastic wrap or a lid.

2. MICROWAVE (high) about 6 minutes or until fish flakes apart easily. Dissolve cornstarch in 1 tablespoon water in 2-cup glass measure. Drain broth from fish into cup; mix well.

3. MICROWAVE (high), uncovered, ¾ to 1¼ minutes or until mixture boils, stirring once. Pour sauce over turbans.

6 Servings, about 150 calories each

TIPS • For other quantities, allow 4 minutes/lb. cooking time.

• The sauce that is made from the cooking juices can be omitted. Just remove turbans with slotted spoon.

• If you omit the mushrooms, add ¼ cup chicken bouillon or dry white wine for cooking liquid.

Patties like these brown and cook quickly on either a browner grill or skillet.

SALMON PATTIES

2 eggs
¼ cup dry bread crumbs
2 tablespoons chopped onion
½ teaspoon grated lemon peel
¼ teaspoon salt
Dash pepper
1 can (16 oz.) salmon, drained and flaked

1. Beat eggs. Stir in remaining ingredients except salmon, mixing thoroughly. Mix in salmon only until combined. Shape into 4 or 5 patties.

2. MICROWAVE (high) browner grill or skillet 4 to 5 minutes. Place patties on hot browner.

3. MICROWAVE (high), uncovered, 1½ minutes or until lightly browned; turn patties over.

4. MICROWAVE (high) 1½ to 2 minutes or until patties are set.

4 to 5 Servings

TIP • Patties are good served with a cheese sauce. Microwave sauce first, then cook patties and reheat sauce for serving.

You need not be dieting to enjoy these attractive and flavorful low calorie fish fillets.

FESTIVE SOLE ROLLS

1 lb. sole or other favorite fish fillets
½ cup chopped unpeeled cucumber or zucchini
1 medium tomato, chopped
¾ teaspoon seasoned salt
Dash pepper
3 tablespoons pasteurized process cheese spread

1. Cut fillets into strips 1 to 1½ inches wide. Curl each piece loosely, leaving a 1½-inch space in center; fasten each roll with toothpick. Place cut-side-down in 8-inch square glass baking dish.

2. Combine cucumber and tomato. Spoon mixture into center of each fillet roll. Sprinkle with salt and pepper. Cover with plastic wrap.

3. MICROWAVE (high) 4 to 5 minutes (6 to 7) or until fish flakes apart easily. Spoon cheese spread onto each. Allow to stand a few minutes to soften cheese.

4 Servings, about 130 calories each

Sole and Shrimp Turbans, page 16.

Festive Sole Rolls.

Mrs. Elizabeth Bowen of Santa Ana, California, reported that she'd never fixed a turkey that tasted as good as this recipe that starts in the microwave and is then completed in a covered Weber-type grill.

BARBEQUED TURKEY—MICRO-WEBER STYLE

14-lb. turkey, thawed
Salt and pepper
¼ teaspoon poultry seasoning
1 large apple, peeled and quartered
1 medium onion, leave whole

1. Be sure turkey is thawed completely. Remove giblets and use as desired. Remove any excess fat from cavity. Wash turkey well; pat dry. Sprinkle cavity with salt, pepper and poultry seasoning. Add apple and onion to main cavity. Sew opening closed. Tie wings to body and legs together with string.

2. Wrap tips of wings and legs with foil to prevent overcooking. Place turkey breast-side-down in roasting pan or baking dish. Cover with waxed paper.

3. MICROWAVE (high) 35 minutes (50), rotating dish once. Turn turkey breast-side-up; remove foil. Cover with waxed paper.

4. MICROWAVE (high) 35 minutes (50), rotating dish once.

5. Place turkey breast-side-up over hot coals in covered grill. Insert meat thermometer (one for use with conventional heat) in breast. Cover grill.

6. GRILL 45 to 60 minutes or until themometer registers 165°, turning turkey over once, if desired. Let stand 15 to 20 minutes before slicing.

12 to 15 Servings

TIPS • Follow manufacturer's instructions for using covered grill.

• For other size turkeys, allow 5 minutes per pound microwave time. Complete on grill as directed.

• Turkey can also be stuffed with favorite dressing or left unstuffed.

This popular dish has an Italian flavor. It is from an article on adapting recipes. The original required about 1 hour of baking.

CHICKEN CACCIATORE

1 medium green pepper, chopped
1 medium onion, thinly sliced
1 tablespoon butter or margarine
1 can (28 oz.) whole tomatoes, undrained
¼ cup all-purpose flour
1 bay leaf
1 tablespoon parsley flakes
1 teaspoon salt
1 teaspoon leaf oregano
1 teaspoon paprika
¼ teaspoon pepper
¼ teaspoon sweet basil
¼ teaspoon garlic powder
½ cup dry red wine or water
2½ to 3-lb. frying chicken, cut-up

1. Combine green pepper, onion and butter in 3-quart glass casserole. Cover with casserole lid.

2. MICROWAVE (high) 9 to 10 minutes or until partially cooked. Add tomatoes and flour; stir until smooth. Stir in remaining ingredients except chicken. Cover.

3. MICROWAVE (high) 5 minutes. Add chicken. Cover.

4. MICROWAVE (high) 20 to 30 minutes or until chicken is tender, stirring once. Allow to stand about 5 minutes before serving with cooked rice or spaghetti.

5 to 6 Servings

TIP • With Combination Oven, microwave in step 2 for 10 to 12 minutes, step 3 for 8 minutes and microwave-bake at 325° for 25 to 30 minutes in step 4.

Broiled chicken is simplified by first steaming in the microwave.

EASY BROILED CHICKEN

2½ to 3-lb. frying chicken, quartered
2 tablespoons lemon juice
½ teaspoon salt
¼ teaspoon paprika
⅛ teaspoon pepper
½ teaspoon prepared mustard
1 teaspoon Worcestershire sauce

1. Rinse chicken with cold water; pat dry. Arrange pieces skin-side-down in 12 x 8-inch glass baking dish with thicker pieces toward corners and smaller pieces in center. Combine remaining ingredients. Brush chicken with about half of mixture. Cover with waxed paper.

2. MICROWAVE (high) 9 minutes. Turn chicken over and rearrange. Brush with remaining lemon mixture. Cover.

3. MICROWAVE (high) 9 to 11 minutes or until just about done. Preheat broiler.

4. Place chicken skin-side-down on broiler rack.

5. BROIL about 3 inches from heat, 5 to 6 minutes or until golden brown. Turn and broil 5 to 6 minutes on other side.

4 Servings, about 200 calories each

TIP • For the least calories, select white meat pieces and let a thin friend enjoy the skin.

A simple blend of seasonings makes this chicken delicious without the addition of extra fat or a sauce. For optimum calorie reduction, remove the skin and select only white-meat pieces. The seasonings are also good sprinkled on a roasting chicken.

CRUSTY SLIMLINE CHICKEN

3-lb. frying chicken, cut up
1 teaspoon garlic salt
1 teaspoon leaf tarragon
1 teaspoon paprika
½ teaspoon salt
¼ teaspoon pepper

1. Wash chicken and pat dry. Combine remaining ingredients. Sprinkle evenly over chicken pieces. Arrange chicken skin-side-up on microwave roasting rack in 12 x 8-inch glass baking dish or on bacon rack. Cover with waxed paper.

2. MICROWAVE (high) 25 to 30 minutes or until chicken is tender, rotating dish once.

5 Servings, about 200 calories each

TIP • With Combination Oven, arrange chicken on rack in broiler pan. Microwave-bake at 375°, uncovered, 20 to 25 minutes.

First, microwave chicken with the seasoned sauce. Then, complete cooking on the grill in 15 to 20 minutes. The chicken is especially moist and the skin never too brown.

CAREFREE BARBECUED CHICKEN

¼ cup olive oil
¼ cup dry white wine or chicken broth
1 small onion, sliced
1 clove garlic, minced
1 teaspoon salt
¼ teaspoon leaf tarragon
⅛ teaspoon pepper
3 to 4-lb. frying chicken, quartered

1. Combine all ingredients except chicken. Arrange chicken skin-side-down in 12 x 8-inch glass baking dish. Brush chicken with part of oil mixture. Cover with waxed paper.

2. MICROWAVE (high) 15 to 20 minutes (about 5 minutes per lb.) or until chicken is just about cooked. About halfway through cooking time, turn chicken pieces over and brush with additional sauce.

3. BARBECUE about 4 inches above hot coals 15 to 20 minutes or until golden brown, turning occasionally and brushing with additional sauce.

4 to 6 Servings

TIP • A combination of half olive oil and half regular oil can be used if the mixture is allowed to stand an hour or two before using.

A vegetable such as asparagus or broccoli spears goes well with the creamy wine sauce in this recipe.

CHICKEN IN WINE SAUCE

2 tablespoons cooking oil
3-lb. frying chicken, cut up
1 can (10¾ oz.) condensed cream of chicken soup
1 can (4 oz.) mushroom pieces, undrained
2 tablespoons flour
½ cup sour cream
¼ cup white wine
2 teaspoons parsley flakes
½ teaspoon salt

1. Heat oil in 10-inch pyroceramic skillet over medium-high heat. Add chicken and brown on all sides, removing pieces as they are browned. Combine remaining ingredients; stir into skillet. Add chicken, placing skin-side-up.

2. MICROWAVE (high), uncovered, 20 to 22 minutes (25 to 30) or until chicken is done, rotating dish once.

5 to 6 Servings

Chicken can be microwaved more quickly than can many meats.

FAVORITE CHICKEN AND RICE

1 cup long-grain white rice
1 can (10¾ oz.) condensed mushroom soup
1½ cups water
1 small onion, chopped
1 tablespoon parsley flakes
½ teaspoon garlic salt
3-lb. frying chicken, cut up
Salt and pepper
¼ cup Parmesan cheese
Paprika

1. Combine rice, soup, water, onion, parsley and garlic salt in presoaked 3 or 4-quart simmer pot or casserole. Place chicken on top, skin-side-down. Sprinkle with salt and pepper. Cover with simmer pot lid.

2. MICROWAVE (high) 25 minutes. Turn chicken over and stir rice. Sprinkle chicken with cheese and paprika. Cover.

3. MICROWAVE (low — 30%) 30 to 35 minutes or until rice is tender.

5 to 6 Servings

TIPS • With Full Power, use 5-minute microwave and 10-minute standing times for cooking time in step 3.

• With Combination Oven, place chicken on rice mixture skin-side-up; sprinkle with cheese and paprika. Microwave-bake at 325° for 35 to 40 minutes.

Favorite Chicken and Rice.

Chicken and dumplings are topped with a creamy sauce in this traditional fricassee recipe.

CHICKEN FRICASSEE WITH DUMPLINGS

1 small onion, sliced
3 to 3½-lb. frying chicken, cut up
⅓ cup all-purpose flour
1½ teaspoons salt
1 teaspoon paprika
¼ teaspoon pepper

Dumplings:
1½ cups unsifted all-purpose flour
2 teaspoons baking powder
¾ teaspoon salt
⅔ cup milk
2 tablespoon cooking oil
1 egg, slightly beaten

Sauce:
2 cups milk
¼ cup all-purpose flour
½ teaspoon salt
1 teaspoon parsley flakes

1. Arrange onion slices in bottom of 12 x 8 or 13 x 9-inch glass baking dish. Rinse chicken pieces with water; coat with mixture of flour, salt, paprika and pepper. Arrange skin-side-up in baking dish, placing larger pieces toward corners of dish. Cover with waxed paper.

2. MICROWAVE (high) 20 to 25 minutes or until tender, rotating dish once.

3. Meanwhile, prepare Dumplings by combining flour, baking powder and salt in mixing bowl. Combine milk, oil and egg. Add to flour mixture; stir just until combined. Drop spoonfuls onto chicken.

4. MICROWAVE (high), uncovered, 6 to 7 minutes or until no longer doughy, rotating dish once. Cover and set aside.

5. Combine milk, flour, salt and parsley for Sauce in 4-cup glass measure.

6. MICROWAVE (high), uncovered, 5 to 6 minutes or until mixture boils, stirring 2 or 3 times during last half of cooking time. Stir in juices from chicken. Serve sauce with chicken and dumplings.

4 to 6 Servings

TIP • When reheating, remove the dumplings and heat chicken until just about serving temperature. Add the dumplings and heat just until dumplings are hot, 1 to 3 minutes. If the dumplings are added for the entire time, they will overcook.

Chipped beef and bacon give these chicken breasts a unique smoky flavor. Extras can be frozen for a quick gourmet meal to serve in the weeks ahead. About 200 calories per piece.

BACON-TOPPED CHICKEN BREASTS

4 whole chicken breasts
3-oz. package chipped or smoked beef
6 strips bacon
1 can (10¾ oz.) condensed mushroom soup
½ cup sour cream
1 tablespoon chopped chives

1. Split and bone each chicken breast. Cut chipped beef into strips and layer evenly in 12 x 8-inch glass baking dish. Place chicken breasts, skin-side-up over beef. Place bacon strips over chicken. Cover with paper towel.

2. MICROWAVE (high) 14 to 16 minutes (26 to 28) or until chicken is just about done. Remove partially cooked bacon strips to paper towel-lined glass plate. Cover with paper towel.

3. MICROWAVE (high) 1½ to 3 minutes (3 to 5) or until crisp. Set aside.

4. Drain juices from chicken. Combine soup, sour cream and chives; spoon onto each chicken breast.

5. MICROWAVE (high), uncovered, 5 to 6 minutes (10 to 11) or until heated through. Crumble bacon and sprinkle over chicken.

6 to 8 Servings

TIPS • Chicken broth for use in soups or sauces can be made from leftover bones and chicken juices. Place bones in 1½-quart glass casserole; add 1 cup water and ½ teaspoon salt. Microwave (high), covered, for 10 minutes. Uncover and cool. Cut any remaining meat from bones and add to broth.

• Individual servings (1 or 2 breasts) can be packaged and frozen. To thaw, microwave (high) 1 breast 4 to 5 minutes (9 to 10) or 2 breasts 6 to 7 minutes (12 to 14), turning pouch over halfway through cooking time. Let stand 5 minutes.

We thank Mrs. Alice Price of Fairfax, Virginia, for sharing this interesting recipe with us. Pockets of crabmeat filling cook right under the skin and add a special flavor to chicken breasts.

CRAB-STUFFED CHICKEN BREASTS

1 can (6½ oz.) crabmeat, drained
1 tablespoon chopped chives
1 egg
3 whole chicken breasts, split (2½ to 3 lbs.)
¼ cup butter or margarine
2 tablespoons soy sauce
¼ teaspoon Worcestershire sauce
Salt

1. Flake crabmeat, removing any shell. Mix in chives and egg with fork. Make a pocket in each half chicken breast by lifting skin just enough to insert 1 rounded tablespoonful crab mixture. Fasten loose skin with toothpick. Arrange skin-side-up in 12 x 8-inch glass baking dish, overlapping as necessary.

2. MICROWAVE (high) butter in small glass dish ½ minute or until melted. Stir in soy and Worcestershire sauces.

3. Drizzle mixture over chicken breasts; sprinkle with salt. Cover with waxed paper.

4. MICROWAVE (high) 25 to 30 minutes or until tender, rotating dish once. Remove toothpicks. If desired, place under broiler a few minutes to crisp skin.

6 Servings

TIP • If desired, bone chicken breasts, leaving skin intact.

Eliminate extra calories in chicken by removing the skin before cooking. Paper toweling is used as the covering to allow the moisture to escape and the coating to retain a crisp texture.

CHEESY CHICKEN BREASTS

2 whole chicken breasts, split and skinned (about 24 ozs.)
2 ozs. Monterey Jack cheese
1 egg, beaten
¼ cup corn flake crumbs
1 tablespoon Parmesan cheese
1 teaspoon parsley flakes
1 teaspoon instant chicken bouillon
¼ teaspoon salt
Dash pepper

1. Cut 3-inch lengthwise slit in thickest part of each chicken breast. Cut cheese into 4 sticks, about ½ x 2½-inches each. Insert cheese stick into opening of each chicken breast. Secure each opening with toothpick. Place breasts bone-side-down on rack in baking dish. Brush skinned side of breasts with egg. Combine remaining ingredients. Sprinkle evenly over chicken. Cover with paper towel.

2. MICROWAVE (high) 10 to 12 minutes (14 to 16) or until done, rotating dish once.

4 Servings, about 210 calories each

TIP • Freeze any extras. To reheat a single frozen, cooked serving, microwave 2 to 2½ minutes.

The flavor of halved Cornish Hens is enhanced with a savory cornbread dressing.

CORNISH HENS WITH CORNBREAD DRESSING

3 tablespoons butter or margarine
1 small onion, chopped
½ cup chopped celery
4 cornish hens, thawed
Salt
8-inch pan cornbread, crumbled
3 slices bread, crumbled
1 teaspoon instant chicken bouillon
1 teaspoon poultry seasoning
½ teaspoon salt
⅛ teaspoon pepper
½ cup water
1 egg, slightly beaten

Glaze:
3 tablespoons butter or margarine
1 teaspoon paprika
1 tablespoon soy sauce

1. Combine butter, onion and celery in 2-quart glass bowl.

2. MICROWAVE (high), uncovered, 3 to 3½ minutes (4½ to 5) or until onion is just about tender; set aside.

3. Remove giblets and neck from each hen. (Set aside to cook as desired.) Wash hens; pat dry. Sprinkle inside of each with salt. Place breast-side-up in 12 x 8 or 13 x 9-inch glass baking dish. Cover with waxed paper.

4. MICROWAVE (high) 20 minutes (30) or until just about done. Cool slightly.

5. Add crumbled breads, seasonings, water and egg to onion mixture; mix well.

6. Remove hens from baking dish, leaving juices in dish. Add dressing mixture to baking dish; mix lightly. Cut each hen in half lengthwise using kitchen or poultry shears. Place cut-side-down on dressing, overlapping as necessary.

7. MICROWAVE (high) butter for Glaze in small glass dish ½ to 1 minute (2 to 2½) or until melted. Stir in paprika and soy sauce. Brush on hens.

8. MICROWAVE (high), uncovered, 15 to 20 minutes or until tender.

6 to 8 Servings

TIPS • Recipe can be prepared several hours ahead through step 7. Complete step 8 when ready to serve.

• To prepare cornbread in microwave, combine a package of mix as directed on package. Spread in 8-inch square glass baking dish. Microwave (high), uncovered, 5 to 6 minutes or until no longer doughy, rotating dish once or twice.

• With Combination Oven, microwave-bake at 350° 25 to 30 minutes in step 8.

Crab-Stuffed Chicken Breasts, page 22.

Duckling is completed in the conventional oven to crisp and brown the skin. Cook a vegetable or other accompaniment in the microwave during this time.

ROAST DUCKLING WITH APRICOT SAUCE

4 to 6-lb. domestic duckling, thawed
Salt and pepper
½ teaspoon leaf marjoram, if desired
2 apples, quartered
1 medium onion, quartered

Sauce:
⅓ cup apricot preserves
2 teaspoons cornstarch
⅓ cup orange juice
1 tablespoon Cointreau, if desired

1. Rinse duckling and pat dry. Set aside giblets to use as desired. Sprinkle inside cavity with salt, pepper and marjoram. Stuff with apples and onion. Secure openings with toothpicks. Wrap tips of legs and wings with small pieces of foil to prevent overcooking. Place breast-side-up in glass baking dish or on roasting rack. Cover with waxed paper.

2. MICROWAVE (high) 3 minutes per pound. Drain off drippings. Turn duck breast-side-down. Cover with waxed paper.

3. MICROWAVE (high) 3 minutes per pound.

4. Preheat conventional oven to 350°.

5. Transfer duckling, breast-side-down to clean baking pan. Place in conventional oven and bake, uncovered, for about 20 minutes or until nicely browned. Turn duckling breast-side-up and continue baking for 20 to 30 minutes longer or until skin is brown and crisp and legs can be moved easily. Allow to stand about 10 minutes before cutting into quarters with kitchen shears.

6. Combine preserves and cornstarch in 2-cup glass measure. Stir in orange juice.

7. MICROWAVE (high), uncovered, 1½ to 2 minutes or until mixture boils, stirring once. Stir in Cointreau. Pour over duckling to serve.

About 4 Servings

TIPS • To thaw a frozen duckling using the microwave, use medium — 50% power and allow 5 minutes per pound with rest periods every 10 minutes.

• The duckling is transferred to a clean pan in step 5 because it is easier to clean 2 lightly soiled pans than one pan with cooked on drippings.

• With Combination Oven, microwave-bake at 375°, uncovered, 6 minutes per pound. Start with breast-side-down; halfway through cooking time turn duckling breast-side-up.

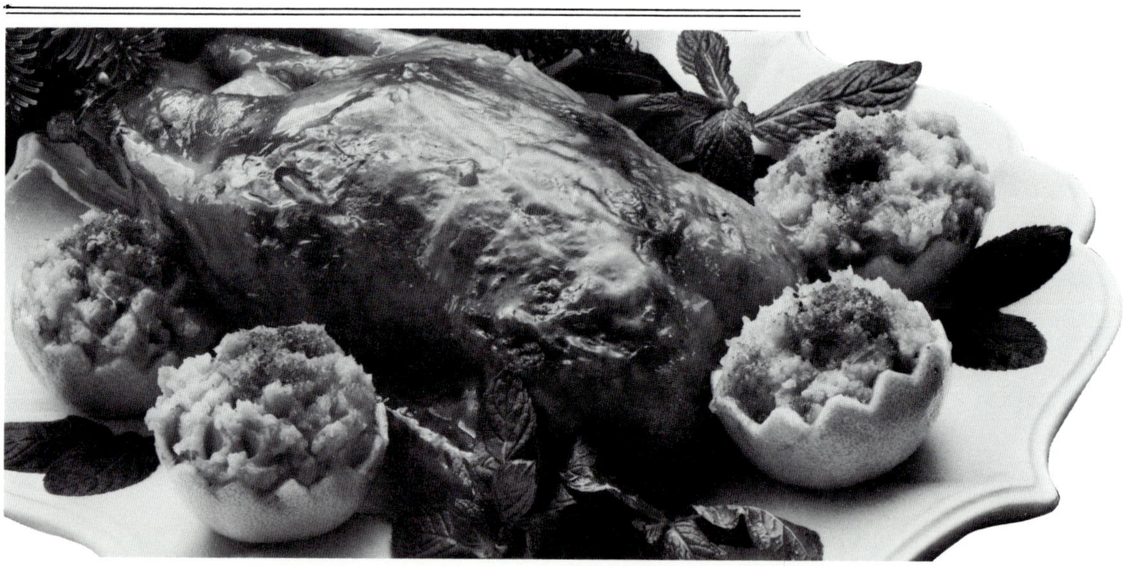

Roast Duckling with Apricot Sauce, this page, and Sweet Potato Filled-Orange Shells, page 88.

Favorite Recipes from

The Microwave Times

Chapter 3

Beef & Pork

Beef Bourguignon, page 29.

An oven cooking bag is a handy container for cooking pot roast. The long, slow simmering gives a fork-tender roast. The carrots and potatoes cook with the meat in the flavorful sauce from the soups.

COUNTRY POT ROAST

3½ to 4-lb. pot roast
1 can (10¾ oz.) condensed mushroom soup
1 envelope (1.37 oz.) dry onion soup mix
5 medium carrots, peeled
5 medium potatoes, peeled

1. Arrange roast in large oven cooking bag or presoaked microwave simmer pot so it lies flat. Top with soups, carrots and potatoes. Close oven bag with rubber band or cover simmer pot with lid. Place the oven bag in a shallow glass baking dish or on a plate. Make several small holes near the closing of the oven bag.

2. MICROWAVE (high) 10 minutes.

3. MICROWAVE (low — 30%) 1½ hours. Carefully turn roast over so vegetables now lie under roast.

4. MICROWAVE (low — 30%) 30 to 60 minutes or until meat is tender.

5 to 6 Servings

TIPS • With Full Power, use segments of 5 minute microwave and 10 minute standing times for step 3 and segments of 5 minute microwave and 15 minutes standing times for step 4.

• With Combination Oven, microwave in step 2 for 10 minutes and in step 3 for 1 hour. Then, microwave-defrost in step 4 for 1 to 1½ hours.

When you desire a slow-cooked, tender pot roast from the microwave, try this method which uses very low power for a long period of time. If you don't have the lower power settings, simmer the roast on a low setting on a burner or surface unit.

BARBECUED BEEF ROAST

2½ to 3-lb. arm or shoulder beef roast
2 tablespoons cooking oil
Salt and pepper
1 cup catsup
¼ cup packed brown sugar
¼ cup Worcestershire sauce
¼ cup vinegar
1 medium onion, chopped
2 tablespoons cornstarch
1 tablespoon lemon juice
1 teaspoon celery seed
¼ teaspoon liquid smoke

1. Brown roast in oil over medium-high heat in 2 to 3-quart pyroceramic casserole; turn to brown all sides. Salt and pepper to taste.

2. Mix remaining ingredients until well blended. Pour over meat. Cover with casserole lid.

3. MICROWAVE (low — 30%) 1½ hours, turning roast over every ½ hour.

4. MICROWAVE (warm —10%) 1 to 1½ hours or until tender, turning roast over every ½ hour.

About 8 Servings

TIPS • About 2 cups of your favorite barbecue sauce can be substituted for sauce ingredients.

• With Combination Oven, microwave-bake at 350° for 15 minutes. Then, bake 1¼ to 1¾ hours or until tender.

Here is a popular recipe for preparing steak on the browner grill. Use the timings for other steaks of similar size and thickness.

GRILLED STEAK WITH SHERRY SAUCE

1½ lb. family steak, cut 1½-inches thick
Meat tenderizer
1 teaspoon whole peppercorns
1 tablespoon butter or margarine, cut into pieces
2 tablespoons dry sherry
1 can (4 oz.) mushroom pieces, drained
Salt
Sour cream

1. Moisten steak with water. Sprinkle both sides with meat tenderizer. Pierce each side several times with fork. Crush peppercorns with rolling pin. Press peppercorns onto both sides of steak. Spread butter on one side of steak.

2. MICROWAVE (high) browner grill or skillet 7 to 8 minutes. Place steak on hot grill, buttered-side-down.

3. MICROWAVE (high), uncovered, 5 to 6 minutes or until browned; turn steak over.

4. MICROWAVE (high) 4 to 5 minutes or until desired doneness. Remove steak from grill. Combine drippings with sherry and mushrooms.

5. MICROWAVE (high), uncovered, 1½ to 2 minutes or until heated. Sprinkle steak with salt; top with sour cream. Spoon sherry sauce over steak.

4 to 5 Servings

Cube steak is a less tender meat which has been tenderized by a machine that cuts through the fibers. Thus, it requires a shorter cooking time than a cut such as round steak.

CUBE STEAK PARMIGIANA

1 lb. cube steaks
3 tablespoons flour
1 egg
2 tablespoons water
¼ cup dry bread crumbs
¼ cup Parmesan cheese
2 tablespoons cooking oil
1 small onion, chopped
1 clove garlic, finely chopped
3 to 4 ozs. sliced Mozzarella cheese
½ cup water
1 can (6 oz.) tomato paste
½ teaspoon Italian seasoning
½ teaspoon salt

1. Coat steaks with flour. Beat together egg and water. Combine crumbs and cheese. Dip steaks into egg mixture, then into crumb mixture.

2. Heat oil in 10-inch pyroceramic skillet over medium heat. Add steaks and brown lightly on both sides. Add onion and garlic. Top steaks with cheese slices. Combine remaining ingredients; pour over steaks. Cover with casserole lid.

3. MICROWAVE (high) 5 minutes. Rotate dish.

4. MICROWAVE (low — 30%) 15 to 20 minutes or until meat is tender.

About 4 Servings

TIPS • With Full Power in step 4, allow meat to stand 10 minutes, microwave 5 minutes; stand 10 minutes and then microwave 2 to 3 minutes.

• With Combination Oven, microwave in step 3 for 5 minutes; use microwave-defrost for time in step 4.

A lower power setting and thin slices contribute to fork-tender meat.

BEEF ROULADEN

8 slices bacon
8 thinly-sliced pieces top round (1½ to 2 lbs. total)
1 medium onion, thinly sliced
⅓ cup all-purpose flour
1 tablespoon instant beef bouillon
¼ teaspoon salt
⅛ teaspoon pepper
1¼ cups water
½ cup dry red wine

1. Layer bacon in 2½ to 3-quart pyroceramic skillet or casserole. Cover with paper towel.

2. MICROWAVE (high) 4 to 5 minutes or until partially cooked. Place a bacon slice on each piece meat. Divide onion slices among meat pieces. Roll up each piece with bacon and onion inside. Fasten with toothpicks. Coat with flour.

3. Place pyroceramic dish with drippings over medium-high heat. Add meat rolls and brown on all sides. Add any remaining flour and the remaining ingredients. Mix lightly. Cover with skillet lid.

4. MICROWAVE (high) 5 minutes. Then, MICROWAVE (low — 30%), covered, 30 to 35 minutes or until tender.

6 to 8 Servings

TIPS • If meat is not thinly-sliced, pound with meat mallet.

• Instead of browning meat on a burner, a microwave browning dish can be used. Preheat dish by microwaving 5 minutes. Add 1 tablespoon bacon drippings and coated meat rolls. Microwave 2 minutes. Turn rolls over and microwave 3 minutes. Add remaining ingredients and continue cooking as directed in step 4.

• With Full Power in step 4, microwave 10 minutes. Let stand 10 minutes. Microwave 6 to 8 minutes. Let stand 5 to 10 minutes.

Family-Style Round Steak, page 29, and Beef Rouladen, this page.

This beef stew becomes special occasion with the addition of bacon and wine flavors. The same cooking method would apply to other beef stew recipes.

BEEF BOURGUIGNON

4 slices bacon
2 lbs. boneless beef stew meat
1/3 cup all-purpose flour
1 teaspoon salt
1/4 teaspoon pepper
1 clove garlic, minced
1 bay leaf
1 tablespoon parsley flakes
1 can (10 1/2 oz.) condensed beef consommé
3/4 cup Burgundy wine
1/2 cup water
5 medium carrots, cut into 1-inch pieces
1 pint (8 ozs.) fresh mushrooms
1 can (16 oz.) whole onions, undrained

1. Place bacon in single layer in 3-quart pyroceramic casserole. Cover with paper towel.

2. MICROWAVE (high) 4 to 5 minutes or until bacon is crisp. Set aside bacon.

3. Place casserole with bacon drippings over medium-high heat. Coat meat cubes with mixture of flour, salt and pepper. Add to drippings and brown on all sides. Add garlic, bay leaf, parsley, consommé, wine, water and any remaining flour mixture. Cover with casserole lid.

4. MICROWAVE (high) 5 minutes or until mixture boils. Then MICROWAVE (low — 30%) 30 minutes, stirring once. Add carrots, mushrooms and onions. Cover.

5. MICROWAVE (high) 5 minutes or until mixture boils. Then, MICROWAVE (low — 30%) 30 to 40 minutes or until meat and vegetables are tender, stirring once. Remove bay leaf before serving.

6 to 8 Servings

TIPS • With Full Power, prepare as directed through step 3. Microwave 5 minutes. Then let stand 10 minutes. Stir and repeat once. Add vegetables. Microwave 5 minutes; let stand 10 minutes. Stir and repeat once or twice or until tender.

• A microwave browning grill or skillet can be used for browning meat. Preheat 5 to 7 minutes or as directed by manufacturer for meats. Add meat and microwave 1 1/2 minutes. Turn meat over and microwave 3 minutes or until meat is browned. Transfer meat to 3-quart glass casserole and continue as directed. If all the meat will not fit on the grill for browning at one time, reheat grill by microwaving about 3 minutes.

Here is a good method for preparing fork-tender round steak.

FAMILY-STYLE ROUND STEAK

1 1/2 to 2-lbs. round steak, cut into serving pieces
3 tablespoons flour
1/4 teaspoon salt
Dash pepper
1 tablespoon cooking oil
1 small onion, sliced
1 can (10 3/4 oz.) condensed mushroom soup

1. Pound steak with meat mallet to help tenderize. Coat pieces with mixture of flour, salt and pepper. Heat oil in pyroceramic skillet or casserole over medium-high heat. Add steak and brown on both sides. Add any remaining flour and remaining ingredients. Cover with skillet lid.

2. MICROWAVE (high) 5 to 5 1/2 minutes or until mixture boils. Then, MICROWAVE (low — 30%) 55 to 70 minutes or until meat is tender, turning meat over once.

About 6 Servings

TIPS • A browning skillet can be used for the prebrowning in step 1. Microwave skillet 5 minutes to preheat. Add meat and microwave 1 1/2 minutes. Turn meat over and microwave 2 minutes. If necessary to reheat skillet, microwave 3 minutes.

• With Full Power, microwave 10 minutes in step 2. Then use periods of 10 minutes rest and 5 minutes microwave for a total of 50 to 60 minutes or until meat is tender.

We receive many questions regarding cooking less tender cuts of meat. Pounding meat before cooking plus slow simmering yields fork-tender round steak. The mild, slightly sauerbraten flavor of the sauce is a favorite.

BAVARIAN ROUND STEAK

1½ lbs. boneless round steak (about ½-inch thick)
3 tablespoons flour
2 tablespoons cooking oil
1 medium onion, sliced
2 cups water
1 envelope (⅝ oz.) brown gravy mix
1 tablespoon brown sugar
1 tablespoon vinegar
1 teaspoon salt
1 teaspoon Worcestershire sauce
¼ teaspoon ground ginger
⅛ teaspoon pepper

1. Cut steak into serving size pieces. Pound steak with meat mallet to help tenderize. Coat meat with flour.

2. Heat oil in 10-inch pyroceramic skillet over medium-high heat. Add steak and brown on both sides. Add onion. Combine remaining ingredients; pour over steak. Cover with skillet lid.

3. MICROWAVE (high) 10 minutes.

4. MICROWAVE (low — 30%) 45 to 55 minutes or until done, rearranging meat once. Serve with boiled potatoes, potato pancakes or noodles.

5 to 6 Servings

TIPS • With Full Power, in step 4, use 3 minutes microwave and 10 minutes stand for periods to equal the 45 to 55 minutes of simmer time.

• With Combination Oven, microwave in step 3 for 10 minutes; use microwave-defrost for time in step 4.

Freeze steak 30 minutes for ease in cutting into strips.

GREEN PEPPER STEAK

1½ lbs. top round steak
3 tablespoons cooking oil
1 medium onion, sliced
1 clove garlic, minced
1½ teaspoons instant beef bouillon
½ teaspoon salt
⅛ teaspoon pepper
2 cups water
1 can (4 oz.) mushroom pieces
2 tablespoons cornstarch
1 green pepper, cut into strips

1. Cut steak into strips ⅛ inch thick and 2 inches long. Heat oil in 2 or 3-quart pryoceramic casserole or skillet over medium-high heat. Add meat, onion and garlic. Brown evenly, stirring occasionally. Add bouillon, salt, pepper and water. Cover with casserole lid.

2. MICROWAVE (high) 5 minutes. Then, MICROWAVE (low — 30%) 50 to 60 minutes or until meat is tender, stirring once.

3. Drain liquid from mushrooms into small dish; stir in cornstarch until smooth. Add cornstarch mixture, mushrooms and green pepper to casserole; stir to combine. Cover.

4. MICROWAVE (high) 4 to 5 minutes or until boiling and green pepper is desired doneness.

5 to 6 Servings

This cut is best microwaved with slow simmering. A simmer pot or casserole dish can be used.

TERIYAKI ROLLED FLANK

1½-lb. flank steak, scored
1 medium onion, thinly sliced
1 clove garlic, minced
1 cup water
⅓ cup soy sauce
2 tablespoons cornstarch
2 tablespoons dry sherry, if desired
2 teaspoons honey
¼ teaspoon ground ginger

1. Top steak with layer of onion slices; sprinkle with garlic. Roll up steak lengthwise; fasten with string. Place seam-side-up in presoaked 3 or 4-quart simmer pot or casserole. Combine remaining ingredients; pour over steak. Cover with lid.

2. MICROWAVE (high) 7 minutes. Then, MICROWAVE (low — 30%) 50 to 60 minutes or until meat is tender, turning meat once.

3. Transfer meat to serving plate. Remove string; cut roll into slices. Serve with sauce.

5 to 6 Servings

TIPS • With Combination Oven, microwave 35 to 45 minutes, turning meat once.

• An oven cooking bag can be used in place of simmer pot or casserole.

Cream of mushroom soup provides additional flavor, a moist texture and creamy sauce for this meat loaf.

SOUPER MEAT LOAF

2 lbs. ground beef
1 small onion, chopped
1 egg
½ cup dry bread crumbs
½ teaspoon salt
1 can (10¾ oz.) condensed mushroom soup
⅓ cup milk

1. Combine meat, onion, egg, bread crumbs, salt and half of soup; mix well. Press into 9 x 5-inch glass loaf dish. Cover with waxed paper.

2. MICROWAVE (high) 18 to 20 minutes or until no longer pink in center, rotating dish 2 or 3 times.

3. Combine remaining soup with milk in glass dish or measuring cup.

4. MICROWAVE (high), uncovered, 2 to 2½ minutes or until boiling. Serve over meat loaf.

6 to 8 Servings

Souper Meat Loaf.

These pizza-topped meat patties can be served open-faced style on toasted English muffin halves or between sliced hamburger buns. If you haven't tried ground beef patties in the microwave, this is an especially attractive and tasty way to learn.

MEATZA PATTIES

1 lb. ground beef
1 egg
2 tablespoons dry bread crumbs
1 teaspoon garlic salt
1/8 teaspoon pepper
1/2 can (6-oz. size) tomato paste
2 tablespoons finely chopped onion
1/2 teaspoon sugar
1/2 teaspoon leaf oregano
1 can (4 oz.) mushroom pieces, drained
1/2 cup (2 ozs.) shredded Mozzarella cheese

1. Combine ground beef, egg, bread crumbs, garlic salt and pepper; mix well. Form into 4 or 5 patties, about 3 inches in diameter. Flatten center of each patty; form a 1/2 inch rim around edges. Arrange on roasting rack in shallow baking dish or on bacon rack.

2. Combine tomato paste, onion, sugar and oregano. Spoon mixture evenly into each patty, spreading to raised edges. Top with mushrooms and cheese.

3. MICROWAVE (high), uncovered, 7 1/2 to 8 1/2 minutes (11 to 13) or until desired doneness, rotating dish once.

4 to 5 Servings

TIPS • Chopped green pepper or sliced pepperoni can be substituted for mushrooms.

• If omitting the use of a roasting rack, use lean ground beef and arrange patties in shallow glass baking dish.

Allow about 6 minutes per pound when cooking meat patties. Since this time is too short for much extra browning, an onion topping is added to the cooked patties.

PARMESAN PATTIES

1 medium onion, sliced
1 tablespoon butter or margarine
1/4 cup sour cream
1/4 teaspoon seasoned salt

Patties:
1 lb. ground beef
1/4 cup dry bread crumbs
1/3 cup Parmesan cheese
1/3 cup milk
1/2 teaspoon salt
1/8 teaspoon pepper

1. Combine onion and butter in small glass dish.

2. MICROWAVE (high), uncovered, 4 to 5 minutes (7 to 8) or until onion is tender, stirring once. Stir in sour cream and seasoned salt; set aside.

3. Combine all ingredients for patties; mix well. Form into 4 patties, about 3/4-inch thick. Place on bacon-meat rack or in shallow glass baking dish. Cover with waxed paper.

4. MICROWAVE (high) 6 to 7 minutes (10 to 12) or until desired doneness, rotating dish once. Top each patty with some of onion mixture.

4 Servings

A traditional favorite that your family is sure to enjoy. Meatballs are simple and delicious in the microwave.

SWEDISH MEATBALLS

1 lb. ground beef
½ lb. lean ground pork
1 small onion, chopped
1 egg
⅓ cup dry bread crumbs
½ teaspoon salt
⅛ teaspoon pepper
⅛ teaspoon nutmeg
½ cup milk
1 cup (8 ozs.) sour cream
¼ cup all-purpose flour
1 teaspoon instant beef bouillon
2 teaspoons parsley flakes
1¾ cups water

1. Mix together ground beef, pork, onion, egg, bread crumbs, salt, pepper, nutmeg and milk. Form into about 24 meatballs, 1½ inches in size. Arrange in 2-quart glass casserole. Cover with waxed paper.

2. MICROWAVE (high) 8 to 9 minutes or until set, rearranging once. Drain.

3. Combine remaining ingredients until smooth; pour over meatballs. Cover.

4. MICROWAVE (high) 7 to 8 minutes or until sauce boils and thickens, stirring once.

About 6 Servings

Homemade sausage has become increasingly popular in recent years. This recipe cooks nicely in the microwave using a lower power setting. The sausage can be stored for up to 3 weeks in the refrigerator or 3 months in the freezer.

HOMEMADE SUMMER SAUSAGE

3 lbs. ground beef
1½ teaspoon peppercorns, crushed
1½ teaspoons mustard seed
1½ teaspoons garlic salt
3 teaspoons tender-quick curing salt
1½ teaspoons liquid smoke

1. Combine all ingredients in large bowl. Mix with hands until well combined. Cover tightly and refrigerate 24 hours.

2. Divide meat mixture into thirds; form each into a smooth roll about 12 inches long. Arrange the 3 rolls on microwave roasting rack in 12 x 8-inch glass baking dish or on bacon rack. Cover with paper towels.

3. MICROWAVE (low — 30%) 20 minutes. Rearrange and turn rolls. Cover.

4. MICROWAVE (low — 30%) 20 to 25 minutes or until meat is set (140°). Cool. Wrap tightly and refrigerate or freeze until sliced for serving.

3 Rolls Sausage

TIPS • With Full Power, microwave 5 minutes and rest 10 minutes. Turn and rearrange sausages. Repeat twice (15 minutes total microwave time).
• With Combination Oven, defrost-bake at 250° on broiler rack, uncovered, for 35 to 40 minutes, turning sausages once.

Homemade Summer Sausage.

Thinly sliced beef and vegetables cook beautifully in the microwave. The combination used in this recipe is indeed delicious.

CANTONESE BEEF WITH VEGETABLES

1 lb. boneless round steak, cut ¾-inch thick
1 medium onion
1 clove garlic, minced
⅓ cup soy sauce
1 medium bunch Chinese cabbage
1 pint (8 ozs.) fresh mushrooms
1 can (8 oz.) water chestnuts, drained
1 package (6 oz.) frozen pea pods
3 tablespoons sliced pimiento
1 cup water
¼ cup cornstarch
1 tablespoon instant beef bouillon
½ teaspoon sugar
Cooked rice

1. Cut steak into strips that will fit feed tube of processor. Partially freeze steak, about 1 hour, until meat becomes firm, but not hard. Insert slicing blade into food processor bowl. Slice meat, using pusher to force through blade. Add onion to feed tube and force through slicing blade. Combine meat, onion, garlic and soy sauce in 3-quart glass casserole. Cover with casserole lid.

2. MICROWAVE (high) 7 to 8 minutes (9 to 10) or until meat is no longer pink, stirring twice. Reinsert slicing blade into food processor. Slice Chinese cabbage, using pusher to force through blade. Repeat with mushrooms and water chestnuts. Add to meat mixture. Cover.

3. MICROWAVE (high) 4 minutes (3 to 5). Stir and add pea pods and pimiento. Cover.

4. MICROWAVE (high) 8 to 9 minutes (11 to 12) or until vegetables are desired doneness, stirring twice.

5. Combine water, cornstarch, bouillon and sugar in 4-cup glass measure. Stir in juices from meat.

6. MICROWAVE (high), uncovered, 6 to 7 minutes (9 to 10) or until mixture boils and thickens, stirring twice. Stir into meat mixture. Serve with rice.

5 to 6 Servings

TIP • If you don't have a food processor, thinly slice partially frozen steak and the vegetables.

In this Oriental-style recipe, the sauce does not come to a boil before the other ingredients are cooked so we cook it separately in step 5. This way, the preparation is faster and we do not overcook and toughen the meat.

BEEF STRIPS WITH SNOW PEAS AND TOMATOES

1 small onion, sliced
1 tablespoon water
1-lb. flank steak, thin-sliced across grain
1 pint (8 ozs.) fresh mushrooms, sliced
1 clove garlic, minced
1 teaspoon sugar
½ teaspoon instant beef bouillon
1½ tablespoons cornstarch
3 tablespoons soy sauce
1 package (6 oz.) frozen pea pods (snow peas)
1 pint (2 cups) cherry tomatoes

1. MICROWAVE (high) onion and water in covered 1½-quart glass casserole 3 minutes. Add meat, mushrooms, garlic, sugar, bouillon, cornstarch and soy sauce; mix lightly. Cover with paper towel.

2. MICROWAVE (high) 8 to 10 minutes or until meat is just about done, stirring twice. Add pea pods. Cover with paper towel.

3. MICROWAVE (high) 2 minutes. Add tomatoes; stir lightly to mix.

4. MICROWAVE (high), uncovered, 1½ to 2 minutes or until heated. Drain juices into glass cup or dish.

5. MICROWAVE (high) sauce, uncovered, 1½ to 2 minutes or until mixture boils and thickens, stirring twice. Pour over beef mixture.

6 Servings, about 195 calories each

TIP • Fresh snow peas can be substituted for frozen.

Chops are small so cook more quickly and require only one power setting.

BARBECUED PORK CHOPS

5 to 6 pork chops (1½ to 2 lbs.)
1 small onion, sliced
½ lemon, sliced
¾ cup barbecue sauce
½ teaspoon salt
Dash pepper
1 clove garlic, minced

1. Arrange chops in 12 x 8-inch glass baking dish. Top each with a few onion slices and a lemon slice. Combine remaining ingredients; pour over chops. Cover with waxed paper.

2. MICROWAVE (medium-high — 70%) 30 to 35 minutes or until tender, rotating dish once.

5 to 6 Servings

TIP • With Full Power, microwave 15 minutes. Rearrange chops and allow to stand 5 minutes. Microwave 5 to 10 minutes or until tender.

Barbecued Pork Chops.

Once a meat such as pork is hot, the cooking should be slowed to simmer by using a lower power or else using standing times along with a full power setting.

SWEET 'N SOUR PORK CHOPS

4 pork chops, cut ½-inch thick (1½ lbs.)
½ teaspoon salt
⅛ teaspoon pepper
1 medium onion, chopped
⅓ cup packed brown sugar
1 can (15¼ oz.) chunk pineapple
¼ cup vinegar
2 tablespoons cornstarch
1 tablespoon soy sauce
1 medium green pepper, cut into strips

1. Brown chops on both sides over medium-high heat in 2-quart pyroceramic skillet. Mix salt, pepper, onion, brown sugar, syrup from pineapple, vinegar, cornstarch and soy sauce. Pour over chops. Cover with skillet lid.

2. MICROWAVE (high) 5 to 6 minutes or until mixture boils.

3. MICROWAVE (medium — 50%) 20 to 25 minutes or until chops are tender. Stir in pineapple and green pepper. Cover.

4. MICROWAVE (medium — 50%) 6 to 8 minutes or until green pepper is tender.

4 Servings

TIPS • A microwave browning skillet can be used for browning chops in step 1. Preheat skillet by microwaving with full power 5 minutes; add chops. Microwave with full power 2 minutes; turn chops. Microwave with full power 3 minutes. Continue with step 1.

• With Full Power, microwave in step 3 for 8 minutes, let stand 5 minutes and repeat once. In step 4, microwave for 5 to 6 minutes.

• With Combination Oven, brown chops as directed. Microwave in step 2 for 6 minutes, in step 3 microwave for 10 minutes, let stand 5 minutes and then microwave 10 minutes. In step 4, microwave for 6 to 7 minutes or until tender.

Pork ribs become tender and remain moist when cooked in a simmer pot with a lower power setting.

RIBS AND KRAUT

1 can (32 oz.) sauerkraut, drained
1 medium apple, chopped
1 clove garlic, minced
2 tablespoons brown sugar
3 lbs. country-style ribs
1 small onion, sliced
¾ teaspoon salt
⅛ teaspoon pepper

1. Combine sauerkraut, apple, garlic and brown sugar in presoaked 3 to 4-quart simmer pot. Arrange ribs and onion slices on sauerkraut. Sprinkle with salt and pepper. Cover with simmer pot lid.

2. MICROWAVE (high) 15 minutes.

3. MICROWAVE (low — 30%) 60 to 70 minutes or until meat is tender, rearranging ribs halfway through cooking time.

About 6 Servings

TIPS • With Full Power, microwave in step 3 for 30 to 40 minutes, rearranging 3 times.

• With Combination Oven, microwave-bake at 325° for about 1 hour, rearranging ribs once.

Ribs and Kraut.

Pork is normally quite tender, but it does require enough cooking to become fork-tender without drying out. The sauce is added after partial cooking.

BARBECUED COUNTRY-STYLE RIBS

- **3 to 3½ lbs. country-style ribs**
- **1 can (15 oz.) tomato sauce**
- **⅓ cup packed brown sugar**
- **⅓ cup vinegar**
- **1 tablespoon prepared horseradish**
- **1 tablespoon Worcestershire sauce**
- **1 clove garlic, minced**

1. Cut meat into single-rib pieces. Arrange in 12 x 8-inch glass baking dish with larger pieces toward ends of dish, smaller pieces in center. Cover with waxed paper.
2. MICROWAVE (high) 15 to 17 minutes or until ribs are no longer pink, turning ribs over and rearranging once. Drain fat.
3. Combine remaining ingredients; brush over ribs using all of sauce. Cover with waxed paper.
4. MICROWAVE (high) 10 to 12 minutes or until done. Let stand 5 to 10 minutes before serving.

About 6 Servings

Cheese soup and caraway make the distinctive sauce for these prebrowned pork cubes.

CHEDDAR AND PORK

- **2 lbs. lean pork cubes**
- **1 small onion, sliced**
- **1 clove garlic, minced**
- **1 can (10¾ oz.) condensed Cheddar cheese soup**
- **½ teaspoon salt**
- **½ teaspoon caraway seed**

1. Heat 2-quart pyroceramic casserole or skillet over medium-high heat. Add meat, onion and garlic; brown well, stirring occasionally. Stir in remaining ingredients. Cover with casserole lid.
2. MICROWAVE (low — 30%) 25 to 30 minutes or until tender, stirring once or twice. Serve over rice, noodles or potatoes.

6 to 8 Servings

TIP • With Full Power, use 5-minute microwave and 10-minute standing times for a total of about 30 minutes.

Breaded meats retain their moistness and brown nicely on a browner.

BREADED PORK CUTLETS

- **½ cup soda cracker crumbs (about 14 crackers)**
- **1 teaspoon parsley flakes**
- **½ teaspoon salt**
- **⅛ teaspoon pepper**
- **1 lb. boneless pork cutlets, cut ½-inch thick**
- **3 tablespoons flour**
- **1 egg, beaten**
- **1 tablespoon butter or margarine**
- **1 small onion, sliced, if desired**

1. Combine cracker crumbs, parsley, salt and pepper on waxed paper or plate. Coat pork with flour. Dip cutlets in egg and then roll in cracker crumb mixture.
2. MICROWAVE (high) browner-grill or skillet 7 to 8 minutes. Divide butter into one pat per cutlet; place a butter piece on each. Place meat on hot browner, buttered-side-down.
3. MICROWAVE (high), uncovered, 1 to 1½ minutes or until lightly browned; turn cutlets over and top with onion slices.
4. MICROWAVE (high), uncovered, 10 to 12 minutes or until meat is tender.

4 to 5 Servings

Breaded Pork Cutlets.

Usually roasts are cooked loosely covered so the surface crusts and browns. However, this roast is cooked covered because of the added vegetables.

CHEESY PORK ROAST SUPPER

3½ to 4-lb. pork roast
5 potatoes, peeled and halved
8 carrots, scrapped and halved
1 small onion, sliced
1 clove garlic, minced
1 can (10¾ oz.) condensed Cheddar cheese soup
½ teaspoon salt
½ teaspoon caraway seed

1. Place roast fat-side-down in 3-quart glass casserole. Add potatoes, carrots, onion and garlic. Cover with casserole lid.

2. MICROWAVE (high) 20 minutes. Turn meat fat-side-up; rearrange vegetables around meat. Combine soup, salt and caraway seed; spoon over meat and vegetables. Cover.

3. MICROWAVE (medium-high — 70%) 30 to 40 minutes or until thermometer inserted in meat registers 170°.

6 to 8 Servings

TIP • With Full Power, microwave in step 3 for 20 minutes with one or two 10-minute standing times during the cooking.

Pork tenderloin is delicious barbecued. When it is started in the microwave oven, only minimal watching and turning are necessary on the grill.

PINEAPPLE-GLAZED PORK TENDERLOINS

1 can (8¼ oz.) sliced pineapple
¼ cup packed brown sugar
1 teaspoon cornstarch
1 teaspoon dry mustard
⅛ teaspoon ground cloves
2 tablespoons vinegar
2 pork tenderloins (about ¾ lb. each)

1. Drain juice from pineapple into glass cup or dish; set aside pineapple. Combine remaining ingredients except pork with pineapple juice in glass dish. Blend until smooth.

2. MICROWAVE (high), uncovered, 1 to 1½ minutes or until mixture boils.

3. Place tenderloins in 12 x 8-inch glass baking dish. Brush with some of the sauce. Cover with waxed paper.

4. MICROWAVE (high) 7 to 9 minutes (about 5 minutes per lb.) or until just about cooked, turning tenderloins once and brushing with additional sauce.

5. BARBECUE about 4 inches above hot coals 15 to 20 minutes or until nicely browned, turning occasionally and brushing with additional sauce. Place pineapple slices on grill during last few minutes. Slice tenderloin across grain; serve with any remaining sauce.

4 to 5 Servings

Full power cooking gives better results than lower power with this dish which combines pork chops and sauerkraut. Chops will tend to be tough if not cooked long enough, and the lower power only extends the cooking time required.

PORK CHOPS 'N KRAUT

3 cups (about 26 ozs.) drained sauerkraut
3 tablespoons brown sugar
1 small onion, chopped
5 to 6 pork chops, cut ½-inch thick
1 can (10¾ oz.) condensed cream of chicken soup

1. Spread sauerkraut in bottom of 12 x 8-inch glass baking dish. Sprinkle with brown sugar and onion. Arrange chops on sauerkraut with larger edges toward sides of dish. Spoon soup over chops. Cover with waxed paper.

2. MICROWAVE (high) 25 to 30 minutes or until chops are tender, rotating dish once. Let stand 5 to 10 minutes.

5 to 6 Servings

Favorite Recipes from

The Microwave Times

Chapter 4

Main Dishes

Deep-Dish Pizza, page 65.

Mrs. Kathleen Wallen of Merced, California, sent us this tasty supper dish for adaption to microwave cooking. Leftovers reheat easily . . . one serving requires only 3/4 to 1 minute.

CRAZY CRUST DINNER

Filling:

1 lb. ground beef
1 medium onion, chopped
2 teaspoons chili powder
1 teaspoon salt
1/4 teaspoon Tabasco sauce
1 can (15 oz.) kidney beans, undrained
1 can (6 oz.) tomato paste

Crust:

1/2 cup all-purpose flour
2 tablespoons yellow cornmeal
1 teaspoon baking powder
1/2 teaspoon salt
1/2 cup sour cream
1/4 cup shortening or softened margarine
1 egg

Topping:

1/2 cup chopped lettuce
1/2 cup chopped tomato
1/2 to 1 cup shredded Cheddar cheese

1. Crumble ground beef into 1½-quart glass casserole. Add onion.

2. MICROWAVE (high), uncovered, 5 to 6 minutes or until meat is set, stirring once. Drain. Stir in remaining Filling ingredients. Cover with casserole lid.

3. MICROWAVE (high) 4 to 5 minutes or until hot and bubbly.

4. Combine all ingredients for Crust; stir until blended (batter will be lumpy). Spoon into greased 8 or 9 inch round glass baking dish. Spread mixture thinly over bottom and thickly up sides of dish. Spoon hot meat mixture into center.

5. MICROWAVE (high), uncovered, 7 minutes. Rotate dish. Then, MICROWAVE (medium — 50%) 7 to 9 minutes or until crust is done. Let stand 5 minutes; cut into wedges. Top with lettuce, tomato, and cheese.

5 to 6 Servings

TIP • With Full Power, in step 5, microwave (high) a total of 10 to 11 minutes, rotating dish once.

Enjoy a serving of this Greek-inspired low calorie casserole. Note that you can prepare it with either zucchini or eggplant.

MOUSSAKA

1/2 lb. lean ground beef or lamb
1 small onion, chopped
1 can (8 oz.) stewed tomatoes, undrained
1 teaspoon parsley flakes
1 teaspoon salt
1/8 teaspoon pepper
5 cups sliced zucchini (1/2-inch thick)
1/2 cup milk
2 eggs
3 tablespoons Parmesan cheese

1. Crumble ground beef into 1-quart glass casserole; add onion.

2. MICROWAVE (high), uncovered, 3 to 4 minutes (5½) or until meat is set, stirring once. Drain. Stir in tomatoes, parsley, salt and pepper.

3. Layer half of zucchini in 8-inch square glass baking dish. Top with half of meat mixture, another layer of zucchini and remaining meat mixture. Cover with waxed paper.

4. MICROWAVE (high) 15 to 17 minutes (16 to 17) or until zucchini is tender, rotating dish once. Beat together milk and eggs. Pour over zucchini. Sprinkle with cheese. Cover with paper towel.

5. MICROWAVE (medium — 50%) 4 to 5 minutes (3 to 4) or until egg mixture is just about set, rotating dish once. Serve cut into squares.

4 Servings, about 230 calories each

TIPS • With Full Power in step 5, microwave 2 minutes. Let stand 5 minutes and microwave 2 to 3 more minutes.

• Eggplant can be substituted for zucchini. Peel 1 medium eggplant and cut into ½-inch thick slices.

Cook noodles conventionally and then layer with a ground beef-tomato sauce and creamy cheese mixture.

COTTAGE BEEF CASSEROLE

- **2 cups egg noodles, cooked**
- **1 lb. ground beef**
- **1 small onion, chopped**
- **1 clove garlic, minced**
- **1 can (8 oz.) tomato sauce**
- **1 teaspoon salt**
- **1/8 teaspoon pepper**
- **1 cup creamed cottage cheese**
- **1 cup sour cream**
- **3/4 cup shredded Cheddar cheese**

1. Cook noodles as directed on package; drain. Crumble ground beef into 2-quart glass casserole. Add onion and garlic.

2. MICROWAVE (high), uncovered, 5 to 6 minutes or until meat is set. Stir to break meat into pieces; drain. Stir in tomato sauce, salt and pepper. Combine cottage cheese and sour cream.

3. Remove half of meat mixture from casserole. Top meat in casserole with cooked noodles, then the cheese-sour cream mixture. Spoon remaining meat mixture over top, spreading to cover. Cover with waxed paper.

4. MICROWAVE (high) 6 minutes. Then, MICROWAVE (medium — 50%) 5 to 7 minutes or until heated through. Top with Cheedar cheese. Let stand, covered, about 5 minutes to melt cheese.

5 to 6 Servings

TIPS • With Full Power, microwave in step 4 a total of 10 to 12 minutes, rotating dish once.

• With Combination Oven, microwave in step 2 for 8 to 9 minutes. Then, microwave-bake, uncovered, in step 4 at 350° for 12 to 15 minutes.

A ground beef casserole that is a low calorie favorite of Mrs. Beth Reber. Enjoy it freshly prepared or freeze for later use. It reheats beautifully.

HAMBURGER-MACARONI CASSEROLE

- **1 lb. ground beef**
- **1 small onion, chopped**
- **1/4 cup chopped green pepper**
- **1 cup uncooked macaroni**
- **1 can (16 oz.) French-cut green beans, undrained**
- **1/2 can (6-oz. size) tomato paste**
- **2 tablespoons vinegar**
- **1 tablespoon Worcestershire sauce**
- **1 teaspoon salt**
- **1 teaspoon prepared mustard**
- **Dash Tabasco sauce**

1. Crumble ground beef into 2-quart glass casserole. Add onion and green pepper.

2. MICROWAVE (high), uncovered, 5 to 6 minutes (9 to 10) or until meat is set. Stir to break meat into pieces; drain.

3. Stir in remaining ingredients. Cover with casserole lid.

4. MICROWAVE (high) 15 to 20 minutes (20 to 25) or until macaroni is tender, stirring 2 or 3 times.

4 Servings, about 370 calories each

Hamburger-Macaroni Casserole.

Meat, potato and a vegetable are all combined in this easy hot dish. Complete your meal with rolls and a salad.

BEEF AND TATER HOT DISH

1 lb. ground beef
1 can (10¾ oz.) condensed mushroom soup
3 tablespoons dry onion soup mix (about ½ envelope)
1 can (16 oz.) cut green beans, drained
½ can (3-oz. size) French fried onions
1 package (16 oz.) frozen precooked potato puffs

1. Crumble ground beef into 2-quart glass casserole.

2. MICROWAVE (high), uncovered, 5 to 6 minutes or until meat is set. Stir to break meat into pieces; drain.

3. Stir in soups and green beans. Spread evenly in dish. Sprinkle with onions and top with potato puffs. Cover with paper towel.

4. MICROWAVE (high) 12 to 14 minutes or until mixture is hot and bubbly.

4 to 6 Servings

TIP • With Combination Oven, microwave in step 2 for 8 to 9 minutes and in step 4 microwave-bake in 350° oven, uncovered, 15 to 20 minutes.

This simple but tasty hot dish came from a "Times" feature article, "When Kids are Cooks".

CHOW MEIN HOT DISH

1 lb. ground beef
¼ cup chopped onion
⅓ cup chopped celery
1 can (10¾ oz.) condensed mushroom soup
1 can (10¾ oz.) condensed chicken gumbo soup
1 cup uncooked instant rice (minute-type)
⅛ teaspoon pepper
1½ cups chow mein noodles

1. Crumble ground beef into 2-quart glass casserole. Add onion and celery. Cover with casserole lid.

2. MICROWAVE (high) 5 to 6 minutes or until meat is no longer pink, stirring once.

3. Stir in soups, rice and pepper. Cover.

4. MICROWAVE (high) 9 to 10 minutes, or until rice is tender, stirring once. Top with noodles.

5. MICROWAVE (high), uncovered, 2 to 3 minutes or until noodles are hot.

4 to 5 Servings

Fresh bean sprouts add flavor and texture to this popular low calorie casserole. About 200 calories per serving.

BEAN SPROUT CASSEROLE

½ lb. ground beef
1 small onion, chopped
1 clove garlic, minced
⅓ cup chopped green pepper
1 tablespoon cornstarch
1 teaspoon instant beef bouillon
1 teaspoon sugar
½ teaspoon salt
⅛ teaspoon pepper
3 tablespoons soy sauce
½ cup water
¼ cup chopped pimiento
1 can (8 oz.) water chestnuts, drained and sliced
3 cups fresh bean or alfalfa sprouts

1. Crumble ground beef into 1½-quart glass casserole. Add onion, garlic and green pepper.

2. MICROWAVE (high), uncovered, 2½ to 3 minutes (5 to 6) or until meat is no longer pink, stirring once. Drain.

3. Stir in remaining ingredients except sprouts. Cover with casserole lid.

4. MICROWAVE (high) 4 to 5 minutes (8 to 9) or until mixture boils, stirring once. Stir in bean sprouts. Cover.

5. MICROWAVE (high) 4 to 5 minutes (8 to 9) or until sprouts are tender-crisp.

3 to 4 Servings

Here is a favorite ground beef and noodle casserole adapted from a recipe sent by Chris Dorsey of Tuscon, Arizona. It is necessary to thoroughly drain ingredients used in recipes such as this one where the cooking time is brief. Since it is not possible in the cooking process to reduce extra liquid, the beef, tomatoes, noodles and spinach must be free of excess juices before combining.

QUADRELTINA CASSEROLE

½ cup finely chopped carrot
½ cup finely chopped onion
¼ cup butter or margarine
¼ cup cooking oil, if desired
2 cloves garlic, minced
1 lb. lean ground beef
3 cups chopped, peeled fresh or canned tomatoes
1 can (6 oz.) tomato paste
2 teaspoons salt
1½ teaspoons oregano leaves
1 teaspoon basil leaves
½ teaspoon thyme leaves
½ teaspoon Tabasco sauce
2 cups noodles, cooked and drained
1 package (10 oz.) frozen chopped spinach
½ cup Parmesan cheese

1. Combine carrot, onion, butter, oil and garlic in 2 or 2½-quart glass casserole. Cover with casserole lid.

2. MICROWAVE (high) 4 to 5 minutes (8 to 9) or until vegetables are tender-crisp, stirring once. Crumble ground beef into casserole.

3. MICROWAVE (high), uncovered, 5 to 6 minutes (10 to 11) or until no longer pink, stirring once.

4. Cut tomatoes into ¾-inch pieces and add to beef along with tomato paste and seasonings.

5. MICROWAVE (high), uncovered, 14 to 16 minutes (30 to 32) or until mixture is bubbly, stirring once.

6. Cook noodles as directed on package. Rinse and drain well.

7. MICROWAVE (high) the spinach in the package 5 to 6 minutes (11 to 12) or until thawed. Drain well.

8. Stir noodles and spinach into beef mixture. Sprinkle with Parmesan cheese.

9. MICROWAVE (high), uncovered, 9 to 11 minutes (20 to 22) or until heated through.

6 to 8 Servings

TIP • Casserole can be prepared through step 8, but do not add Parmesan cheese. Cover and refrigerate. To heat, microwave (high) 12 to 14 minutes or until hot, stirring 2 or 3 times. Sprinkle with cheese and microwave 1 to 2 minutes.

This pizza-flavored hot dish is an all-time favorite of our staff. Prepare this for a quick family supper.

PIZZA HOT DISH

1 lb. ground beef
1 small onion, chopped
1 clove garlic, minced
1 can (6 oz.) tomato paste
1 can (4 oz.) mushroom pieces, drained
½ to 1 cup (2 to 4 ozs.) chopped pepperoni
½ cup sliced ripe or green olives
⅓ cup chopped green pepper
1 teaspoon salt
¼ teaspoon leaf oregano
⅛ teaspoon pepper
2 cups water
2 cups uncooked noodles
1 cup (4 ozs.) shredded Mozzarella cheese
¼ cup Parmesan cheese

1. Crumble ground beef into 2-quart glass casserole; add onion and garlic.

2. MICROWAVE (high), uncovered, 5 to 6 minutes or until meat is set, stirring once. Drain.

3. Stir remaining ingredients except cheeses into meat mixture. Cover with casserole lid.

4. MICROWAVE (high) 15 to 17 minutes or until noodles are tender, stirring 2 or 3 times. Sprinkle with cheeses.

5. MICROWAVE (high), uncovered, 1 to 1½ minutes or until cheeses are melted.

5 to 6 Servings

These round steak strips are first simmered and then rolled up in tortillas for an enchilada-like dish.

BEEF-E-LADAS

- **1½ lbs. boneless round steak, cut ½-inch thick**
- **1 package (1½ oz.) enchilada sauce mix**
- **1 medium onion, sliced**
- **2 tablespoons flour**
- **1 teaspoon salt**
- **½ teaspoon chili powder**
- **2 cups water**
- **10 to 12 flour tortillas**
- **1 cup (4 ozs.) Monterey Jack cheese**
- **2 cups shredded lettuce**
- **1 tomato, chopped**

1. Cut steak into strips ½-inch wide and 1-inch long. Combine meat and dry sauce mix in 2-quart glass casserole.

2. MICROWAVE (high), uncovered, 5½ to 6½ minutes or until meat is no longer pink, stirring once. Stir in onion, flour, salt, chili powder and water. Cover with casserole lid.

3. MICROWAVE (high) 5 minutes. Then, MICROWAVE (low — 30%) 50 to 60 minutes or until meat is tender, stirring once.

4. Using a slotted spoon, spoon meat into the center of each tortilla. Fold edges over to secure meat inside. Place in 12 x 8-inch glass baking dish. Pour sauce over tortillas. Sprinkle with cheese.

5. MICROWAVE (high), uncovered, 5 to 6 minutes or until bubbly. Garnish with shredded lettuce and chopped tomato.

5 to 6 Servings

TIPS • With Full Power in step 3, use segments of 5 minute microwave and 10 minutes standing time.

• With Combination Oven, microwave in step 2 for 10 to 12 minutes, in step 3, microwave 7 minutes and use microwave-defrost for low power time. In step 5, microwave 10 to 12 minutes.

Beef-E-Ladas.

Mrs. Edward Frowd of Mission Viejo, California, requested help in adapting this layered Mexican casserole. The cheese topping is added the last few minutes since it will become tough and rubbery if overcooked.

MEXICAN CASSEROLE

1½ lbs. ground beef
1 medium onion, chopped
1 can (10¾ oz.) condensed cream of chicken soup
1 can (10 oz.) chopped tomatoes with green chilies
1 can (8 or 10 oz.) enchilada sauce
½ cup sliced ripe olives
2 tablespoons chopped green chilies
1 teaspoon salt
½ teaspoon leaf oregano
⅛ teaspoon pepper
⅛ teaspoon cumin
⅛ teaspoon garlic powder
⅛ teaspoon chili powder
8 to 10 flour tortillas, torn into pieces
2 cups (8 ozs.) shredded Cheddar cheese
1 cup (4 ozs.) shredded Monterey Jack cheese

1. Crumble ground beef into 2-quart glass casserole; add onion.

2. MICROWAVE (high),uncovered, 7 to 8 minutes (10 to 11) or until meat is set, stirring once. Drain. Stir in remaining ingredients except tortillas and cheeses. Cover with casserole lid.

3. MICROWAVE (high) 8 to 10 minutes (12 to 14) or until mixture is hot and bubbly, stirring once. Stir in Cheddar cheese. Layer half of tortilla pieces in 12 x 8-inch glass baking dish. Top with half of meat mixture, remaining tortillas and remaining meat mixture.

4. MICROWAVE (high), uncovered, 7 minutes (10). Sprinkle with Jack cheese.

5. MICROWAVE (high), uncovered, 2 to 3 minutes (4 to 5) or until cheese is melted and mixture is hot.

8 to 10 Servings

TIP • If tortillas are frozen, microwave on paper toweling 1½ to 2 minutes to thaw.

This colorful taco salad variation, pictured on the cover, is from an issue on low calorie dishes. Serve each salad with 2 corn muffins and a wedge of melon for a 525-calorie meal.

TACO SALADS

4 medium tomatoes
3 cups torn lettuce
½ lb. lean ground beef
1 small onion, chopped
3 tablespoons chili sauce
⅛ teaspoon garlic salt
⅛ teaspoon cayenne pepper
Dash pepper
¼ cup shredded Cheddar cheese
⅓ cup coarsley crushed taco chips
3 tablespoons taco sauce

1. Remove stem from each tomato. Place tomato stem-side-down. Cut almost through each tomato to form 6 wedges. Divide lettuce among 4 serving plates. Top with tomato, separating wedges slightly to form cup shape. Set aside.

2. Crumble ground beef into 1-quart glass casserole; add onion.

3. MICROWAVE (high), uncovered, 3 to 3½ minutes (5 to 6) or until meat is set, stirring once. Drain. Stir in chili sauce, garlic salt and peppers. Cover with casserole lid.

4. MICROWAVE (high) 1 to 2 minutes (2 to 3) or until heated through.

5. Spoon meat mixture into center of each tomato. Top with cheese, taco chips and taco sauce. If desired, garnish with sliced olives.

4 Servings, about 245 calories each

This delicious main dish features the popular flavor of lasagna, but with fewer calories.

ZUCCHINI ITALIANO

4 medium zucchini (about 1½ lbs.)
½ lb. extra lean ground beef
1 clove garlic, minced
1 teaspoon Italian seasoning
1 teaspoon salt
1 can (8 oz.) tomato sauce
¾ cup low-calorie cottage cheese
1 egg
½ cup (2 ozs.) shredded Mozzarella cheese

1. Cut zucchini in half lengthwise. Using a grapefruit spoon, scoop out interior of zucchini leaving a ¼-inch shell. Turn shells cut-side-down in 12 x 8-inch glass baking dish. Cover with waxed paper.

2. MICROWAVE (high) 5 minutes or until partially cooked. Let stand covered. Finely chop zucchini removed from centers.

3. Crumble beef into 1-quart glass casserole.

4. MICROWAVE (high), uncovered, about 3 minutes or until meat is set, stirring once. Drain. Stir in garlic, Italian seasoning, salt, tomato sauce and chopped zucchini. Cover with casserole lid.

5. MICROWAVE (high) 5 minutes.

6. Combine cottage cheese and egg. Drain excess liquid from zucchini shells. Turn each shell cut-side-up in baking dish. Fill centers with cottage cheese mixture. Spoon meat mixture over zucchini. Cover with waxed paper.

7. MICROWAVE (high) 6 to 10 minutes or until heated through and zucchini shells are tender-crisp. Sprinkle with cheese.

8. MICROWAVE (high), uncovered, 2 to 2½ minutes or until cheese is melted.

4 Servings, about 195 calories each

TIP • To Make Ahead, prepare through step 6. Complete when ready to serve.

Zucchini replaces the traditional noodles in this popular dish. For an "under 500 calorie meal", just add a roll and green salad.

ZUCCHINI LASAGNA

6 cups sliced zucchini
½ lb. ground beef
1 can (8 oz.) tomato sauce
1 teaspoon Italian seasoning
1 teaspoon salt
⅛ teaspoon garlic powder
1 cup dry curd cottage cheese
1 egg
¼ cup dry bread crumbs
¾ cup (6 ozs.) shredded Mozzarella cheese

1. Place zucchini in 8-inch square glass baking dish; cover with waxed paper.

2. MICROWAVE (high) 7 to 8 minutes (10 to 12) or until tender-crisp. Drain and set aside.

3. Crumble ground beef into 1-quart glass casserole.

4. MICROWAVE (high), uncovered, 2 to 3 minutes (3 to 4) or until meat is set. Stir to break meat into pieces; drain. Stir in tomato sauce, Italian seasoning, salt and garlic powder. Combine cottage cheese and egg.

5. Remove half of zucchini from baking dish. Arrange remainder evenly in baking dish. Sprinkle with half of bread crumbs. Spoon on half of meat mixture and cottage cheese mixture; spread evenly. Sprinkle with half of Mozzarella cheese. Repeat with remaining zucchini, bread crumbs, meat and cottage cheese. Cover with waxed paper.

6. MICROWAVE (high) 10 to 12 minutes (13 to 15) or until heated in center. Sprinkle with remaining Mozzarella cheese.

7. MICROWAVE (high), uncovered, 2 to 3 minutes (2½ to 3½) or until cheese is melted.

4 Servings, about 300 calories each

Even those not fond of spinach will enjoy this recipe for lasagna. It doesn't contain meat, but most people are not even aware of that because of the hearty flavor. Notice in the Tips that it can be prepared ahead, too.

POPEYE'S LASAGNA

6 to 8 lasagna noodles
2 tablespoons butter or margarine
1 medium onion, chopped
1 clove garlic, minced
1 can (8 oz.) tomato sauce
1 can (6 oz.) tomato paste
¾ cup water
1 tablespoon instant beef bouillon
1 teaspoon sugar
½ teaspoon basil leaves
½ teaspoon leaf oregano
⅛ teaspoon pepper
12 ozs. fresh spinach leaves (about 9 cups)
2 cups creamed cottage cheese
2 eggs
3 cups (12 ozs.) shredded Mozzarella cheese
⅓ cup Parmesan cheese

1. Cook noodles as directed on package. Drain; cool in cold water. Combine butter, onion and garlic in 1½-quart glass casserole.

2. MICROWAVE (high), uncovered, 3 to 3½ minutes or until tender, stirring once. Stir in tomato sauce and paste, water, bouillon, sugar, basil, oregano and pepper. Cover with casserole lid.

3. MICROWAVE (high) 8 to 9 minutes or until mixture boils several minutes, stirring once. Set aside.

4. Wash spinach and remove large stems. Place in 2-quart glass cassrole. Cover with plastic wrap.

5. MICROWAVE (high) 3½ to 4 minutes or until steaming hot. Drain well by pressing leaves to drain juices. Chop coarsley by using knife or kitchen shears. Stir in cottage cheese and eggs.

6. To assemble, layer half of noodles in bottom of 12 x 8-inch glass baking dish. Top with half of sauce mixture, all of spinach mixture, 2 cups Mozzarella cheese and the remaining noodles and sauce mixture. Cover with waxed paper.

7. MICROWAVE (high) 5 minutes. Then, MICROWAVE (medium-high — 70%) 12 to 15 minutes or until heated in center (150 to 160°). Remove waxed paper. Sprinkle with remaining cheese.

8. MICROWAVE (high), uncovered, 3 to 4 minutes or until cheese is melted. Let stand 5 to 10 minutes before cutting and serving.

8 Servings, about 380 calories each

TIPS • With Full Power, microwave in step 7 for 12 minutes. Then let stand 5 minutes, microwave 5 minutes, stand 3 minutes and microwave 3 minutes.

• Frozen chopped spinach can be substituted for fresh. Use a 10-oz. package and microwave in package 3½ to 4½ minutes or until thawed. Omit cooking in step 5.

• Lasagna can be assembled ahead and then refrigerated. To heat, increase time in step 7 to 10 minutes on high and 15 to 17 minutes on medium-high.

• With Combination Oven, microwave in step 2 for 4 to 5 minutes, step 3 for 13 to 15 minutes and in step 5 for 8 to 10 minutes. Then, for step 7, microwave-bake at 350°, uncovered, for 12 to 15 minutes. Add cheeses and continue baking 5 minutes.

Popeye's Lasagna.

Both calorie and cholesterol-watchers will want to try this recipe. Our tasters found the flavor very appealing and it may well become one of your favorites, too. Serve it with ½ cup cooked noodles or a baked potato and a tossed salad for an "under 500 calorie" meal.

HAMBURGER STROGANOFF

1 lb. ground beef
1 pint (8 ozs.) fresh mushrooms, sliced
1 medium onion, chopped
3 tablespoons flour
2 teaspoons instant beef bouillon
½ teaspoon salt
½ teaspoon prepared mustard
⅛ teaspoon pepper
1 cup water
½ cup buttermilk or plain yogurt
2 teaspoons parsley flakes

1. Crumble ground beef into 1½-quart glass casserole. Add mushrooms and onion.

2. MICROWAVE (high), uncovered, 7 to 8 minutes (11 to 12) or until meat is set, stirring twice. Drain. Stir in flour, bouillon, salt, mustard, pepper and water. Cover with casserole lid.

3. MICROWAVE (high) 7 minutes (10 to 11), stirring once. Stir in buttermilk and parsley. Cover.

4. MICROWAVE (high) 2 to 3 minutes (3 to 4) or until hot.

4 Servings, about 260 calories each

Hamburger Stroganoff.

Use ground beef for an economical stroganoff-flavored hot dish. It's super quick and easy since the noodles require no precooking.

BEEF-NOODLE STROGANOFF

1 lb. ground beef
1 small onion, chopped
½ cup finely chopped celery
1 can (10½ oz.) condensed beef broth
¼ cup water
1 tablespoon dried parsley flakes
¼ teaspoon salt
¼ teaspoon pepper
1 can (4 oz.) mushroom pieces, undrained
4 cups uncooked noodles (about 5 oz.)
1 cup (8 ozs.) sour cream
1 teaspoon prepared mustard

1. Crumble ground beef into 2-quart glass casserole. Add onion and celery.

2. MICROWAVE (high), uncovered, 5 to 6 minutes or until meat is set. Stir to break meat into pieces; drain fat.

3. Stir in broth, water, parsley, salt, pepper, mushrooms and noodles. Cover with casserole lid.

4. MICROWAVE (high) 12 to 14 minutes or until noodles are just about tender, stirring 2 or 3 times. Stir in sour cream and mustard. Cover.

5. MICROWAVE (high) about 2 minutes or until heated through.

5 Servings

TIP • The stirring in step 4 is important to assure that all noodles become tender by being in the liquid during part of the cooking time.

Fork-tender pork chops require long, slow simmering. Here they simmer with the rice which also requires about the same time to become tender.

SPANISH RICE WITH CHOPS

4 pork chops, cut ⅝-inch thick
1 tablespoon cooking oil
¼ cup chopped onion
⅓ cup chopped green pepper
1 teaspoon salt
½ teaspoon chili powder
⅛ teaspoon pepper
1 cup uncooked long or medium-grain rice
1 can (16 oz.) tomatoes, undrained
2 cups water

1. Heat oil in 2-quart pyroceramic skillet over medium-high heat. Add chops and brown on both sides. Add remaining ingredients; cover with casserole lid.

2. MICROWAVE (high) 15 minutes. Then, MICROWAVE (low — 30%) 40 to 50 minutes or until chops are tender, rearranging once.

4 Servings

TIPS • With Full Power, microwave 15 minutes. Then use 10 minute microwave and 10 minute standing times for about 40 minutes.

• With Combination Oven, microwave 45 to 55 minutes, omitting standing times.

Mrs. Charles Cook of Manhattan Beach, California, used her leftover Easter ham for this recipe she prepares in the fluted ring dish. It is elegant in appearance and would be a delicous entrée for a brunch or luncheon.

HAM RING WITH CREAMED EGGS

1 cup chopped celery
½ cup chopped onion
1 tablespoon water
3 cups ground cooked ham (about 1½ lbs.)
2 cups cooked rice
2 eggs, slightly beaten
1 can (10¾ oz.) condensed mushroom soup (reserve half for sauce)
Dash red (Cayenne) pepper
½ cup mayonnaise or salad dressing

Creamed Eggs:
¼ cup butter or margarine
¼ cup all-purpose flour
¼ teaspoon salt
1 tablespoon prepared mustard
2 cups milk
Remaining mushroom soup
1 cup shredded Cheddar cheese
5 hard-cooked eggs, shelled and sliced
Pimiento strips, if desired

1. Combine celery, onion and water in large glass mixing bowl. Cover with plastic wrap.

2. MICROWAVE (high) 3 to 3½ minutes or until just about tender. Mix in ham, rice, eggs, soup (half a can), pepper and mayonnaise. Spoon into lightly greased 5-cup fluted ring dish, pressing mixture into dish. Cover with waxed paper.

3. MICROWAVE (high) 14 to 16 minutes or until set, rotating dish 3 or 4 times. Let stand covered.

4. MICROWAVE (high) butter for Creamed Eggs in 1½-quart glass casserole. Stir in flour, salt and mustard. Blend in milk and soup. Cover with casserole lid.

5. MICROWAVE (high) 7 to 9 minutes or until mixture boils and thickens, stirring twice during last half of cooking time. Stir in cheese and eggs. Cover.

6. MICROWAVE (high) 1 to 2 minutes or until heated.

7. Unmold ham ring onto serving plate. Fill center with creamed eggs; serve remaining sauce in bowl. Garnish with pimiento.

About 8 Servings

Fresh asparagus spears are wrapped in ham slices and then smothered with a flavorful egg sauce. An ideal recipe for a brunch or luncheon, or even a summer supper.

ASPARAGUS IN HAM BLANKETS

2 tablespoons butter or margarine
1 tablespoon flour
1 teaspoon instant chicken bouillon
1 teaspoon parsley flakes
¼ teaspoon dry mustard
Dash pepper
1 cup half & half cream
¼ cup Parmesan cheese
3 hard-cooked eggs, chopped
1 lb. fresh asparagus
8 thin slices cooked ham

1. MICROWAVE (high) butter in 4-cup glass measure ½ to 1 minute (1 to 2) or until melted. Stir in flour, bouillon, parsley, mustard and pepper. Stir in cream.

2. MICROWAVE (high), uncovered, 3 to 4 minutes (5 to 7) or until mixture boils, stirring occasionally during last half of cooking time. Stir in Parmesan cheese and eggs.

3. Wash and trim woody portion from asparagus. Place spears in 10 x 6-inch glass loaf dish; cover with plastic wrap.

4. MICROWAVE (high) 4½ to 5½ minutes (9 to 11) or until tender, rearranging once. Uncover and cool slightly.

5. Divide asparagus spears among ham slices. Roll up each; secure with toothpick if necessary. Place on serving plate.

6. MICROWAVE (high), uncovered, 2 to 3 minutes (4 to 5) or until ham is heated. Top with egg sauce.

7. MICROWAVE (high), uncovered, 1 to 2 minutes (2 to 3) or until heated. Serve on toasted English muffins or rice.

8 Servings, about 240 calories each

TIP • Frozen asparagus spears can be substituted for fresh. Use a 10-oz. package. Microwave in package 6 to 7 minutes for step 4.

Extra ham and chicken will never taste like "leftovers" when combined in a dish like this that can be enjoyed now or frozen for a later date.

CURRIED CHICKEN AND HAM

1 cup sliced fresh or canned mushrooms
1 small onion, chopped
¼ cup chopped green pepper
1½ teaspoons curry powder
⅓ cup butter or margarine
⅓ cup all-purpose flour
½ teaspoon salt
1 cup chicken broth or bouillon
1 cup milk
2 cups cubed, cooked chicken or turkey
2 cups cubed, cooked ham
½ cup slivered almonds or shredded coconut, if desired

1. Combine mushrooms, onion, green pepper, curry powder and butter in 1½-quart glass casserole.

2. MICROWAVE (high), uncovered, 3 to 4 minutes (6 to 7) or until onion is transparent, stirring once. Stir in flour, salt, broth and milk.

3. MICROWAVE (high), uncovered, 7 to 8 minutes (14 to 15) or until mixture boils and thickens, stirring once or twice. Stir in chicken and ham.

4. MICROWAVE (high), uncovered, 3 to 4 minutes (6 to 7) or until heated through. Sprinkle with almonds or coconut. Serve with rice.

About 5 Servings

TIP • To thaw a 1-cup serving, microwave (high) 3½ to 4½ minutes (8 to 9) or until hot, rearranging contents once.

Chicken, asparagus and cauliflower combine for a flavorful, colorful combination.

CHICKEN-ASPARAGUS ORIENTAL

1 lb. boned and skinned chicken breasts, cut into bite-sized pieces
3 tablespoons soy sauce
2 tablespoons dry sherry
1 medium head cauliflower
1 package (8 oz.) frozen cut asparagus
1 can (8½ oz.) water chestnuts, drained and sliced
1 tablespoon cornstarch
1 teaspoon instant chicken bouillon
½ teaspoon salt
¼ cup water

1. Combine chicken, soy sauce and sherry in 2-quart glass casserole. Mix to coat evenly. Cover with casserole lid.

2. MICROWAVE (high) 5 minutes. Separate cauliflower into flowerettes; cut into ¼-inch slices. Add cauliflower, asparagus and water chestnuts to chicken mixture. Cover.

3. MICROWAVE (high) 10 to 12 minutes or until cauliflower is tender-crisp, stirring once. Combine remaining ingredients in 2-cup glass measure. Stir in juices from chicken.

4. MICROWAVE (high), uncovered, 1½ to 2 minutes or until mixture boils, stirring once. Pour over chicken mixture.

6 Servings, about 190 calories each

TIP • Fresh asparagus can be substituted for frozen.

An ideal one-dish entrée for a company buffet or luncheon.

SUPERB CHICKEN AND RICE

1 cup uncooked long or medium-grain rice
2 cups water
1 teaspoon salt
2½ to 3 cups cubed, cooked chicken
1 can (4 oz.) mushroom pieces, undrained
1 can (8 oz.) water chestnuts, drained and sliced
1 can (10¾ oz.) condensed cream of chicken soup
1 can (10¾ oz.) condensed mushroom soup
¼ cup dry sherry or water
2 tablespoons chopped pimiento
⅛ teaspoon pepper
2 cans (15 ozs. each) cut asparagus, drained

1. Combine rice, water and salt in 1½-quart glass casserole. Cover with casserole lid.

2. MICROWAVE (high) 6 to 7 minutes or until mixture boils. Let stand 10 minutes. Cover.

3. MICROWAVE (high) 4 to 5 minutes. Let stand 5 minutes. Fluff with fork. Spread in 12 x 8-inch glass baking dish.

4. Combine chicken, mushrooms, water chestnuts, soups, sherry, pimiento and pepper. Top rice with asparagus. Then, spoon chicken mixture onto asparagus, spreading evenly. Cover with waxed paper.

5. MICROWAVE (high) 10 to 12 minutes or until heated through, rotating dish once.

About 6 Servings

Chow Mein is always a favorite. Vegetables cook to a tender-crispness in the microwave.

CHICKEN CHOW MEIN

1 cup chopped celery
1 medium onion, chopped
1 green pepper, cut into thin strips
2 tablespoons butter or margarine
1 can (16 oz.) bean sprouts, drained
1 can (4 oz.) mushroom pieces, undrained
2 tablespoons chopped pimiento
2 cups cubed, cooked chicken
1¾ cups water
2 teaspoons instant chicken bouillon
3 tablespoons cornstarch
3 tablespoons soy sauce

1. Combine celery, onion, green pepper and butter in 2-quart glass casserole. Cover with casserole lid.

2. MICROWAVE (high) 9 to 10 minutes or until vegetables are tender-crisp. Add bean sprouts, mushrooms, pimiento and chicken; set aside.

3. Combine water, bouillon, cornstarch and soy sauce in 4-cup glass measure; mix well.

4. MICROWAVE (high), uncovered, 6 to 7 minutes or until mixture boils and thickens, stirring once or twice during last half of cooking time. Add to vegetables. Cover.

5. MICROWAVE (high) 5 to 7 minutes or until heated, stirring once. Serve with Chinese noodles or cooked rice.

5 to 6 Servings

Cottage cheese adds creaminess and nutritional value to this family favorite.

CHICKEN-NOODLE CASSEROLE

1 small onion, chopped
½ cup chopped celery
¼ cup butter or margarine
¼ cup all-purpose flour
1 teaspoon salt
¾ teaspoon poultry seasoning
⅛ teaspoon pepper
½ cup milk
3 cups (24 ozs.) small curd cottage cheese
3 cups cooked noodles (about 2½ cups uncooked)
3 cups cubed, cooked chicken or turkey
1 package (10 oz.) frozen peas
⅓ cup corn flake crumbs, if desired

1. Combine onion, celery and butter in 2½ or 3-quart glass casserole. Cover with casserole lid.

2. MICROWAVE (high) 5 to 6 minutes or until tender.

3. Blend in flour, salt, poultry seasoning and pepper. Stir in milk. Mix in remaining ingredients except corn flake crumbs. Cover.

4. MICROWAVE (high) 20 to 25 minutes or until mixture is hot and bubbly, stirring once or twice. Sprinkle with crumbs.

About 6 Servings

TIP • For 3 cups cooked chicken, microwave about 2 lbs. chicken pieces in covered dish for 10 to 12 minutes.

This recipe from Mrs. J. A. Glatthaar of West Chester, Ohio, is perfect for those meal occasions for two. Since rice boils over easily, a standing time is used to complete the cooking.

CHICKEN PILAF FOR TWO

1 tablespoon butter or margarine
1 to 1¼ lbs. chicken pieces (legs or thighs)
⅓ cup long or medium-grain rice
2 to 4 tablespoons chopped onion
1 teaspoon instant chicken bouillon
¼ teaspoon salt
⅔ cup water

1. Melt butter in 1½-quart pyroceramic skillet over medium-high heat. Add chicken pieces and brown on all sides. Remove chicken to plate (or use the overturned lid). Stir rice, onion, bouillon, salt and water into skillet. Top with chicken pieces, skin-side-up. Cover with skillet lid.

2. MICROWAVE (high) 2 to 3 minutes or until mixture boils. Let stand 5 minutes. Then, MICROWAVE (high) 10 to 12 minutes or until rice is tender and chicken is done. Let stand 5 minutes.

2 Servings

TIPS • If omitting the prebrowning in step 1, combine rice mixture in casserole. Top with chicken. Sprinkle chicken with paprika. Increase first microwave time in step 2 to 5 to 6 minutes. Continue as directed.

• With Combination Oven, microwave in step 2 for 5 to 6 minutes. Let stand 5 minutes. Then, microwave 10 to 12 minutes.

Leftover turkey can be transformed into a delectable combination. Served with rice and a tossed salad, this recipe makes an attractive and easy dinner for any microwaver.

TURKEY-GREEN BEAN BAKE

2 packages (10 ozs. each) frozen French-cut green beans
1½ lbs. sliced turkey (6 servings)
⅓ cup butter or margarine
1 small onion, chopped
1 cup sliced fresh mushrooms
⅓ cup all-purpose flour
½ teaspoon salt
½ teaspoon leaf thyme
1 can (13¾ oz.) chicken broth
2 tablespoons dry sherry, if desired
2 tablespoons butter or margarine
¼ cup slivered almonds
1 tablespoon parsley flakes
½ cup dry bread crumbs

1. MICROWAVE (high) beans in paper packages 10 to 12 minutes (14 to 15) or until tender. Drain.

2. Arrange turkey slices in 12 x 8-inch glass baking dish. Top with beans; set aside.

3. Combine ⅓ cup butter, the onion and mushrooms in 4-cup glass measure.

4. MICROWAVE (high), uncovered, 3 to 4 minutes (4 to 5) or until onion is partially cooked. Blend in flour, salt, thyme and broth.

5. MICROWAVE (high), uncovered, 3½ to 4 minutes (6 to 7) or until mixture boils and thickens, stirring once. Stir in sherry. Pour mixture over beans.

6. Combine 2 tablespoons butter and the almonds in 2-cup glass measure.

7. MICROWAVE (high), uncovered, 3 to 4 minutes (6 to 7) or until almonds are toasted, stirring once. Stir in parsley and bread crumbs. Sprinkle over turkey mixture. Cover with paper towel.

8. MICROWAVE (high) 7 to 9 minutes (11 to 12) or until heated through.

About 6 Servings

TIPS • This casserole can be prepared ahead through step 5 and the topping can be prepared as directed in steps 6 and 7. To serve, sprinkle topping on casserole and microwave as directed if at room temperature, or 10 to 12 minutes if mixture has been refrigerated.

• If you have both ham and turkey on hand, combine the two for this recipe. Alternate slices in the baking dish and reduce salt in sauce to ¼ teaspoon.

• Frozen chopped broccoli or cut asparagus can be substituted for the beans.

Here's a recipe that is perfect for disguising poultry leftovers.

TURKEY AND DRESSING BAKE

¼ cup slivered almonds
1 tablespoon butter or margarine
⅓ cup dry bread crumbs
1 teaspoon dried parsley
½ cup chopped celery
1 medium onion, chopped
¼ cup butter or margarine
4 cups (7-oz. pkg.) cubed herb-seasoned stuffing mix
1 can (4 oz.) mushroom pieces, drained
1 tablespoon dried parsley
3 to 4 cups cubed, cooked turkey or chicken
1 can (10¾ oz.) condensed mushroom soup
1 cup milk
2 eggs

1. MICROWAVE (high) almonds and butter in uncovered small glass dish 2 to 3 minutes or until toasted. Stir in bread crumbs and parsley; set aside.

2. Combine celery, onion and butter in 1-quart glass casserole.

3. MICROWAVE (high), uncovered, 4 to 5 minutes or until tender, stirring once.

4. Layer stuffing cubes, mushrooms, parsley, turkey and onion mixture in 12 x 8-inch glass baking dish. Combine soup, milk and eggs; pour over mixture. Mix lightly to evenly moisten stuffing cubes. Sprinkle with crumb mixture. Cover with paper towel.

5. MICROWAVE (high) 10 minutes, rotating dish once. Then, MICROWAVE (medium — 50%) 6 to 7 minutes or until heated through.

5 to 6 Servings

TIP • With Full Power, microwave in step 5 for 10 minutes. Let stand 5 minutes. Then microwave 2 to 4 minutes.

A tasty turkey casserole for two. It makes 2 servings and can be prepared in 1 dish or divided into 2 dishes. If desired, heat 1 for serving now and freeze the other for another time.

NEXT DAY TURKEY CASSEROLE

1 package (10 oz.) frozen chopped broccoli
Salt
1 tablespoon butter or margarine
1 tablespoon flour
¼ teaspoon salt
⅛ teaspoon ground thyme
1 cup milk
⅓ cup shredded Cheddar cheese
1 cup cooked turkey (cut into thin strips)
2 teaspoons butter or margarine
1 tablespoon dry bread crumbs
1 tablespoon Parmesan cheese

1. MICROWAVE (high) broccoli in package 5 to 6 minutes (10 to 11) or until hot. Drain and place in 1-quart glass casserole; sprinkle with salt. Set aside.

2. MICROWAVE (high) 1 tablespoon butter in 2-cup glass measure ½ to 1 minute (2) or until melted. Stir in flour, salt and thyme until smooth. Stir in milk.

3. MICROWAVE (high), uncovered, 2½ to 3½ minutes (7 to 8) or until mixture boils and thickens slightly, stirring occasionally during last half of cooking time. Stir in cheese.

4. Arrange turkey evenly over broccoli; top with sauce.

5. MICROWAVE (high) 2 teaspoons butter in small glass dish ½ to 1 minute (2 to 3) or until melted. Stir in bread crumbs and Parmesan cheese. Sprinkle on casserole.

6. MICROWAVE (high), uncovered, 3½ to 4½ minutes (7 to 8) or until hot.

2 to 3 Servings

TIPS • Leftover gravy can be substituted for the sauce that is prepared in steps 2 and 3.

• Casserole can be prepared in 2 individual casseroles. Heat 1 casserole in step 6 for 2 to 3 minutes. If 1 casserole is frozen, microwave, covered with paper towel, 4 minutes. Allow to stand 5 minutes and then microwave 2 to 2½ minutes or until hot.

Wild rice requires slow simmering to become tender and fluffy.

CHICKEN-RICE CASSEROLE

½ cup wild rice
1 cup water
½ cup long or medium-grain white rice
1 envelope (1.37 oz.) dry onion soup mix
1 can (10¾ oz.) condensed cream of chicken soup
1 can (10¾ oz.) condensed cream of celery soup
1 can (4 oz.) mushroom pieces, drained
3 whole chicken breasts, split

1. Combine wild rice and water in 1½-quart glass casserole. Cover with casserole lid.

2. MICROWAVE (high) 5 to 6 minutes or until mixture boils. Let stand 1 hour, covered.

3. Stir in white rice, soups and mushrooms. Cover.

4. MICROWAVE (high) about 15 minutes or until mixture is hot and rice starts to swell, stirring twice.

5. Pour rice mixture into 12 x 8-inch glass baking dish, spreading evenly. Dip skin side of chicken into rice mixture and then place skin-side-up over the rice. Cover with waxed paper.

6. MICROWAVE (high) 22 to 25 minutes or until chicken and rice are tender, rearranging chicken once if necessary. Remove waxed paper. For additional browning, place dish under preheated broiler or browning element for a few minutes.

About 6 Servings

TIP • With Combination Oven, microwave in step 2 for 5 to 6 minutes and in step 4 for about 20 minutes. In step 6, microwave-bake at 350°, uncovered, for 20 to 25 minutes.

Susan Scheerer of Minneapolis, Minnesota, shared one of her elegant company dishes with us. This has been a popular seminar recipe and one that is ideal for making ahead.

MICROWAVED CHICKEN DIVINE

2 whole chicken breasts, split
2 packages (10 ozs. each) frozen broccoli spears
8 ozs. pasteurized processed cheese
1 can (10¾ oz.) condensed mushroom soup
½ teaspoon salt
¼ teaspoon rosemary
⅛ teaspoon pepper
1 teaspoon Worcestershire sauce
2 tablespoons dry sherry or chicken broth
¾ to 1 cup crumbled croutons

1. Place chicken breasts in 12 x 8-inch glass baking dish. Cover with waxed paper.

2. MICROWAVE (high) 10 to 12 minutes or until tender; uncover and allow to cool.

3. MICROWAVE (high) broccoli in packages 9 to 10 minutes or until thawed. Drain and set aside.

4. Remove chicken from baking dish. Remove skin and bones; cut chicken into pieces. Arrange broccoli in baking dish and top with chicken. Crumble cheese over chicken. Combine soup, salt, rosemary, pepper, Worcestershire sauce and sherry; pour over chicken. Sprinkle with croutons.

5. MICROWAVE (high), uncovered, 10 to 12 minutes or until heated in center, rotating dish once.

4 to 5 Servings

TIP • To prepare ahead, prepare through step 4, except omit croutons. To heat, cover with waxed paper and microwave as directed. Uncover and sprinkle with croutons. Microwave 2 to 3 minutes.

Fish cooks perfectly in the microwave. This recipe also features zucchini and rice for a scrumptious main dish.

FISHERMAN'S FANCY

2 cups cooked rice
1 teaspoon parsley flakes
¼ cup all-purpose flour
1½ teaspoons salt
1 teaspoon dill weed
1 cup milk
2 tablespoons butter or margarine
1 lb. fresh fish fillets, cut into 1-inch pieces
1½ cups halved and sliced unpeeled zucchini
1 tablespoon chopped pimiento
2 tablespoons white wine

1. Combine rice and parsley in 8-inch round glass baking dish. Press mixture into bottom of dish. Set aside.

2. Combine flour, salt, dill weed and milk in 1½-quart glass casserole; add butter and fish. Cover with casserole lid.

3. MICROWAVE (high) 6 to 6½ minutes or until sauce is thickened and fish flakes easily, stirring once.

4. Stir in remaining ingredients; pour over rice. Cover with waxed paper.

5. MICROWAVE (high) 4 to 6 minutes or until zucchini is desired doneness, rotating dish once.

4 to 6 Servings

TIPS • A firm textured fish such as pike or cod will retain piece shape and size better than a more delicate fish like sole.

• For 2 cups cooked rice, use ½ cup regular white rice or 1 cup instant rice. Cook as directed on package.

Crêpes are first prepared using a conventional method. They are then filled with our favorite tuna filling and microwaved until hot.

FAVORITE TUNA CREPES

Crêpes:

- **2 eggs**
- **1 cup unsifted all-purpose flour**
- **1/8 teaspoon salt**
- **1 cup plus 2 tablespoons milk**
- **2 tablespoons butter or margarine, melted**

Filling and Topping:

- **1 can (12 oz.) tuna, drained**
- **2 tablespoons instant minced onion**
- **1/2 cup mayonnaise or salad dressing**
- **1 can (10¾ oz.) condensed cream of celery soup**
- **1/2 cup milk**
- **1 cup shredded Cheddar cheese**
- **Parsley flakes**

1. Beat eggs just until mixed. Beat in flour, salt and milk. Blend in butter. Allow mixture to stand at room temperature 1 hour for bubbles to disappear.

2. Cook crêpes in favorite crêpe pan as directed by manufacturer. Stack cooked crêpes on plate. (There should be 10 to 12 crêpes.)

3. Combine tuna, onion and mayonnaise; set aside. Combine soup, milk and cheese in glass bowl.

4. MICROWAVE (high), uncovered, 3 to 3½ minutes (5 to 6) or until bubbly and cheese is melted, stirring once. Spoon about 2 tablespoons tuna mixture down center of each crêpe. Roll up with filling inside. Place rolls in 12 x 8-inch glass baking dish. Top crêpes with cheese sauce. Cover with waxed paper.

5. MICROWAVE (high) 10 to 12 minutes (18 to 20) or until center is heated. Sprinkle with parsley flakes.

5 to 6 Servings

Favorite Tuna Crêpes.

Mrs. Marcia Bernick shared one of her family's favorite luncheon casseroles in one of our first issues of "The Times".

TUNA-BROCCOLI LUNCHEON CASSEROLE

¼ cup sliced almonds
1 tablespoon butter or margarine
2 packages (10 ozs. each) frozen chopped broccoli
1 can (10 oz.) white tuna, drained
1 can (4 oz.) button mushrooms, drained
½ cup dry bread crumbs
½ cup sliced water chestnuts
½ cup shredded Cheddar cheese
1 can (10¾ oz.) condensed mushroom soup
½ cup milk
¼ cup salad dressing or mayonnaise
¼ teaspoon salt
2 tablespoons chopped pimiento

1. Combine almonds and butter in small glass dish.

2. MICROWAVE (medium-high — 70%), uncovered, 5 to 6 minutes or until toasted, stirring once. Set aside.

3. MICROWAVE (high) broccoli in paper packages 9 to 10 minutes or until thawed; drain if necessary. Arrange broccoli in 12 x 8-inch glass baking dish. Sprinkle tuna, mushrooms, half of bread crumbs, the water chestnuts and cheese evenly over top. Combine soup, milk, salad dressing, salt and pimiento; pour over tuna mixture. Add remaining bread crumbs to toasted almonds. Sprinkle over casserole.

4. MICROWAVE (high), uncovered, 8 minutes. Then, MICROWAVE (medium — 50%) 6 to 8 minutes or until heated through.

4 to 6 Servings

TIPS • To Prepare Ahead, prepare through step 3. Complete step 4 just before serving.

• With Full Power, microwave almonds 4 to 5 minutes, stirring occasionally. Microwave, covered with paper towel, in step 4 for 12 to 14 minutes, rotating dish twice.

• If broccoli is in a 20-oz. plastic package, remove from package and place in covered baking dish for cooking in step 3.

Tuna-Broccoli Luncheon Casserole.

This recipe for stuffed peppers is a favorite of Mrs. Richard Kurkowski of Grant, Nebraska. We found the combination of tuna and peppers tasty.

TUNA-STUFFED PEPPERS

5 medium green peppers
2 cans (7 ozs. each) tuna, drained
1/3 cup sweet pickle relish
2 hard-cooked eggs, chopped
2 teaspoons lemon juice, if desired
1/4 teaspoon salt
2/3 cup mayonnaise or salad dressing
2/3 cup cubed American cheese
Paprika

1. Cut peppers in half lengthwise; remove core and seeds. Arrange cut-side-down in 12 x 8-inch glass baking dish. Cover with plastic wrap.

2. MICROWAVE (high) 6 to 8 minutes (8 to 10) or until steaming hot and tender-crisp, rearranging once. Drain on paper toweling. Arrange cut-side-up in baking dish or on glass serving plate.

3. Combine remaining ingredients, except paprika. Spoon into pepper halves. Sprinkle with paprika. Cover with plastic wrap.

4. MICROWAVE (high) 8 to 9 minutes (10 to 12) or until heated through (175°).

About 5 Servings

One of our readers, Mrs. Betty Steinhaus, shared some tips for low calorie microwave ideas. This recipe is one of her favorites when watching calories.

TUNA AND RICE QUICHE

1 package (10 oz.) frozen chopped broccoli
1½ cups cooked rice
3/4 cup shredded Cheddar cheese
3 eggs
1/3 cup milk
3/4 teaspoon salt
1 can (6½ oz.) water-packed tuna, drained

1. MICROWAVE (high) broccoli in paper package (place on paper towel or remove outer waxed wrap) 5 to 6 minutes or until just about tender. Drain.

2. Combine rice, half the cheese and 1 egg. Press evenly over bottom and ½ inch up sides of 9-inch glass pie plate or quiche dish. Beat remaining 2 eggs with milk and salt. Top rice mixture with broccoli and tuna; mix lightly. Pour egg mixture over tuna.

3. MICROWAVE (medium-high —70%), uncovered, 14 to 15 minutes, rotating once. Sprinkle with remaining cheese.

4. MICROWAVE (medium-high — 70%), uncovered, 2 to 3 minutes or until center is just about set. Serve cut into wedges.

4 Servings, about 300 calories each

TIPS • With Full Power, microwave in step 3 for 8½ minutes and in step 4 for 11 to 12 minutes.

• With Combination Oven, microwave in step 1 for 7 to 8 minutes, in step 3 for 11 to 12 minutes and in step 4 for 2 to 3 minutes.

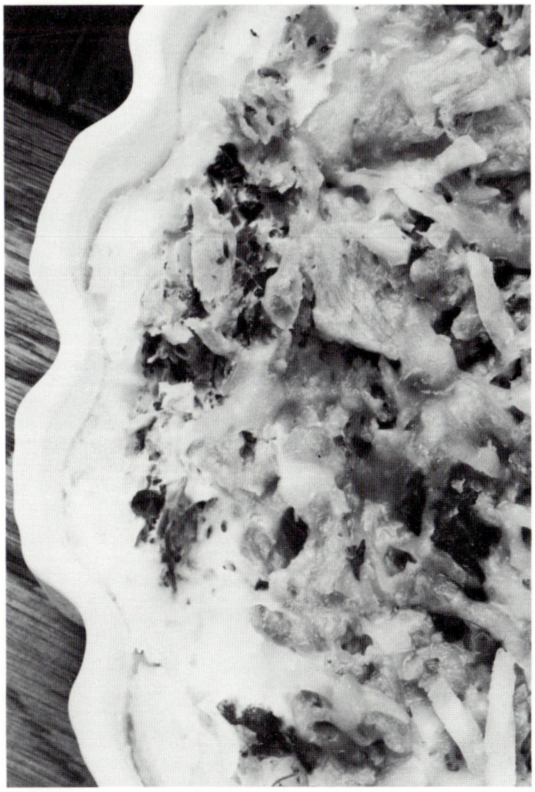

Tuna and Rice Quiche.

Layered casserole mixtures cook or heat more evenly with a lower power setting.

TUNA-CHEESE SANDWICH BAKE

5 slices whole wheat or white bread, cubed
2/3 cup shredded Cheddar cheese
1/3 cup sliced green olives
4 green onions, sliced
1 can (6½ oz.) tuna, drained
1/3 cup mayonnaise or salad dressing
1¼ cups milk
2 eggs, beaten
2 medium tomatoes, chopped
1/3 cup shredded Cheddar cheese

1. Layer bread cubes, 2/3 cup cheese, the olives and onions in 8-inch square glass baking dish. Combine tuna and mayonnaise; spoon onto bread mixture.

2. MICROWAVE (high) milk in 2-cup glass measure 1½ minutes; beat in eggs. Pour over tuna mixture. Cover with waxed paper.

3. MICROWAVE (medium — 50%) 15 to 17 minutes or until center is set, rotating dish once. Sprinkle with tomatoes and remaining cheese. Cover with waxed paper.

4. MICROWAVE (medium — 50%) 3 to 3½ minutes or until cheese is melted.

4 to 6 Servings

TIPS • With Full Power, microwave in step 3 for 5 minutes, let stand 5 minutes and microwave 5 minutes. In step 4, microwave for 2½ to 3 minutes.

• With Combination Oven, omit cooking in step 2. Microwave in step 3 for 12 to 13 minutes and in step 4 for 6 to 7 minutes.

Hash brown potatoes and eggs make a popular brunch or supper dish. We think you'll enjoy this new version of an old standby.

SUPPER OMELET

2 medium potatoes, peeled
1 small onion
2 tablespoons butter or margarine
4 eggs
¼ cup milk
¾ teaspoon salt
1/8 teaspoon pepper
¼ medium green pepper
1 medium tomato, quartered

1. Insert shredding blade into food processor bowl. Shred potatoes, using pusher to force through blade. Place potatoes in sieve; rinse thoroughly with cold water and drain. Reinsert shredding blade. Shred onion by forcing through blade with pusher. Combine potatoes and onion in 9-inch glass pie plate. Cover with waxed paper.

2. MICROWAVE (high) 6 to 7 minutes (8 to 9) or until potatoes are tender, stirring once. Stir in butter. Insert metal blade into food processor bowl. Add eggs, milk, salt and pepper. Process until well mixed. Cut green pepper into quarters; add to eggs. Process until chopped. Add tomato. Process with on-off motion until chopped. Pour over potatoes; mix lightly to combine. Cover with waxed paper.

3. MICROWAVE (high) 2 minutes (4). Stir to move cooked edges to center. Cover.

4. MICROWAVE (high) 2 to 3 minutes (4 to 5) or until just about set in center, rotating dish once. Let stand a few minutes. Cut into wedges to serve.

3 to 4 Servings

TIP • If you don't have a food processor, shred potatoes and onion and chop the green pepper and tomato. Combine eggs and milk with a beater.

Here's a hearty recipe to serve at a brunch buffet. The potato-base can be varied in many ways: substitute asparagus for peas, omit cubed ham and serve with baked ham or grilled sausages, substitute cooked seafood or chicken for ham.

BRUNCH-STYLE SOUR CREAM POTATOES

1 package (24 oz.) frozen hash browns
8 hard-cooked eggs
1 package (10 oz.) frozen peas
2 tablespoons butter or margarine
2 tablespoons flour
1 cup milk
1 tablespoon chopped chives
1 teaspoon salt
⅛ teaspoon pepper
1 cup sour cream
1 teaspoon prepared mustard
¼ teaspoon salt
2 to 3 cups cubed, cooked ham (¾ to 1 lb.)
Paprika

1. MICROWAVE (high) potatoes in package 12 minutes. Meanwhile cook eggs conventionally (don't cook eggs in the shell with microwaves because they will explode). Transfer potatoes to 12 x 8-inch glass baking dish, breaking potato mixture into pieces and rearranging. Add peas. Cover with waxed paper.

2. MICROWAVE (high) 5 to 6 minutes or until potatoes are tender. Set aside.

3. MICROWAVE (high) butter in 4-cup glass measure ½ to 1 minute or until melted. Blend in flour. Gradually blend in milk.

4. MICROWAVE (high), uncovered, 2½ to 3½ minutes or until mixture boils, stirring 2 or 3 times during last half of cooking time. Stir in chives, 1 teaspoon salt, the pepper and sour cream.

5. Remove shells from eggs; halve each egg lengthwise. Carefully remove yolk and place in bowl. Mash yolks with fork. Mix in mustard, ¼ teaspoon salt and ¼ cup of sour cream sauce. Fill egg whites with yolk mixture; set aside.

6. Add ham and remaining sour cream sauce to potatoes; stir lightly to mix. Cover with waxed paper.

7. MICROWAVE (medium-high — 70%) 10 to 12 minutes or until heated through. Arrange eggs on potato mixture, making indentations for each. Sprinkle with paprika. Cover with waxed paper.

8. MICROWAVE (medium-high — 70%) 3 to 4 minutes or until eggs are heated.

About 8 Servings

TIPS • With Full Power, microwave in step 7 for 5 to 7 minutes, stirring once, and in step 8 for 2 to 3 minutes.

• To Make Ahead, prepare through step 6. When ready to serve, complete steps 7 and 8. If mixture has been refrigerated, increase time in step 7 to 18 to 20 minutes.

Brunch-Style Sour Cream Potatoes.

Serve this pretty quiche as an hors d'oeuvre or as the main portion of a light meal. Superb for year round entertaining.

PARTY QUICHE

9-inch unbaked pastry shell
1 small onion, chopped
2 tablespoons butter or margarine
1 package (10 oz.) frozen chopped spinach
2 tablespoons flour
½ teaspoon salt
¼ teaspoon pepper
¼ teaspoon nutmeg
2 eggs
1¼ cups half & half cream
¼ cup Parmesan cheese
2 tablespoons chopped pimiento

1. MICROWAVE (high) pricked pastry shell 4 to 5 minutes or until no longer doughy, rotating plate once. Set aside.

2. MICROWAVE (high) onion and butter in uncovered glass bowl 3 to 4 minutes or until tender.

3. MICROWAVE (high) spinach in package 5 to 6 minutes or until thawed; drain. Add to onion mixture along with flour, salt, pepper and nutmeg. Beat in eggs; mix in remaining ingredients.

4. Pour into pastry shell.

5. MICROWAVE (high), uncovered, 6 to 8 minutes or until center is just about set, rotating dish once.

6 Meal or 12 Hors d'Oeuvre Servings

TIP • To make ahead, prepare through step 3. Complete steps 4 and 5 just before serving. Or, cook ahead and reheat for serving.

An easy to make, tasty and nutritional brunch dish. Or, serve it for lunch with a tossed salad.

CHEESE PIE

5 slices bread, buttered
Garlic salt
6 slices bacon
1 medium onion, chopped
1 tablespoon bacon drippings
1 cup (4 ozs.) shredded Cheddar cheese
1 cup (4 ozs.) shredded Swiss cheese
2 tablespoons flour
1½ cups milk
2 eggs

1. Sprinkle buttered bread with garlic salt. Cut slices in half diagonally. Arrange slices buttered-side-down in 9 or 10-inch glass pie plate forming a crust. Layer bacon in glass dish. Cover with paper towel.

2. MICROWAVE (high) 3½ to 4½ minutes or until crisp; set aside.

3. MICROWAVE onion and drippings in uncovered glass dish 2 to 3 minutes or until tender. Mix in cheeses, flour and crumbled bacon. Sprinkle into bread-lined pan. Beat together milk and eggs. Pour over cheese mixture.

4. MICROWAVE (medium-high — 70%), uncovered, 12 to 15 minutes or until knife inserted near center comes out clean.

About 5 Servings

TIP • With Full Power, microwave milk 3 minutes or until steaming hot before mixing with eggs. Microwave in step 4 for 6 to 8 minutes, rotating dish twice.

This recipe has the makings of Mexican tostadas served pizza-style. If your family enjoys Mexican foods, we're sure this will be a favorite. Serve with a fruit and cottage cheese salad.

GIANT TOSTADA

1¾ cups unsifted all-purpose flour
2 tablespoons yellow cornmeal
2 teaspoons baking powder
1 teaspoon salt
½ cup milk
¼ cup cooking oil
1 tablespoon yellow cornmeal
1 lb. ground beef
1 small onion, chopped
1 package (1¼ to 1¾ oz.) taco seasoning mix
½ cup water
1 can (16 oz.) refried beans
1½ cups (6 ozs.) shredded Cheddar cheese
1 cup shredded lettuce
1 tomato, chopped
Taco sauce, if desired

1. Combine flour, 2 tablespoons cornmeal, the baking powder and salt in mixing bowl. Add milk and oil; stir until dough clings together to form a ball. Turn onto lightly floured surface; knead 5 times. Roll dough between sheets of waxed paper to a 12-inch round. Cut a piece of cardboard about 12 inches square. Sprinkle surface with 1 tablespoon cornmeal. Peel top waxed paper from dough; invert dough onto cardboard. Remove other sheet of waxed paper. Turn under edge of dough and pinch to form a standing rim. Prick bottom several times with fork.

2. MICROWAVE (high), uncovered, 5 to 6 minutes (7 to 8) or until no longer doughy, rotating cardboard once or twice. Set aside. Crumble ground beef into 1-quart glass casserole; add onion.

3. MICROWAVE (high), uncovered, 5 to 6 minutes (7 to 8) or until meat is set. Stir to break meat into pieces; drain. Stir in taco seasoning and water.

4. MICROWAVE (high), uncovered, 3 to 4 minutes (5 to 7) or until most of liquid is absorbed. Spoon beans onto crust; spread evenly. Top with meat mixture, spreading evenly. Sprinkle with cheese.

5. MICROWAVE (high), uncovered, 3 to 4 minutes (4 to 5) or until hot and cheese is melted, rotating once. Top with lettuce, tomato and taco sauce. Cut into wedges.

5 to 6 Servings

Giant Tostada.

Solve the problem of "soggy" pizza crust by precooking the crust before adding the topping. A shelf or elevated cooking device allows the moisture on the crust to escape. Be sure to include the sauerkraut in the topping. It's super!

MICROWAVED PIZZA WITH WHOLE WHEAT CRUST

½ cup whole wheat flour
½ cup all-purpose flour
1 teaspoon baking powder
½ teaspoon salt
⅓ cup milk
3 tablespoons cooking oil

Sauce:
½ can (8-oz. size) tomato sauce
2 tablespoons catsup
2 tablespoons chopped onion
¾ teaspoon oregano leaves
¼ teaspoon leaf basil
⅛ teaspoon garlic powder

Topping:
¼ cup Parmesan cheese
1 cup drained sauerkraut
1 cup favorite cooked meat*
1 cup (4 ozs.) shredded Mozzarella cheese

1. Combine flours, baking powder and salt in mixing bowl. Stir in milk and oil until dough leaves sides of bowl and forms a ball. Knead 4 to 5 times; shape into a ball.

2. Place ball of dough between squares of waxed paper. Roll to an 11-inch circle. Peel off top sheet of waxed paper. Place dough (still on waxed paper) on oven shelf**.

3. MICROWAVE (high), uncovered, 4 minutes. Invert dough onto rack; carefully peel off waxed paper.

4. MICROWAVE (high) 1½ to 2 minutes or until dough is no longer doughy. Remove crust (leave on shelf) from oven.

5. Combine ingredients for Sauce; spoon onto crust, spreading to edges. Sprinkle evenly with Parmesan cheese, sauerkraut, meat and cheese. Return shelf with pizza to oven.

6. MICROWAVE (high), uncovered, 5½ to 6½ minutes or until cheese is melted, rotating pizza once.

11-inch Pizza

TIPS • *For meat, use ½ lb. ground beef, cooked, drained and seasoned; 1 cup (4 ozs.) sliced brown 'n serve sausage; about 2 ozs. sliced pepperoni or 1 cup canned, drained seafood.

• **If you do not have a oven shelf, you can improvise. Just cut a piece of heavy cardboard at least 12 inches square. Then cut several 1 to 1½ inch holes in cardboard. Elevate cardboard in oven by placing on four paper or glass cups.

• The crust can be prepared through step 4, cooled, wrapped tightly and frozen. The sauce can also be combined and frozen, but it is best to reduce the seasonings or wait and add them after freezing. To use, spread the frozen crust with thawed sauce (microwave about 2 minutes to thaw). Top with favorite meats and cheeses and microwave as directed in step 6.

• With Combination Oven, place pizza on metal oven shelf and microwave in step 3 for 6 to 7 minutes, step 4 for 1 to 2 minutes and step 6 for 8 to 10 minutes.

Microwaved Pizza with Whole Wheat Crust.

This pizza needs some extra browning for a crisp crust.

DEEP-DISH PIZZA

1¼ cups warm water
1 package active dry yeast
¼ cup cornmeal
1 tablespoon sugar
1 tablespoon butter or margarine
¾ teaspoon salt
2¾ to 3 cups unsifted all-purpose flour

Topping:
1½ cups (6 ozs.) shredded Mozzarella cheese
1 cup (4 ozs.) chopped brown 'n serve sausage, uncooked
1 can (4 oz.) mushroom pieces, drained
1 cup favorite pizza sauce
½ cup Parmesan cheese

1. Combine water and yeast in large mixing bowl. Stir to combine. Allow to stand a few minutes until yeast is dissolved. Add cornmeal, sugar, butter, salt and 1½ cups flour. Beat well. Stir in remaining 1¼ to 1½ cups flour to form a stiff dough.

2. Turn out onto floured surface; knead 1 to 2 minutes or until smooth. Place dough in greased glass bowl; cover with plastic wrap.

3. MICROWAVE (warm — 10%) 5 minutes. Let stand 10 minutes. Repeat once. Let stand until doubled in size. Punch down dough. Divide in half. Press each half into greased 8-inch square or round glass baking dish, pressing dough halfway up sides of dish.

4. MICROWAVE (warm — 10%) 2 minutes. Let stand 10 minutes or until almost doubled in size. Top each dough portion with half of cheese, sausage and mushrooms. Spoon half of pizza sauce onto each. Sprinkle each with half of Parmesan cheese.

5. (Preheat oven or toaster oven to 425°.)

6. MICROWAVE (high) one pizza at a time, uncovered, 5 minutes, rotating dish once. Transfer to oven.

7. BAKE one or two pizzas at a time 10 to 12 minutes or until nicely browned and bubbly. Let stand a few minutes before cutting into squares or wedges.

6 to 8 Servings

Breads need only a short microwave time to heat. They become tough if the microwave time is too long.

PIZZA BUNS

1 lb. ground beef
2 tablespoons finely chopped onion
½ teaspoon salt
⅛ teaspoon pepper
¾ cup pizza sauce
1 cup (4 ozs.) shredded Mozzarella cheese
8 to 10 hamburger buns, split

1. Crumble ground beef into 1½-quart glass casserole. Add onion. Cover with casserole lid.

2. MICROWAVE (high) 5 to 6 minutes or until no longer pink, stirring once. Drain.

3. Stir in salt, pepper and pizza sauce. Cover with casserole lid.

4. MICROWAVE (high) 5 to 6 minutes or until hot and bubbly. Stir in ½ cup of the cheese.

5. Arrange bottom half of buns on glass plate. Spoon meat mixture onto buns. Sprinkle with remaining ½ cup cheese. Top with other half of buns.

6. MICROWAVE (high), uncovered, 1 to 1½ minutes or until cheese just starts to melt.

8 to 10 Sandwiches

Use your favorite pizza toppings for these quick snacks. Kids will love to heat their own for a quick after-school or party time treat.

INDIVIDUAL PIZZAS

6 hamburger buns, split and toasted
1 can (6 oz.) tomato paste
2 tablespoons finely chopped onion
½ teaspoon leaf oregano
½ teaspoon sugar
Dash pepper
Dash Tabasco sauce
Dash garlic powder
3½ ozs. sliced pepperoni
½ cup sliced olives
1 cup (4 ozs.) shredded Mozzarella cheese

1. Toast hamburger buns under broiler. Combine remaining ingredients except pepperoni, olives and cheese. Spoon mixture onto toasted bun halves, dividing evenly. Spread evenly over surface. Top each bun half with equal amounts of pepperoni, olives and cheese. If desired, wrap sandwiches tightly, stacking as necessary; label and freeze up to 2 months.

2. To serve, place desired number of pizzas on paper plate or napkin-lined glass plate.

3. MICROWAVE (high), uncovered, until cheese is just about melted, rotating plate once during cooking if necessary:
1 pizza - ½ to 1 minute
2 pizzas - 1 to 1½ minutes
3 pizzas - 1½ to 2 minutes
4 pizzas - 2 to 2½ minutes
5 pizzas - 2 to 2½ minutes

12 Pizzas

TIPS • Use minimum time for freshly made pizzas; maximum time for frozen ones. If desired, use 1 cup pizza sauce for tomato paste and seasonings.

• With Combination Oven, place pizzas on baking sheet or broiler pan. Microwave-broil 2 inches from heat 2 to 3 minutes or until cheese is bubbly.

Individual Pizzas.

Pocket bread halves make great holders for meals. Here we've used a salmon salad mixture, but other favorites would also be good.

POCKETS OF SALMON

1 can (7¾ oz.) salmon, drained and flaked
¾ cup chopped cucumber
3 hard-cooked eggs, chopped
¾ cup alfalfa sprouts
2 tablespoons finely chopped onion
1 cup (4 ozs.) shredded Cheddar cheese
½ cup mayonnaise or salad dressing
½ teaspoon prepared mustard
⅛ teaspoon pepper
4 pocket bread rounds

1. Combine all ingredients except bread in bowl; mix until moistened.

2. Slice bread rounds in half vertically. Open pockets and spoon mixture evenly into each. Place in single layer on large glass or plastic serving tray.

3. MICROWAVE (high), uncovered, 3 to 4 minutes (4 to 6) or until filling is heated and cheese starts to melt, rotating once.

8 Sandwiches

TIPS • For 4 sandwiches, microwave 2 to 2½ minutes.

• A 6½-oz. can tuna, drained, can be substituted for salmon.

Chapter 5

Favorite Recipes from

The Microwave Times

Soups & Salads

Vichyssoise, page 69.

This variation of a popular standby combines both chicken and beef bouillon. The result is a lighter flavor that makes a pleasant beginning for hearty entrées. A processor makes quick slicing of the onions.

FRENCH ONION SOUP

¼ cup butter or margarine
3 to 4 medium onions, thinly sliced (3 to 4 cups)
1 tablespoon instant chicken bouillon
1 can (10½ oz.) condensed beef bouillon
1½ cups water
1 tablespoon Worcestershire sauce
6 slices French bread, toasted
¼ cup Parmesan cheese
½ cup (2 ozs.) shredded Swiss cheese

1. Combine butter and onions in 2-quart glass casserole. Cover with casserole lid.

2. MICROWAVE (high) 15 to 20 minutes (23 to 25) or until onions are tender, stirring once. Stir in bouillons, water and Worcestershire sauce. Cover.

3. MICROWAVE (high) 9 to 10 minutes (11 to 12) or until hot.

4. Spoon into 6 individual soup dishes. Top each with a slice of toast. Sprinkle evenly with cheeses.

5. MICROWAVE (high), uncovered, 2 to 3 minutes (5 to 6) or until cheese melts. Or, place dishes under broiler or browning unit to melt and lightly brown cheese.

About 6 Servings

TIPS • Soup can be prepared ahead through step 4. To serve, increase time in step 5 to 6 to 8 minutes.

• If all soup dishes do not fit in oven at one time, microwave in two steps, heating three at a time and using about half the time in step 5.

This soup was shared by one of our readers, Elizabeth Walters. Try it for lunch or supper. We think it is delicious!

CREAMY BROCCOLI-TUNA CHOWDER

¼ cup butter or margarine
1 medium onion, chopped
¼ cup all-purpose flour
1½ teaspoons salt
½ teaspoon celery salt
⅛ teaspoon pepper
3 cups milk
1 can (7 oz.) tuna, drained
1 package (10 oz.) frozen chopped broccoli
2 tablespoons chopped chives
1 cup (8 ozs.) sour cream

1. Combine butter and onion in 2-quart glass casserole.

2. MICROWAVE (high), uncovered, 4 to 5 minutes (5 to 6) or until tender, stirring once. Blend in flour, salt, celery salt and pepper. Stir in milk.

3. MICROWAVE (high), uncovered, 7 to 8 minutes (12 to 14) or until mixture boils and thickens, stirring 3 or 4 times. Add tuna, broccoli and chives. Cover with casserole lid.

4. MICROWAVE (high) 11 to 12 minutes (13 to 15) or until broccoli is just about tender, stirring twice. Stir in sour cream. Cover.

5. MICROWAVE (high) 2 to 3 minutes (4 to 6) or until hot.

5 to 6 Servings

TIP • If desired, substitute a 7-oz. can chunky ham for tuna, reducing salt to ½ teaspoon.

Rivels, or rice-like particles, are said to have originated in Pennsylvania Dutch country. Cooks of the area pressed together egg, flour and salt with their fingers and let the bits drop into simmering soups, stews and chowders. This recipe is from our 1976 Bicentennial issue.

CHICKEN AND RIVEL CHOWDER

3 to 3½-lb. frying chicken, cut up
1 large onion, sliced
1 cup sliced celery
3 teaspoons salt
¼ teaspoon pepper
5 cups water
1 can (12 oz.) cut corn, undrained

Rivels:
1 cup unsifted all-purpose flour
¼ teaspoon salt
1 large egg
½ to 1 tablespoon milk

1. Combine chicken, onion, celery, 3 teaspoons salt, the pepper and water in 4-quart glass casserole. Cover with casserole lid.

2. MICROWAVE (high) 12 to 13 minutes or until mixture starts to boil.

3. MICROWAVE (medium — 50%) 60 to 70 minutes or until chicken is tender. Remove chicken pieces to plate to cool.

4. Combine flour and salt in mixing bowl; make a well in center. Add egg; gradually mix into flour with fork until mixture is crumbly and size of small peas, adding milk as necessary.

5. Add corn to chicken broth. Stir in "rivels" mixture. Cover.

6. MICROWAVE (high) 4 to 5 minutes. Meanwhile, cut chicken from bones; add chicken to soup.

7. MICROWAVE (high) 3 to 4 minutes or until heated through. If desired, garnish with parsley.

5 to 6 Servings

TIPS • With Full Power, let mixture stand in step 3 for 15 minutes. Then, microwave 20 minutes and let stand 15 minutes. Rearrange chicken and microwave 20 minutes.

• With Combination Oven, microwave 1¼ hours for steps 2 and 3. Continue with remaining steps, using timings as directed.

This smooth, creamy potato soup is traditionally served chilled, but is equally delicious warm. When leeks are not available, you can substitute green onions.

VICHYSSOISE

4 medium potatoes, peeled and quartered
½ cup sliced leeks or green onions
3 cans (13¾ ozs. each) chicken broth
1 cup whipping cream or half and half
1½ teaspoons salt
⅛ teaspoon pepper
Chopped chives

1. Combine potatoes, leeks and 1 can chicken broth in 3-quart glass casserole. Cover with casserole lid.

2. MICROWAVE (high) 13 to 15 minutes or until potatoes are tender. Cool slightly.

3. Transfer potato mixture to blender container. Process at medium speed until smooth, adding additional broth if necessary. Return to casserole, 3-quart serving bowl or soup tureen. Stir in remaining broth, the cream, salt and pepper. Cover and refrigerate. Serve in chilled soup bowls, garnished with chives.

8 to 10 Servings

TIPS • For a hot soup, microwave Vichyssoise 12 to 15 minutes or until heated.

• The soup can be prepared several days ahead.

One of our most popular features combined the food processor and microwave. This easy soup was from that feature. If you don't have a food processor, chop the vegetables to desired thickness using a knife. Or, combine vegetables with the water in a blender container and process until desired size.

QUICK VEGETABLE-CREAM SOUP

1 small potato, peeled
1 small carrot, peeled
1 flowerette cauliflower
1 sprig parsley
1-inch section onion
1 tablespoon butter or margarine
½ teaspoon instant chicken bouillon
½ cup water
1 cup milk
¼ teaspoon salt
Dash pepper
¼ cup shredded Cheddar or American cheese

1. Insert metal blade into food processor bowl. Cut potato and carrot into 1-inch pieces; add to bowl along with cauliflower, parsley and onion. Process to desired size with on-off motion.

2. Place vegetables in 1-quart glass casserole. Add butter, bouillon and water. Cover with casserole lid.

3. MICROWAVE (high) 4 to 5 minutes (8 to 10) or until vegetables are desired doneness, stirring once. Stir in remaining ingredients. Cover.

4. MICROWAVE (high) 2 to 3 minutes (3 to 4) or until hot and cheese is melted.

1 to 2 Servings

Canned soups simplify this recipe that just requires heating to serving temperature. Small portions are delicious as "meal-starters", or try larger servings for light meals.

SEAFOOD BISQUE

1 package (6 oz.) frozen cooked shrimp and crabmeat
1 can (10¾ oz.) condensed mushroom soup
1 can (10¾ oz.) condensed cream of asparagus soup
1 cup half and half cream
1½ cups milk
½ teaspoon Worcestershire sauce
Dash Tabasco sauce
1 tablespoon snipped parsley
3 tablespoons dry sherry

1. MICROWAVE (high) frozen shrimp and crabmeat in package 1½ to 2 minutes (2 to 3) or until just about thawed; set aside.

2. Combine remaining ingredients in 2-quart glass casserole. Stir in shrimp and crabmeat. Cover with casserole lid.

3. MICROWAVE (high) 8 to 10 minutes (14 to 16) or until steaming hot, stirring twice during last half of cooking time. If desired, garnish with additional snipped parsley.

6 to 8 Servings

TIPS • A 6-oz. can of crabmeat or shrimp can be substituted for the frozen seafood.

• Soup can be prepared through step 2 several hours ahead; then, just heat at serving time.

Spicy, hearty chili makes a great family supper. To further develop the flavors, make chili a few hours ahead and then bring to serving temperature at meal time.

CHILI

1 medium onion, chopped
½ cup chopped green pepper
½ cup chopped celery
1 tablespoon water
1 lb. ground beef
1 can (28 oz.) whole tomatoes, undrained
1 can (8 oz.) tomato sauce
2 cans (15½ ozs. each) kidney beans, undrained
2 to 3 teaspoons chili powder
1 teaspoon salt
⅛ teaspoon Cayenne pepper
⅛ teaspoon garlic powder

1. Combine onion, green pepper, celery and water in 3-quart glass casserole. Cover with casserole lid.

2. MICROWAVE (high) 6½ to 7 minutes (13 to 14) or until vegetables are partially cooked. Crumble ground beef; add to casserole.

3. MICROWAVE (high), uncovered, 6 to 7 minutes (9 to 10) or until meat is set. Stir in remaining ingredients. Cover.

4. MICROWAVE (high) 18 to 20 minutes (25 to 28) or until hot and bubbly and flavors are blended, stirring once or twice.

5 to 6 Servings

This combination of simmered dried fruits and spice makes a unique addition to breakfasts or brunches as well as a refreshing meal starter or ending. The cranberry juice enhances the fruits with an attractive amber glow.

FESTIVE FRUIT SOUP

8 ozs. dried prunes
4 ozs. each dried pears, apricots and apples
½ cup golden raisins
2 cups (1 pint) cranberry juice
5 cups water
⅓ cup honey
2 tablespoons quick-cooking tapioca
1 stick cinnamon

1. Combine all ingredients in 3-quart glass casserole. Cover with casserole lid.

2. MICROWAVE (high) 25 to 30 minutes (45 to 50) or until fruit is tender, stirring twice. Let stand covered about 15 minutes. Remove cinnamon stick. Serve warm or cold.

About 10 Cups

TIP • Apple or orange juice can be substituted for cranberry juice.

This basic recipe for cranberry sauce includes the addition of flavorful spices.

SPICY CRANBERRY SAUCE

1 package (16 oz.) fresh or frozen cranberries (4 cups)
1 cup water
5 whole cloves
5 whole allspice
1 stick cinnamon
2 cups sugar

1. Rinse cranberries. Combine cranberries, water, cloves, allspice and cinnamon stick in 2-quart glass casserole. Cover with casserole lid.

2. MICROWAVE (high) 6 to 7 minutes (10 to 12) or until cranberries begin to pop, stirring once. Stir in sugar.

3. MICROWAVE (high), uncovered, 5 to 6 minutes (6 to 7) or until mixture starts to thicken and all cranberries are popped. Cool and remove spices. Serve warm or cold. Store in covered container in refrigerator.

4 Cups

Chicken salad is simple to make any time of the year when the chicken is cooked in the microwave oven.

CHICKEN AND RICE SALAD

2 whole chicken breasts, halved
1 package (6 oz.) chicken-flavored rice mix
1 jar (6 oz.) marinated artichoke hearts
3 green onions, sliced
½ cup chopped green pepper
½ cup sliced black olives
½ teaspoon curry powder
½ cup mayonnaise or salad dressing

1. Arrange chicken breasts on roasting rack or in shallow glass baking dish. Cover with waxed paper.

2. MICROWAVE (high) 14 to 16 minutes or until done; set aside.

3. Combine rice mix (with seasonings) and amount of water specified on package in 1½-quart glass casserole (omit butter). Cover with casserole lid.

4. MICROWAVE (high) 4½ to 5½ minutes or until mixture boils. Let stand 10 minutes.

5. MICROWAVE (high) 2 to 4 minutes or until liquid is absorbed. Cool.

6. Stir in remaining ingredients including marinade from artichokes. Cube chicken and add to rice. Refrigerate until served.

4 to 5 Servings

TIPS • If you omit the chicken, you have a delicious rice salad to serve with chicken, salmon or lamb.

• Some brands of rice may require additional microwave time in step 4.

Here is a shortcut way to potato salad. You can vary by using other favorite potato salad dressings . . . just be sure to cool the potatoes before adding a mayonnaise-type dressing.

SIMPLE POTATO SALAD

2 packages (12 ozs. each) frozen hash browns
½ cup salad oil (part olive oil if desired)
¼ cup white wine or water
1 tablespoon dried parsley flakes
2 tablespoons vinegar
1 teaspoon instant beef bouillon
1 teaspoon salt
½ teaspoon leaf tarragon
½ teaspoon bouquet garni, if desired
¼ teaspoon pepper

1. Place potatoes in 1½ to 2-quart glass casserole. Cover with casserole lid.

2. MICROWAVE (high) 12 to 14 minutes or until thawed and tender, stirring once or twice.

3. Combine remaining ingredients. Pour over warm potatoes; mix lightly. Serve salad warm or cold.

5 to 6 Servings

Chicken and Rice Salad.

Fresh garden greens are topped with a delicate dressing that flavors as it "wilts." The cooked bacon and hot dressing are easily prepared in the microwave.

WILTED SPINACH SALAD

12 ozs. fresh spinach
6 green onions, sliced
6 radishes, sliced
1 to 2 hard-cooked eggs, sliced
2 slices bacon
1½ tablespoons sugar
3 tablespoons vinegar
1 tablespoon water
½ teaspoon salt
⅛ teaspoon pepper

1. Wash spinach; tear into bite-sized pieces. Add onions and radishes. Refrigerate tightly covered. Cook eggs conventionally; cool and remove shells.

2. Place bacon in single layer in glass dish. Cover with waxed paper.

3. MICROWAVE (high) 3 to 4 minutes or until crisp. Remove bacon; set aside. Add remaining ingredients to drippings.

4. MICROWAVE (high), uncovered, ¾ to 1 minute or until mixture boils. Pour over greens in salad bowl; toss lightly. Sprinkle with sliced egg and crumbled bacon.

4 to 6 Servings

TIP • To make ahead, prepare through step 3. Complete step 4 just before serving.

Wilted Spinach Salad.

This salad has always been a special favorite, using whatever fresh fruits are plentiful and in season. The custard-like dressing is easily cooked in the microwave.

OVERNIGHT FRUIT SALAD

20 large marshmallows, quartered, or
2 cups miniature marshmallows
1 can (20 oz.) pineapple chunks
1 can (11 oz.) mandarin oranges, drained
2 cups seedless grapes
2 large apples, cored and chopped

Dressing:
2 eggs, slightly beaten
2 tablespoons sugar
2 tablespoons pineapple juice
2 tablespoons white vinegar
½ teaspoon dry mustard
½ cup whipping cream, whipped

1. Quarter large marshmallows using kitchen shears dipped in hot water. Drain pineapple, reserving 2 tablespoons juice for dressing. Combine marshmallows and remaining fruit in large bowl; mix lightly to combine. Cover and refrigerate 6 to 12 hours.

2. Beat together eggs, sugar, pineapple juice, vinegar and mustard in 2-cup glass measure.

3. MICROWAVE (high), uncovered, 2 to 2½ minutes or until thickened, stirring every 30 seconds. Cool.

4. Shortly before serving, drain any excess liquid from fruit. Add cooled dressing and whipped cream to fruit. Fold together until evenly mixed. Refrigerate until served.

6 to 8 Servings

TIP • Other fruit combinations can be used. Prepare about 8 cups fruit mixture for this amount of dressing.

Cranberry Gelatin Mold.

This makes a pretty two-toned red cranberry gelatin salad.

CRANBERRY GELATIN MOLD

1½ cups water
1 package (6 oz.) cherry-flavored gelatin
1 can (11 oz.) mandarin oranges
1 can (8 oz.) crushed pineapple
1 can (16 oz.) whole cranberry sauce
¼ cup mayonnaise or salad dressing
¼ cup sour cream

1. MICROWAVE (high) water in glass mixing bowl 3½ to 4½ minutes or until boiling.

2. Stir in gelatin until dissolved. Drain oranges and pineapple into measuring cup. Add water to make 1 cup. Stir into gelatin mixture. Stir in cranberry sauce. Chill until thickened.

3. Combine mayonnaise and sour cream. Slowly blend in about 1 cup of gelatin mixture. Pour into 8-cup mold. Refrigerate until just set.

4. Add oranges and pineapple to remaining gelatin. Carefully spoon over gelatin in mold. Refrigerate until set, about 4 hours. Unmold onto serving plate.

8 to 10 Servings

Use fruit and their juices to make your own quick gelatin desserts. Just allow about double the setting time as when using a gelatin mix.

RASPBERRY-PEAR SALAD

1 bottle (32 oz.) cranapple juice (4 cups)
2 envelopes unflavored gelatin
1 package (10 oz.) frozen sweetened raspberries
1 can (8 oz.) crushed pineapple, undrained
3 to 4 fresh pears, cored and chopped

1. Measure ½ cup juice into 1-cup measure. Sprinkle in gelatin. Stir and let stand until gelatin softens, about 5 minutes. Pour remaining juice into 2-quart glass mixing bowl.

2. MICROWAVE (high), uncovered, 6 to 8 minutes (8 to 10) or until steaming hot. Stir in softened gelatin until dissolved. Add frozen raspberries. Stir occasionally until raspberries are thawed. Stir in pineapple. Refrigerate until mixture is slightly thickened, about 3 to 4 hours.

3. Stir in pears. Pour into 8-inch square dish or an 8-cup ring mold. Refrigerate until set, about 3 hours. Cut into squares or unmold onto serving plate.

8 to 12 Servings

TIP • Other fruits can be used, but avoid fresh or frozen pineapple (unless you first cook it) since it prevents gelatin from setting.

Favorite Recipes from

The Microwave Times

Chapter 6

Vegetables

Gardener's Special Platter, page 78.

In our Bicentennial issue, we included interesting bits of history with each recipe. Artichokes were a favorite of Martha Washington's and her personal cookbook reveals several recipes for their use.

ARTICHOKES WITH TARRAGON BUTTER

1 medium artichoke
1 clove garlic, if desired
2 tablespoons water
1 teaspoon lemon juice
2 tablespoons butter or margarine
1 teaspoon lemon juice
½ teaspoon chives
¼ teaspoon tarragon leaves

1. Cut off 1 inch straight across top of rinsed artichoke. Remove any loose or damaged leaves around bottom; trim off bottom stem. Snip off thorny part of each outer leaf using kitchen shears.

2. Place artichoke in 4-cup glass measure. Add garlic. Combine water and 1 teaspoon lemon juice. Drizzle over artichoke. Cover with plastic wrap.

3. MICROWAVE (high) 3½ to 4½ minutes or until leaves can be easily pulled from stem and bottom is easily pierced with a fork. Let stand covered.

4. MICROWAVE (high) remaining ingredients in small glass dish ¾ to 1 minute or until bubbly. Before serving, remove "choke" or prickly area in center of artichoke with spoon. Serve by pulling leaves from artichoke, dipping thick end in butter and scraping off soft pulp by pulling between teeth. Once leaves are removed, enjoy the artichoke heart.

About 2 Servings

TIP • For 2 artichokes, microwave 6 to 7 minutes; 3 artichokes, microwave 8 to 9 minutes. If you don't have enough 4-cup glass measuring cups, wrap artichokes tightly in waxed paper, or place in large covered casserole.

Fresh and frozen green beans are a little difficult to adapt to microwave cooking because they require slow cooking to become tender without toughening. A lower power setting helps overcome the problem.

SNAP BEANS WITH BACON

2 slices bacon
1 medium onion, chopped
1 lb. fresh green beans, trimmed and snapped
2 tablespoons water
1 tablespoon sugar
2 tablespoons vinegar
½ teaspoon salt
Dash pepper

1. Arrange bacon in 1-quart glass casserole; cover with paper towel.

2. MICROWAVE (high) 2½ to 3½ minutes or until crisp. Remove bacon and set aside.

3. Add onion, beans and water to drippings. Cover with casserole lid.

4. MICROWAVE (high) 5 minutes. Then, MICROWAVE (medium — 50%) 10 to 15 minutes or until beans are desired tenderness. Combine sugar, vinegar, salt and pepper; add to beans. Cover.

5. MICROWAVE (high) 1 to 1½ minutes or until heated through. Crumble bacon and sprinkle over top.

4 to 5 Servings

TIP • With Full Power in step 4 microwave 5 minutes and let stand 5 minutes. Repeat once. Then, microwave 2 to 3 minutes or until desired tenderness.

For added convenience the broccoli is cooked in the package before combining with the other ingredients.

BROCCOLI SPECIAL

- **1 package (10 oz.) frozen broccoli spears**
- **1 can (10¾ oz.) condensed cream of chicken soup**
- **½ cup sour cream**
- **¼ cup finely shredded carrot**
- **1 tablespoon flour**
- **1 tablespoon instant minced onion**
- **¼ teaspoon salt**
- **⅛ teaspoon pepper**
- **2 tablespoons butter or margarine**
- **¾ cup herb-seasoned stuffing cubes**

1. MICROWAVE (high) frozen broccoli in package 3 to 4 minutes or until thawed; drain. Cut broccoli spears into 1-inch pieces.

2. Combine soup, sour cream, carrot, flour, onion, salt and pepper in 1-quart glass casserole. Add broccoli; mix lightly.

3. MICROWAVE (high) butter in glass dish ½ to 1 minute or until melted. Stir in stuffing cubes. Spoon over broccoli.

4. MICROWAVE (high), uncovered, 7 to 8 minutes or until bubbly in center.

5 to 6 Servings

TIPS • If desired, 2 packages broccoli can be used with this amount of sauce. Add 2 additional minutes microwave time in steps 1 and 4. Also, frozen chopped broccoli can be substituted for spears.

• With Combination Oven, microwave in step 1 for 5 to 6 minutes and microwave-bake at 350° in step 4 for 10 to 12 minutes.

Both creamed onions and broccoli are delicious accompaniments for many meals. Here we combine the two for a double treat.

CHEESY BROCCOLI-ONION CASSEROLE

- **2 packages (10 ozs. each) frozen chopped broccoli**
- **1 can (10¾ oz.) condensed mushroom soup**
- **1 can (16 oz.) whole onions, drained**
- **½ teaspoon seasoned salt**
- **4 ounces processed cheese spread, sliced**
- **2 tablespoons butter or margarine**
- **⅓ cup dry bread crumbs**

1. MICROWAVE (high) broccoli in covered 1½-quart glass casserole 10 to 12 minutes or until thawed. Drain. Stir in soup, onions and salt; arrange evenly in dish. Top with cheese slices.

2. MICROWAVE (high) butter in glass dish ½ minute or until melted. Stir in crumbs; sprinkle over cheese.

3. MICROWAVE (high), uncovered, 10 to 12 minutes or until heated through, rotating dish once or twice.

6 to 8 Servings

TIP • To Make Ahead, prepare through step 2. Complete step 3 when ready to serve.

Cheesy Broccoli-Onion Casserole.

Tomatoes cook more quickly than the other vegetables so are added toward the end of the cooking time. A seasoned butter sauce is drizzled over the vegetables after cooking.

GARDENER'S SPECIAL PLATTER

1½ lbs. fresh broccoli
½ medium head cauliflower
2 medium zucchini
3 tablespoons butter or margarine
½ teaspoon garlic salt
¼ teaspoon thyme leaves
2 medium tomatoes, cut into wedges
¼ cup Parmesan cheese

1. Trim broccoli; cut into pieces about 2½ inches long and with stalks about ¼-inch thick. Arrange toward edge of 12-inch glass serving plate with flower ends toward center of dish. Cut cauliflower into similar-sized flowerettes. Place between broccoli stalks. Slice zucchini and mound in center of plate. Cover all with plastic wrap. Combine butter, garlic salt and thyme in glass dish. (Can stand several hours at room temperature.)

2. MICROWAVE (high) 9 to 11 minutes (12 to 14) or until vegetables are just about tender.

3. MICROWAVE (high) butter mixture about 1 minute (3) or until melted. Drain excess liquid from vegetables. Remove plastic wrap. Arrange tomato wedges over other vegetables. Drizzle vegetables with butter; sprinkle with Parmesan cheese.

4. MICROWAVE (high), uncovered, 1½ to 2 minutes (2 to 3) or until tomatoes are heated.

6 to 8 Servings

Cabbage is superb cooked in the microwave. It retains a pretty delicate green color and there is no strong aroma to linger throughout the house.

CREAMY CABBAGE

1 medium head cabbage
2 tablespoons water
1 package (3 oz.) cream cheese
2 tablespoons milk
½ teaspoon salt
½ teaspoon celery seed
Dash pepper

1. Shred cabbage into 1½-quart glass casserole. Add water. Cover with casserole lid.

2. MICROWAVE (high) 7 to 9 minutes or until desired doneness, stirring once. Add remaining ingredients. Cover.

3. MICROWAVE (high) 1 to 2 minutes or until cheese is softened. Stir lightly to mix. If desired, garnish with paprika.

5 to 6 Servings

Orange marmalade and butter add a simple glaze to carrots. A standing time is added during the cooking to allow the carrots to become tender without overcooking.

GLAZED CARROTS

3 cups sliced carrots
1 tablespoon water
1 tablespoon butter or margarine
1 tablespoon orange marmalade
¼ teaspoon salt

1. Combine carrots and water in 1-quart glass casserole. Cover with casserole lid.

2. MICROWAVE (high) 5 minutes. Let stand 5 to 10 minutes. Then, MICROWAVE (high) 3 to 5 minutes or until tender. Drain. Add remaining ingredients.

3. MICROWAVE (high) 1 to 2 minutes or until butter is melted.

5 Servings

TIP • If orange marmalade is not on hand, substitute apple jelly or 1 teaspoon honey.

A whole head of cauliflower cooks easily in the microwave.

REGAL CAULIFLOWER

1 medium head cauliflower
1 tablespoon water
1 tablespoon butter or margarine
1 tablespoon flour
½ cup milk
¼ teaspoon salt
⅛ teaspoon dry mustard
1 tablespoon snipped parsley
2 tablespoons mayonnaise or salad dressing
⅓ cup cooked or canned shrimp

1. Trim most of leaves from head of cauliflower, but leave head whole. Cut and remove a cone-shaped section from the center core to help the center cook more quickly. Place cauliflower stem-side-down in 2-quart glass casserole. Add water. Cover with lid or overturned casserole.

2. MICROWAVE (high) 8 to 9 minutes or until just about tender. Set aside.

3. MICROWAVE (high) butter in 2-cup glass measure ½ minute or until melted. Blend in flour; stir in milk, salt and mustard.

4. MICROWAVE (high), uncovered, 1 to 1½ minutes or until mixture boils, stirring once or twice. Stir in remaining ingredients. Place head of cauliflower on glass serving plate. Sprinkle lightly with salt. Spoon sauce over cauliflower.

5. MICROWAVE (high), uncovered, ½ to 1 minute or until heated through.

6 to 8 Servings

Mrs. Ann Canning of Sepulveda, California, describes this as a vegetable favorite which everyone seems to like.

SAUCY MUSTARD CAULIFLOWER

1 medium head cauliflower
1 to 2 tablespoons water
½ cup mayonnaise or salad dressing
1 teaspoon finely chopped onion
1 teaspoon prepared mustard
½ cup (2 ozs.) shredded Cheddar cheese

1. Trim most of leaves from cauliflower, but leave head whole. Cut and remove a cone-shaped section from center core to help the center cook. Place cauliflower stem-side-down in 2-quart glass casserole. Add water. Cover with lid or overturned casserole.

2. MICROWAVE (high) 8 to 9 minutes or until just about tender. Combine remaining ingredients except cheese. Place cauliflower on glass serving plate. Spread with mayonnaise mixture.

3. MICROWAVE (high), uncovered, 1 to 2 minutes or until heated. Sprinkle with cheese. Let stand a few minutes before serving.

6 to 8 Servings

Regal Cauliflower.

This recipe illustrates how to cook frozen vegetables in a homemade butter sauce.

CORN IN SAVORY BUTTER SAUCE

¼ cup sliced green onions (including tops)
1 package (10 oz.) frozen cut corn
¼ cup butter or margarine
1 teaspoon cornstarch
½ teaspoon sugar
¼ teaspoon salt
¼ teaspoon tarragon leaves
Dash pepper

1. Combine all ingredients in 1-quart glass casserole; cover with casserole lid.

2. MICROWAVE (high) 6 to 7 minutes (10 to 12) or until corn is tender and sauce bubbly, stirring 2 or 3 times.

About 4 Servings

Corn can be cooked right in the husk or wrapped in waxed paper. Since the outside ears will cook faster, it is best to rearrange the ears about halfway through the cooking time. For other quantities, allow about 2 minutes/ear.

BUTTERED CORN IN THE HUSK

4 ears fresh corn on the cob
¼ cup butter or margarine
¼ teaspoon garlic or regular salt

1. Pull husk back about ¾ of the way and remove silk.

2. MICROWAVE (high) butter in small glass dish about ¾ minute or until melted. Add salt. Brush mixture over each ear. Pull husk back around corn. Arrange ears evenly in microwave oven.

3. MICROWAVE (high) 8 to 10 minutes or until corn has a bright color, rearranging ears once. Serve with any remaining butter.

4 Servings

Custard mixtures like scalloped corn are easier to cook with a lower power setting. This recipe uses garden fresh corn and zucchini, and is a test kitchen favorite.

SCALLOPED CORN AND ZUCCHINI

4 medium ears fresh corn on the cob
2 tablespoons water
1 large zucchini, shredded (about 2 cups)
½ cup crushed soda crackers
2 green onions, sliced
1 cup milk
2 eggs, beaten
1 teaspoon sugar
½ teaspoon salt
⅛ teaspoon pepper
2 tablespoons butter or margarine

1. Cut corn from cob to make about 2 cups. Place in 1½-quart glass casserole; add water. Cover with casserole lid.

2. MICROWAVE (high) 6 to 7 minutes or until corn is tender. Stir in zucchini, crackers and onions; set aside.

3. MICROWAVE (high) milk in 2-cup glass measure 1½ minutes. Beat in eggs, sugar, salt and pepper. Stir into corn mixture. Cut butter into pieces and place on corn.

4. MICROWAVE (medium — 50%), uncovered, 4 minutes; stir. Then, MICROWAVE (medium — 50%), uncovered, 10 to 11 minutes or until center is set.

4 to 6 Servings

TIPS • Frozen corn can be substituted for fresh; use a 10-oz. package.

• With Full Power, microwave in step 4 for a total of 10 to 11 minutes, rotating dish 2 or 3 times.

• With Combination Oven, microwave in step 2 for 9 to 10 minutes and in step 4 microwave-bake at 350° for 14 to 16 minutes.

Buttered Corn in the Husk, page 80, Cheese 'N Bacon-Topped Tomatoes, page 89 and Gardener's Delight, page 82.

Cornmeal thickens the custard-like base for this corn pudding. Broccoli adds bits of bright green color as well as additional nutrients. The stirring during cooking assures an evenly cooked product in minimum time.

COLORFUL CORN PUDDING

1 package (10 oz.) frozen chopped broccoli
2 cups milk
3 tablespoons butter or margarine
1½ teaspoons salt
¼ teaspoon pepper
2 tablespoons finely chopped onion
½ cup white or yellow cornmeal
3 eggs
½ teaspoon baking powder
1 can (8 oz.) cream-style corn
Paprika

1. MICROWAVE (high) broccoli in package 4 to 5 minutes (5½ to 6) or until thawed; drain well. Set aside.

2. Combine 1½ cups of the milk with the butter, salt, pepper and onion in 4-cup glass measure.

3. MICROWAVE (high), uncovered, 4½ to 5 minutes (7 to 8) or until milk is hot. Combine remaining ½ cup milk and cornmeal. Slowly stir mixture into hot milk.

4. MICROWAVE (high), uncovered, 2½ to 3 minutes (4½ to 5) or until mixture thickens, stirring 2 or 3 times.

5. Beat eggs and baking powder in 1½-quart glass casserole until frothy. Slowly blend in the hot cornmeal mixture. Stir in corn and broccoli until well mixed.

6. MICROWAVE (high), uncovered, 11 minutes (15), stirring every 3 minutes. Spread evenly in dish; sprinkle with paprika.

7. MICROWAVE (high), uncovered, 3 to 4 minutes (6½ to 7) or until center is just about set.

About 8 Servings

We have printed many good vetegable recipes, but this is a special favorite. Not only is it colorful, the taste combination is very appealing.

GARDENER'S DELIGHT

3 medium ears fresh corn
1 small onion, chopped
¼ cup chopped green pepper
1 medium zucchini, sliced
¼ cup butter or margarine
2 teaspoons sugar
¾ teaspoon salt
⅛ teaspoon pepper
¼ teaspoon ground cumin, if desired
1 large tomato, chopped

1. Cut corn from ears, using sharp knife. Place in 1½-quart glass casserole. Add onion and green pepper. Cover with casserole lid.

2. MICROWAVE (high) 2 minutes or until heated. Add remaining ingredients, except tomato. Cover.

3. MICROWAVE (high) 7 to 9 minutes or until just about tender, stirring once. Add tomato. Cover.

4. MICROWAVE (high) 2 to 3 minutes or until tomato is heated.

4 to 5 Servings

The flavors and colors of corn and green beans go well together. Here, they are accented with a cheese sauce. Beans require longer cooking than corn so are started first. Then, both vegetables continue to cook while the sauce is cooking.

CHEESY CORN AND BEANS

2 cups cut or snapped fresh green beans
¼ cup water
2 cups cut fresh corn
2 tablespoons flour
½ teaspoon salt
¼ teaspoon dry mustard
⅛ teaspoon pepper
¾ cup milk
2 tablespoons butter or margarine
½ cup cubed American or Cheddar cheese

1. Combine green beans and water in 1½-quart glass casserole. Cover with casserole lid.

2. MICROWAVE (high) 6 minutes (12); stir. Let stand, covered, 5 minutes. Stir in corn; cover.

3. MICROWAVE (high) 5 minutes (10), stirring once. Stir in flour, salt, mustard, pepper and milk; add butter. Cover.

4. MICROWAVE (high) 4 to 5 minutes (8 to 9) or until mixture boils and thickens, stirring once. Stir in cheese. Cover.

5. MICROWAVE (high) 1 to 1½ minutes (2 to 3) or until cheese is melted. Stir to combine.

5 to 6 Servings

TIP • To thaw a ⅔-cup serving, microwave (high) 3 to 4 minutes (7 to 8) or until hot, rearranging contents once.

Here is a vegetable combination that is exceptionally attractive yet "ordinary" enough to appeal to most family's taste preferences. The larger bags are usually more economical when cooking in quantities.

SPECIAL OCCASION VEGETABLES

1 package (about 16 ozs.) frozen cut corn
1 package (about 16 ozs.) frozen cut green beans
¼ cup butter or margarine
½ teaspoon garlic salt
1 teaspoon seasoned salt
½ teaspoon leaf thyme

1. Place vegetables in 2-quart glass casserole. Cover with casserole lid.

2. MICROWAVE (high) 13 to 15 minutes (25 to 30) or until just about tender, stirring once; drain.

3. Add remaining ingredients.

4. MICROWAVE (high), uncovered, 2 to 2½ minutes (4 to 5) or until butter is melted. Stir to evenly mix seasonings with vegetables.

8 to 10 Servings

TIP • If green beans are not a favorite at your house, substitute peas or chopped broccoli.

Onion shells make attractive holders for a delicious creamed spinach mixture. They can serve as the garnish for a meat platter or as a unique vegetable dish.

FESTIVE FILLED ONIONS

4 medium onions
1 package (10 oz.) frozen chopped spinach
¼ cup milk
2 tablespoons flour
½ teaspoon salt
2 tablespoons butter or margarine
½ cup (2 ozs.) shredded Cheddar cheese
1 tablespoon butter or margarine
3 tablespoons dry bread crumbs

1. Peel onions and halve each crosswise. Place cut-side-down in 8-inch round glass baking dish. Cover with waxed paper.

2. MICROWAVE (high) 7 to 9 minutes or until onions are tender-crisp. Remove centers from onions and set aside for use in other dishes. Separate onion halves into about two shells each, leaving 2 to 3 layers of onion in each. Place shells cut-side-up in baking dish. Set aside.

3. MICROWAVE (high) spinach in covered glass bowl 5 to 6 minutes or until thawed. Drain well. Combine milk, flour and salt; stir into hot spinach. Add butter.

4. MICROWAVE (high), uncovered, 2 to 2½ minutes or until thickened. Stir in cheese.

5. MICROWAVE (high) 1 tablespoon butter in small glass dish about ½ minute or until melted. Stir in bread crumbs.

6. Spoon spinach mixture into onion shells; top with buttered crumbs. Cover with waxed paper.

7. MICROWAVE (high) 3 to 4 minutes or until heated through.

8 to 10 Servings

TIPS • When onions have been refrigerated, microwave in step 7 for 4 to 5 minutes.

• Onions can be prepared ahead through step 6. Complete step 7 when ready to serve.

Festive Filled Onions.

Dress up frozen peas with mushrooms and water chestnuts.

GARDEN PEAS

- **1/3 cup chopped celery**
- **3 green onions, sliced**
- **1/4 cup chopped green pepper**
- **1 tablespoon butter or margarine**
- **1 can (4 oz.) mushroom pieces, drained**
- **1 can (8 oz.) water chestnuts, drained and sliced**
- **1 package (10 oz.) frozen peas**
- **1/2 teaspoon seasoned salt**

1. Combine celery, green onions, green pepper and butter in 1-quart glass casserole. Cover with casserole lid.

2. MICROWAVE (high) 5 to 6 minutes or until tender. Stir in remaining ingredients. Cover.

3. MICROWAVE (high) 7 to 9 minutes or until peas are tender.

About 6 Servings

When new potatoes are left whole, a peeled strip around center or piercing with a fork prevents bursting.

BUTTERED DILL POTATOES

- **1 1/2 lbs. new potatoes**
- **3 tablespoons butter or margarine**
- **2 tablespoons snipped parsley**
- **1 tablespoon lemon juice**
- **1/2 teaspoon salt**
- **1/2 teaspoon dill weed**

1. Scrub and rinse potatoes. Pare 1-inch strip around center of each potato. Place in 1 1/2-quart glass casserole. Add butter. Cover with casserole lid.

2. MICROWAVE (high) 9 to 11 minutes or until just about tender, rearranging once. Let stand a few minutes. Add remaining ingredients. Mix lightly to coat potatoes. Cover.

3. MICROWAVE (high) 2 minutes or until heated through.

5 to 6 Servings

Capture the natural sweetness of pea pods by picking them just before microwaving.

PEA PODS WITH CHESTNUTS

- **1 lb. (6 cups) fresh pea pods (snow peas)**
- **2 tablespoons butter or margarine**
- **1 tablespoon soy sauce**
- **1/2 cup sliced water chestnuts**

1. Wash pea pods; combine with butter in 1 1/2-quart glass casserole. Cover with casserole lid.

2. MICROWAVE (high) 5 to 6 minutes or until just about tender, stirring once. Add soy sauce and chestnuts. Cover.

3. MICROWAVE (high) 1 to 2 minutes or until desired doneness.

5 to 6 Servings

Frozen potatoes make easy starters for microwave potato dishes. They are also very convenient for small quantities.

CHEESY QUICK AU GRATINS

- **1 package (12 oz.) frozen shredded hash browns**
- **2/3 cup milk**
- **1/2 cup (2 ozs.) shredded Cheddar or American cheese**
- **1 tablespoon butter or margarine**
- **1/2 teaspoon salt**
- **Pepper**

1. Place hash browns in 1-quart glass casserole. Cover with casserole lid.

2. MICROWAVE (high) 7 to 8 minutes (10 to 12) or until tender, stirring once to break into pieces. Mix in remaining ingredients.

3. MICROWAVE (high), uncovered, 2 to 3 minutes (4 to 5) or until hot and bubbly. If desired, sprinkle with paprika.

2 to 3 Servings

TIP • Three cups shredded peeled potato can be substituted for frozen hash browns. Rinse shredded potatoes thoroughly in cold water; drain well. Microwave as directed in steps 2 and 3.

A little water provides ample moisture to cook the potatoes for this hot potato salad combination.

GARDEN FRESH POTATOES

1½ lbs. new potatoes
2 tablespoons water
½ cup sour cream
¼ cup mayonnaise or salad dressing
3 green onions, sliced
½ teaspoon salt
Dash pepper
5 radishes, sliced

1. Scrub and rinse potatoes. Halve small potatoes; quarter larger potatoes. Place in 1½-quart glass casserole. Add water. Cover with casserole lid.

2. MICROWAVE (high) 8 to 10 minutes or until just about tender, rearranging once. Let stand a few minutes. Drain. Combine remaining ingredients, except radishes. Add to potatoes. Mix lightly to coat evenly; garnish with radishes.

5 to 6 Servings

This recipe is from one of LaVerne Yarnell's customers, Charlotte Synder. The cubed potatoes are coated with a cheese mixture and then browned in the browner skillet.

"BROWNER" BROASTED POTATOES

¼ cup Parmesan cheese
¼ cup all-purpose flour
½ teaspoon salt
¼ teaspoon pepper
4 medium potatoes, peeled
½ cup butter or margarine, softened

1. Combine cheese, flour, salt and pepper in paper or plastic bag. Cut potatoes into ½-inch cubes. Place ¼ of potatoes at a time in bag; shake to coat evenly. Repeat with remaining potatoes.

2. MICROWAVE (high) 10-inch browner skillet 4 to 5 minutes. Add butter and potatoes.

3. MICROWAVE (high), uncovered, 10 to 12 minutes or until potatoes are browned and tender, stirring 3 or 4 times.

4 to 5 Servings

Pea Pods with Chestnuts and Buttered Dill Potatoes, page 84.

Jackie Coakley of Canoga Park, California, asked for help in converting this favorite recipe to microwave preparation. The quantity of butter and sour cream can easily be adjusted to fit personal tastes.

THOSE POTATOES

6 medium potatoes
1¼ teaspoons salt
2 cups (16 oz. carton) sour cream
4 to 5 green onions, sliced
¼ to ½ cup butter or margarine

1. Scrub and trim potatoes (do not peel). Cut potatoes into ¼-inch thick slices (about 8 cups). Layer potatoes in 2-quart glass casserole, sprinkling layers with salt. Cover with casserole lid.

2. MICROWAVE (high) 20 to 25 minutes or until tender, stirring 2 or 3 times. Spoon sour cream onto potatoes; sprinkle with onions. Stir lightly to combine.

3. MICROWAVE (high) butter in glass dish ½ to 1 minute or until melted. Drizzle over potatoes. Mix lightly just until partially combined (too much mixing causes a curdled appearance). Garnish with sliced green onion tops, if desired.

6 to 8 Servings

TIPS • With other potato quantities, follow basic cooking for baked potatoes. Increase or decrease other ingredients according to number of potatoes used.
• With Combination Oven, microwave-bake at 325° for 20 to 25 minutes in step 2.

This potato recipe is colorful and attractive as well as good tasting. The microwave oven is used for three steps—to cook the bacon, cook the potatoes and then to heat the completed dish.

POTATOES ROYALE

4 slices bacon
4 medium potatoes, peeled
¼ cup chopped onion
¼ cup water
½ cup mayonnaise or salad dressing
⅓ cup sour cream
1 cup (4 ozs.) shredded Cheddar cheese
¼ cup sliced stuffed green olives
½ teaspoon salt
Dash pepper

1. Place bacon between layers of paper toweling on glass plate. Cover with paper towel.

2. MICROWAVE (high) 3 to 4 minutes (8 to 9) or until crisp; set aside.

3. Slice potatoes into casserole; add onion and water. Cover with casserole lid.

4. MICROWAVE (high) 12 to 14 minutes (14 to 15) or until potatoes are tender, stirring twice. Drain. Combine remaining ingredients; add to potatoes. Mix lightly to combine. Crumble bacon; sprinkle over top.

5. MICROWAVE (high), uncovered, 1½ to 2 minutes (3 to 4) or until heated through.

About 4 Servings

These potatoes freeze beautifully and taste freshly prepared.

TWICE BAKED POTATOES

4 large potatoes
½ to ⅔ cup milk
2 tablespoons butter or margarine
1 teaspoon chopped chives
½ teaspoon salt
Dash pepper
½ cup shredded American or Cheddar cheese
Paprika

1. Scrub and pierce potato skins with fork.

2. MICROWAVE (high) 12 to 14 minutes or until potatoes are just about tender, turning and rearranging potatoes once or twice. Cool enough to handle.

3. Cut potatoes in half lengthwise; scoop out insides into mixing bowl, leaving about ¼ inch potato in shell. Mash potato well. Blend in milk to make a fluffy consistency. Beat in butter, chives, salt and pepper. Fill potato shells. Top with cheese; sprinkle with paprika.

4. MICROWAVE (high), uncovered, 3 to 4 minutes or until potatoes are heated through.

6 to 8 Servings

TIP • Potatoes can be prepared through step 3, wrapped tightly and frozen for up to 3 months. To serve, place frozen potatoes spoke-fashion on plate. Microwave (high) 8 to 10 minutes.

Potatoes need not be high in calories. Here we add a golden coating of butter and crunchy corn flake crumbs.

CRUNCHY POTATO SLICES

1 tablespoon butter or margarine
¼ teaspoon onion salt
3 medium potatoes, peeled
¼ cup corn flake crumbs

1. MICROWAVE (high) butter in glass dish ½ minute or until melted. Stir in onion salt.

2. Cut potatoes into ½-inch slices. Brush each slice with butter; sprinkle with crumbs. Arrange in shallow baking dish. Cover with paper towel.

3. MICROWAVE (high) 8 to 10 minutes or until potatoes are tender.

4 Servings, about 115 calories each

TIP • For ease in coating with crumbs, shake a few potato slices at a time in crumbs in a plastic bag.

Frozen hash browns make this recipe quick and easy. Combined with the sauce, they are supreme.

CREAMY POTATO BAKE

1 package (24 oz.) frozen hash browns
1 package (12 oz.) frozen hash browns
2 tablespoons chopped onion
2 cups milk
¼ cup all-purpose flour
¼ cup butter or margarine
2 teaspoons salt
⅛ teaspoon pepper
1 tablespoon parsley flakes
½ cup sour cream

1. Combine hash browns and onion in 12 x 8-inch glass baking dish. Cover with waxed paper.

2. MICROWAVE (high) 16 to 18 minutes or until potatoes are tender, rearranging and stirring once or twice. Set aside.

3. Combine milk and flour in 4-cup glass measure. Add butter.

4. MICROWAVE (high), uncovered, 4 to 5 minutes or until mixture boils, stirring occasionally. Stir in salt, pepper, parsley and sour cream. Pour over potatoes in baking dish. Stir to combine. Cover with waxed paper.

5. MICROWAVE (high) 5 to 7 minutes or until heated through.

8 to 10 Servings

TIPS • For an extra special flavor, sprinkle Parmesan cheese over potatoes before microwaving in step 5.

• When potatoes have been refrigerated, microwave in step 5 for 10 to 12 minutes.

This is a simple make-ahead method for serving mashed potatoes. Use the smaller quantity of cottage cheese when serving with gravy. When not serving gravy, we think you'll prefer the light, creamy texture from the larger quantity of cheese.

MASHED POTATO FAVORITE

6 medium potatoes, peeled and quartered
½ cup water
¾ to 1 cup milk
⅓ cup butter or margarine, cut into pieces
½ to 1 cup creamed cottage cheese
4 to 6 green onions, chopped
1½ teaspoons salt
Paprika

1. Combine potatoes and water in large glass mixing bowl or 2-quart casserole. Cover with plastic wrap or lid.

2. MICROWAVE (high) 15 to 20 minutes (23 to 25) or until potatoes are tender, stirring 2 or 3 times. Drain. Mash potatoes until smooth using potato masher or mixer. Beat in milk until consistency is thick and creamy. Mix in butter until melted and blended. Stir in cottage cheese, onions and salt. Spoon into 1½-quart glass casserole. Sprinkle with paprika. Cover with casserole lid.

3. MICROWAVE (high) 7 to 8 minutes (10 to 12) or until heated through (160°).

6 to 8 Servings

TIPS • Potatoes can be prepared ahead through step 2 and refrigerated; increase microwave time in step 3 to 12 to 14 minutes.

• Instant mashed potatoes can be substituted for raw potatoes. Prepare a 6-serving recipe following directions on package. Reduce salt in step 2 to ½ teaspoon.

Raisins and cranberry sauce team with yams for a colorful side dish.

CANDIED YAMS

7 medium yams or sweet potatoes
½ cup packed brown sugar
6 tablespoons butter or margarine
½ teaspoon salt
⅓ cup raisins
½ cup whole cranberry sauce

1. MICROWAVE (high) yams on paper toweling 18 to 20 minutes or until tender, rearranging once or twice. Cool.

2. Combine brown sugar, butter and salt in 2½-quart glass casserole.

3. MICROWAVE (high), uncovered, 2½ to 3 minutes or until hot and bubbly, stirring once. Stir in raisins and cranberry sauce.

4. Peel yams; cut into 1-inch slices. Add to casserole, carefully coating with brown sugar mixture. Cover with casserole lid.

5. MICROWAVE (high) 5 to 6 minutes or until heated through, stirring once.

8 to 10 Servings

TIP • When mixture has been refrigerated, microwave in step 5 for 10 to 11 minutes.

Candied Yams.

Orange shells make attractive servers for these light and tasty sweet potatoes.

SWEET POTATO-FILLED ORANGE SHELLS

4 fresh oranges
1 can (18 oz.) vacuum-packed sweet potatoes
¼ cup butter or margarine, softened
¼ cup packed brown sugar
¼ teaspoon ginger

1. Cut oranges in half crosswise. With grapefruit knife, carefully cut around orange pulp and remove from shell. If desired, cut a decorative edge on each orange shell. Arrange shells on glass serving plate and set aside.

2. Remove membrane from orange sections by cutting along membrane of each section. Discard membrane; reserve orange sections.

3. Mash sweet potatoes until smooth. Beat in butter, brown sugar and ginger. Fold in orange sections. Pile mixture into orange shells. Top each with a little brown sugar; sprinkle with cinnamon.

4. MICROWAVE (high), uncovered, 4 to 5 minutes (5 to 7) or until heated through (160°), rotating plate once.

8 Servings

When you are looking for a change from sliced tomatoes, try this savory idea which adds flavor and interest with minimal calories.

CRUMB-TOPPED TOMATOES

5 tomatoes
¼ cup dry bread crumbs
2 tablespoons Parmesan cheese
¼ teaspoon garlic salt
¼ teaspoon leaf basil

1. Cut tomatoes in half horizontally. Arrange cut-side-up on glass serving plate. Combine remaining ingredients; spoon onto tomato halves.

2. MICROWAVE (high), uncovered, 3 to 4 minutes (5 to 6) or until heated, rotating plate once.

5 Servings, about 60 calories each

Microwave fresh spinach and mushrooms for a nutritional and colorful vegetable dish.

SAUTEED SPINACH AND MUSHROOMS

1 cup sliced fresh mushrooms
1 small onion, sliced
2 tablespoons butter or margarine
12 ozs. fresh spinach, rinsed and drained (9 cups)
1 tablespoon lemon juice
1/8 teaspoon salt

1. Combine mushrooms, onion and butter in 1½ or 2-quart glass casserole.

2. MICROWAVE (high), uncovered, 3 minutes, stirring once. Add spinach. Cover with casserole lid.

3. MICROWAVE (high) 5 to 6 minutes or until tender. Add lemon juice and salt; mix lightly.

4 to 5 Servings

TIP • Add lemon juice to vegetable juices rather than directly to leaves so the acid will not bleach the green color.

Tomatoes can be quickly heated in the microwave. Heat just until they are warm, yet still hold their shape.

CHEESE 'N BACON-TOPPED TOMATOES

6 slices bacon
1/3 cup shredded Cheddar cheese
1 teaspoon sesame seed
4 tomatoes

1. Layer bacon between paper toweling on plate or in shallow baking dish. Cover with paper towel.

2. MICROWAVE (high) 4 to 5 minutes or until crisp. Cool slightly; crumble bacon into small dish. Mix in cheese and sesame seed. Core tomatoes; slice each in half horizontally. Arrange in circle on glass serving plate, cut-side-up. Top each with spoonful of bacon mixture.

3. MICROWAVE (high), uncovered, 1½ to 2 minutes or until heated, rotating dish once if necessary.

4 Servings

TIP • The bacon topping can be sprinkled over sliced tomatoes on toast for easy bacon, cheese and tomato sandwiches.

This makes a versatile dish. Serve as a hot vegetable, use as a topping on roast chicken or pork, add some cooked rice for a meatless casserole or serve it cold as a salad.

RATATOUILLE

1 medium eggplant, peeled and cubed (5 cups)
3 medium zucchini, sliced (3 cups)
1½ teaspoons salt
1 medium onion, sliced
1 clove garlic, minced
1 tablespoon olive oil
1 green pepper, cut into strips
4 tomatoes, chopped
½ teaspoon leaf basil
¼ teaspoon pepper
1 tablespoon Parmesan cheese

1. Combine eggplant and zucchini in collander or bowl lined with paper toweling, sprinkling each layer of vegetables with salt. Let stand 20 to 30 minutes to remove excess liquid.

2. Combine onion, garlic and olive oil in 2½-quart glass casserole. Cover with casserole lid.

3. MICROWAVE (high) 4 minutes or until onion is limp. Drain eggplant and zucchini; add to casserole along with green pepper. Cover with paper towel.

4. MICROWAVE (high) 8 minutes, stirring once. Stir in tomatoes, basil and pepper.

5. MICROWAVE (high), uncovered, 6 to 8 minutes or until vegetables are tender-crisp, stirring once. Sprinkle with Parmesan cheese.

6 Servings, about 100 calories each

TIP • The olive oil is added primarily for flavor. If you wish to omit it, just add 1 tablespoon water to the onion for cooking.

ACORN SQUASH

1. Prick the skin of 2 whole medium-sized acorn squash and place them in the microwave oven, allowing space between. (No baking dish is necessary.)

2. MICROWAVE (high) 10 minutes. Turn each squash over; rearrange if one is cooking faster than the other. Then, MICROWAVE (medium — 50%) 5 to 7 minutes or until tender and soft to the touch. Cool enough to handle.

3. Cut each in half, either lengthwise or crosswise; scoop out seeds. Place squash halves cut-side-up in glass serving dish or on glass plate. Fill with desired filling.

4. MICROWAVE as directed in filling recipe until the filling is cooked and/or heated through.

4 Servings

TIPS • For 1 squash, microwave 6 minutes, then complete as directed with medium setting. For 3 squash, microwave 12 minutes, then complete as directed.
• With Full Power, microwave 1 squash 8 to 10 minutes, 2 squash 12 to 14 minutes and 3 squash 16 to 18 minutes. Turn squash and rearrange 2 or 3 times during cooking. Allow to stand 5 minutes before cutting in half.

Smoky sausages and maple syrup team for a hearty addition to acorn squash.

SAUSAGE-FILLED ACORNS

3 acorn squash
1 package (12 oz.) smokie link sausages (precooked type)
6 tablespoons maple syrup

1. Cook squash as directed. Cut in half and remove seeds. Cut sausages into 1-inch pieces. Divide among squash halves. Spoon a tablespoon of syrup into each half.

2. MICROWAVE (high), uncovered, 5 to 6 minutes or until heated through.

6 Servings

Fruit and brown sugar combine nicely with the squash flavor.

PEACHY ACORNS

2 acorn squash
Salt
¼ cup butter or margarine
¼ cup packed brown sugar
¼ cup slivered almonds
1 can (16 oz.) sliced peaches, drained

1. Cook squash as directed. Cut in half and remove seeds. Sprinkle lightly with salt. Combine butter, brown sugar and almonds in small glass mixing bowl.

2. MICROWAVE (medium-high — 70%), uncovered, 4 to 5 minutes or until almonds are lightly toasted, stirring once. Divide peaches among squash halves. Spoon nut mixture over each. Cover with waxed paper.

3. MICROWAVE (high) about 4 minutes or until steaming hot.

4 Servings

TIP • With Full Power, microwave in step 2 for 3 to 4 minutes, stirring twice.

These make a nice compliment for chicken or pork.

ACORNS WITH ONIONS 'N STUFFING

2 acorn squash
Salt
1 package (10 oz.) frozen onions in cream sauce
¼ cup butter or margarine
1 cup crumbled stuffing mix
2 tablespoons water

1. Cook squash as directed. Cut in half and remove seeds. Sprinkle lightly with salt. Make small slit in top side of onion cooking pouch.

2. MICROWAVE (high) onions 4 to 5 minutes or until thawed. Divide onions among squash halves.

3. MICROWAVE (high) butter in small glass dish ½ to 1 minute or until melted. Stir in stuffing and water. Spoon over onions. Cover with paper towel.

4. MICROWAVE (high) about 4 minutes or until steaming hot.

4 Servings

Favorite Recipes from

The Microwave Times

Chapter 7

Breads

Beer Bread, page 97.

Mrs. C. E. Lewis of Bullhead City, Arizona, asked us to adapt her favorite muffin recipe to microwave cooking. Store the batter in the refrigerator and cook just the amount needed. Perfect for after-school and coffee treats as well as meals.

FAVORITE BRAN MUFFINS

1 cup water
2 cups all-bran cereal
2 large shredded wheat biscuits, crumbled
½ cup butter or margarine
1½ cups packed brown sugar
2 eggs
2½ cups unsifted all-purpose flour
2 teaspoons soda
½ teaspoon salt
2 cups buttermilk
1 cup raisins or chopped dates
1 cup chopped nuts

1. MICROWAVE (high) water in glass measure 2 to 3 minutes or until boiling. Combine cereals in large mixing bowl; add hot water and stir until moistened. Cut butter into pieces; stir into cereal mixture. Mix in brown sugar; beat in eggs. Add remaining ingredients; stir until combined.

2. Spoon batter into paper-lined microwave muffin pan or glass custard cups, filling about ½ full.

3. MICROWAVE (high) 6 muffins at a time, uncovered, 1¾ to 2½ minutes or until no longer doughy, rotating once. Extra batter can be stored in refrigerator up to 1 month.

42 to 48 Muffins

TIPS • When microwaving only 3 muffins, allow 1¼ to 1¾ minutes.

• With Combination Oven, microwave 6 muffins at a time for 5 to 6 minutes or 12 muffins at a time for 9 to 10 minutes.

This muffin batter can be refrigerated for quick and easy muffins any time of the day. This recipe was in our "cooking for two" feature; for larger quantities, simply double or triple recipe.

REFRIGERATOR OATMEAL MUFFINS

1 egg
⅓ cup packed brown sugar
¼ cup cooking oil
¼ cup buttermilk or sour milk
½ cup all-purpose flour
⅓ cup rolled oats
½ teaspoon baking powder
¼ teaspoon soda
¼ teaspoon salt

Topping:
Brown sugar
Chopped nuts
Nutmeg

1. Beat egg; beat in brown sugar, oil and buttermilk. Stir in remaining ingredients except Topping just until moistened.

2. Spoon batter into paper-lined microwave muffin pan or custard cups, filling cups ½ full.

3. Sprinkle each muffin with a little brown sugar, some nuts and nutmeg.

4. MICROWAVE (high), uncovered, until no longer doughy, rotating cups once:
1 muffin - ½ to ¾ minute
2 muffins - ¾ to 1¼ minutes
4 muffins - 1¼ to 1½ minutes
6 muffins - 1½ to 2 minutes
Store any leftover batter in refrigerator up to 1 week. When ready to use, cook muffins as directed.

About 8 Muffins

TIPS • With Combination Oven for 6 muffins, microwave, 2½ to 3 minutes.

• For sour milk, add 1 teaspoon vinegar to ¼ cup milk. Let stand a few minutes.

Serve this muffin variation for breakfast or as a delicious mealtime addition.

CRANBERRY-ORANGE MUFFINS

½ cup butter or margarine
½ cup sugar
1 egg
¼ cup orange juice or milk
1 cup unsifted all-purpose flour
¾ teaspoon baking powder
¼ teaspoon grated orange peel
¼ cup whole cranberry sauce

1. MICROWAVE (high) butter in glass mixing bowl about ½ minute or until softened.

2. Blend in sugar; beat in egg. Stir in orange juice, flour, baking powder and orange peel just until smooth.

3. Spoon batter into about 12 paper-lined microwave muffin or custard cups, filling half full. Top each with about 1 teaspoon cranberry sauce.

4. MICROWAVE (high) 6 muffins at a time, uncovered, 2 to 2½ minutes or until no longer doughy, rotating once.

About 12 Muffins

Cranberry-Orange Muffins.

Muffins are a natural for preparation in the microwave. This quick and easy recipe was included in our food processor issue. See the "Tips" if you don't have a processor.

CARROT-GRANOLA MUFFINS

½ cup packed brown sugar
¼ cup butter or margarine
1 egg
1 medium carrot, peeled and cut into 3 pieces
½ cup buttermilk or sour milk
¾ cup unsifted all-purpose flour or whole wheat flour
½ cup granola cereal
¾ teaspoon baking powder
¼ teaspoon salt
¼ teaspoon soda

1. Insert metal blade into food processor bowl. Place brown sugar and butter in processor bowl. Process with short on-off motion until creamy. Add egg, carrot and buttermilk; process until carrot is in fine pieces. Add remaining ingredients; process just until combined.

2. Spoon batter into paper-lined microwave muffin pan or custard cups, filling ½ full. If desired, sprinkle tops with additional granola.

3. MICROWAVE (high) 6 muffins at a time, uncovered, 2 to 3 minutes (4 to 5) or until no longer doughy, rotating once or twice. Repeat with remaining batter.

12 Muffins

TIPS • If you don't have a food processor, shred the carrot and add along with buttermilk. Or, combine the egg, buttermilk and carrot in blender and process until carrot is in fine pieces. Add to creamed mixture along with flour mixture.

• With Combination Oven, microwave 6 muffins at a time for 4 to 5 minutes, rotating once.

This light bran batter has bits of fresh, colorful cranberries. Without the cranberries, the batter can be stored up to 2 weeks in the refrigerator. Once the berries are added, the batter should be used within 3 days. Use the recipe year around by substituting raisins or chopped dates for cranberries.

STORE AND BAKE HOLIDAY MUFFINS

1 cup quick-cooking rolled oats
1 cup all-bran cereal
1 cup buttermilk or sour milk
⅔ cup packed brown sugar
½ cup cooking oil
2 eggs
1 cup unsifted all-purpose flour
1 teaspoon baking powder
½ teaspoon soda
½ teaspoon salt
1 teaspoon grated orange peel, if desired
1 cup coarsely chopped cranberries

1. Combine oats, cereal and buttermilk in large bowl. Blend in brown sugar, oil and eggs. Stir in remaining ingredients, mixing just until moistened. (Batter can be cooked immediately or refrigerated in covered container for up to 3 days.)

2. Spoon batter into paper-lined microwave muffin cups, filling half full.

3. MICROWAVE (high), uncovered, until no longer doughy, rotating once:
1 muffin - 30 to 45 seconds
3 muffins - 1 to 1¼ minutes
6 muffins - 2 to 2½ minutes

22 to 26 Muffins

TIPS • For other variations, add ½ cup chopped nuts with cranberries. Or, substitute chopped dates or raisins for cranberries.

• For miniature muffins, line empty egg carton with miniature cupcake liners (this size is usually available in gourmet cook shops). Fill cups half full. Microwave (high) 12 at a time, uncovered, 1 to 1½ minutes. For 2 cartons (24 muffins), microwave 2 to 2½ minutes, rotating cartons once or twice. Recipe makes about 100 miniature muffins.

• With Combination Oven, microwave 6 regular-size muffins 3 to 4 minutes or 12 muffins 4 to 5 minutes.

Bev Dillon of Central Point, Oregon, shared one of her favorite bread recipes. Use the microwave oven for proofing the bread dough as well as cooking the loaves.

NO-KNEAD OATMEAL BREAD

½ cup warm water
2 packages active dry yeast
1½ cups water
1 cup quick-cooking rolled oats
⅓ cup shortening or margarine
½ cup light molasses
1 tablespoon salt
2 eggs
6 cups unsifted all-purpose flour
2 tablespoons wheat germ or rolled oats

1. Soften yeast in warm water; let stand. Combine 1½ cups water and the oats in large glass mixing bowl.

2. MICROWAVE (high), uncovered, 3 to 3½ minutes or until mixture boils. Stir in shortening, molasses and salt. Cool slightly. Beat in eggs and 2 cups of the flour. Stir in softened yeast. Add 2 more cups flour; beat well. Stir in remaining 2 cups flour until well mixed. Cover with plastic wrap.

3. MICROWAVE (warm — 10%) 10 minutes. Let stand 20 minutes or until doubled in size. Stir down dough. Divide evenly between two greased 9 x 5-inch glass loaf dishes or two 1½-quart glass casseroles. Sprinkle surface with wheat germ.

4. MICROWAVE (warm — 10%), both loaves at once, uncovered, 10 minutes. Let stand 10 to 15 minutes or until just about doubled in size. Place one loaf in microwave oven; set aside other loaf.

5. MICROWAVE (medium — 50%), one loaf at a time, uncovered, 8 minutes. Rotate dish.

6. MICROWAVE (high) 1½ to 2½ minutes or until surface springs back when lightly touched. Cool 5 minutes; turn out of dish. Repeat cooking process with other loaf.

2 Loaves

With lower power, the very low "warm" setting can be used to speed proofing of yeast doughs. Most yeast breads cook more evenly with a lower power setting. The flavor of this bread is super.

BRAIDED BARBECUE BREAD

1¼ cups warm water
1 package active dry yeast
2 tablespoons sugar
2 tablespoons butter or margarine, softened
½ teaspoon salt
¼ teaspoon garlic salt
¼ teaspoon liquid smoke
⅛ teaspoon chili powder
⅛ teaspoon paprika
1 egg
2 cups unsifted all-purpose flour
1¾ to 2¼ cups unsifted whole wheat flour

Topping:
1 tablespoon butter or margarine
1 tablespoon Parmesan cheese
¼ teaspoon garlic salt
⅛ teaspoon paprika

1. Dissolve yeast in warm water in large mixing bowl. Stir in remaining ingredients except whole wheat flour and topping. Beat until smooth. Stir in whole wheat flour to form a stiff dough.

2. Turn onto floured surface; knead until smooth and elastic, about 5 minutes. Place in greased bowl, turning to grease top. Cover with plastic wrap.

3. MICROWAVE (warm — 10%) 10 minutes. Let stand 10 minutes or until doubled in size. Punch down dough.

4. Divide dough into thirds. Form each portion into strips about 18 inches long by rolling between hands. Place strips side by side; pinch strips together at one end. Braid strips together. Place on paper towel-covered cardboard (cut to fit inside microwave) bringing ends of braid together to form a ring; pinch ends to seal.

5. MICROWAVE (high) butter for topping in small glass dish ¾ to 1 minute or until melted. Brush braid with butter. Combine remaining Topping ingredients; sprinkle on braid.

6. MICROWAVE (warm — 10%), uncovered, 10 minutes. Let stand 10 minutes or until doubled in size.

7. MICROWAVE (medium — 50%), uncovered, 10 to 11 minutes or until edges spring back when lightly touched, rotating cardboard once. Cool.

1 Loaf

TIPS • With Full Power, proof bread in warm room until doubled in size (steps 3 and 6). In step 7, microwave for 3 minutes, let stand 5 minutes, rotate cardboard and microwave 2½ to 3½ minutes.

• With Combination Oven, microwave-defrost in step 3 for 2 minutes, let stand 10 minutes, microwave-defrost another 2 minutes and let stand 10 minutes or until doubled in size. For step 6, microwave-defrost for 2 minutes, let stand 10 minutes, microwave-defrost for 1 minute and let stand 10 minutes. In step 7, microwave for 5 to 7 minutes.

Braided Barbecue Bread.

This convenient and popular coffee cake utilizes frozen bread dough. Double the convenience by using the microwave to thaw and proof the frozen dough.

CARAMEL BUBBLE LOAF

1 loaf frozen bread dough
3 tablespoons butter or margarine
⅓ cup packed brown sugar
2 tablespoons chopped nuts
2 tablespoons butter or margarine
¼ cup sugar
1 teaspoon cinnamon

1. To thaw dough, place frozen dough in greased glass bowl. Cover with plastic wrap.

2. MICROWAVE (warm — 10%) 10 minutes. Let stand 10 minutes.

3. MICROWAVE (warm — 10%) 5 minutes. Let stand 10 minutes.

4. MICROWAVE (warm — 10%) 5 minutes. Let stand 5 to 10 minutes or until thawed. Divide dough into 24 pieces; form each into a smooth ball.

5. MICROWAVE (high) 3 tablespoons butter in 10 or 12-cup fluted glass or plastic cake dish ¾ to 1 minute or until melted. Tilt dish to coat evenly with butter. Sprinkle with brown sugar and nuts.

6. MICROWAVE (high) 1 to 1½ minutes or until bubbly; set aside.

7. MICROWAVE (high) 2 tablespoons butter in glass dish ¾ to 1 minute or until melted. Stir in sugar and cinnamon.

8. Layer 8 balls of dough on caramel mixture in dish. Spoon ⅓ of sugar mixture over balls. Repeat with two more layers of balls and sugar mixture. Cover with plastic wrap.

9. MICROWAVE (warm — 10%) 10 minutes. Let stand 10 minutes or until dough is doubled in size. Remove covering.

10. MICROWAVE (medium — 50%), uncovered, 10 to 12 minutes or until dough springs back when touched lightly, rotating dish once. Cool 10 minutes; invert onto serving plate.

One Loaf

TIPS • With Combination Oven, microwave-defrost in steps 2-4 for 2 minutes and let stand 10 minutes for each step. In steps 5-7, microwave 2 to 3 minutes each. In step 9, microwave-defrost 2 minutes, let stand 10 minutes, microwave-defrost 1 minute and let stand 10 minutes. In step 10, microwave 7 to 8 minutes or until dough springs back when lightly touched.

• A 3-quart glass casserole can be used for fluted cake dish. Place a drinking glass, top-side-up in center of dish before adding bread dough.

Nut breads in loaf shapes are difficult to cook with full power without overcooking the ends before the center is done. A lower power setting helps overcome this uneveness.

ZUCCHINI-NUT BREAD

3 eggs
2 cups sugar
1 cup cooking oil
1 tablespoon vanilla
2 cups shredded zucchini (unpeeled)
2 cups unsifted all-purpose flour
1 tablespoon cinnamon
1½ teaspoons soda
1¼ teaspoons salt
¼ teaspoon baking powder
1 cup chopped nuts
2 tablespoons graham cracker crumbs

1. Beat eggs until light and frothy. Stir in remaining ingredients, except graham cracker crumbs, until blended.

2. Grease two 8 x 4-inch glass or plastic loaf dishes. Sprinkle with graham cracker crumbs. Divide batter between dishes.

3. MICROWAVE (high) one loaf at a time, uncovered, 2 minutes; rotate dish.

4. MICROWAVE (medium — 50%) 8 to 9 minutes or until toothpick inserted near center comes out clean. Repeat with second loaf. Cool 10 minutes. Remove from pan. Cool completely.

2 Loaves

TIPS • With Full Power, microwave in steps 3 and 4 for 4 minutes, let stand 3 minutes, rotate dish and microwave 2 to 3 minutes or until toothpick inserted near center comes out clean.

• With Combination Oven, microwave-bake both loaves together in preheated 350° oven for 11 to 12 minutes.

Carol Hayes of Yucca Valley, California, sent this interesting quick bread recipe to be adapted to microwave cooking. The beer gives it a distinctive yeast bread taste. Cornmeal and corn flake crumbs are used for an attractive crust.

BEER BREAD

2 cups unsifted self-rising flour
1 cup unsifted all-purpose flour
3 tablespoons sugar
1 can (12 oz.) beer
Yellow cornmeal

1. Combine flours and sugar in mixing bowl. Stir in beer until smooth.

2. Grease 8 x 4-inch glass loaf dish; coat dish with cornmeal, shaking out excess. Spoon batter into dish. Sprinkle lightly with additional cornmeal.

3. MICROWAVE (medium — 50%), uncovered, 9 minutes, rotating dish once.

4. MICROWAVE (high), uncovered, 2 to 3 minutes or until no longer doughy. Cool 5 minutes; turn out of dish. For a golden brown top, brush baked loaf with melted butter and then sprinkle with corn flake crumbs.

1 Loaf

TIPS • With Full Power, microwave in step 3 for 5 minutes; let stand 3 minutes and then microwave as directed in step 4.

• We found self-rising flour produced the best loaf. However, you can also get a good product using just all-purpose flour. You must reduce the amount of flour to 2½ cups and add 3 tablespoons cornstarch, 3 teaspoons baking powder and 1½ teaspoons salt as well as the sugar and beer. In step 4, increase the microwave time to 3½ to 4½ minutes.

• With Combination Oven, bake in preheated 350° oven for 30 minutes. Then, microwave-bake 3 to 5 minutes.

Sour Cream Scones.

This recipe for scones published in our Bicenntenial issue quickly became a favorite of our readers and staff.

SOUR CREAM SCONES

2 cups unsifted all-purpose flour
2 tablespoons sugar
3 teaspoons baking powder
1 teaspoon salt
¼ teaspoon soda
¼ cup shortening
½ cup raisins
¼ cup milk
½ cup sour cream
1 egg, slightly beaten
Cinnamon-sugar

1. Combine flour, sugar, baking powder, salt and soda. Cut in shortening until crumbly. Stir in raisins, milk, sour cream and egg until mixture is moistened.

2. Turn onto floured surface and knead dough 10 to 12 times. Divide dough in half. Pat each half into a 6-inch circle with top slightly rounded. Brush surface with a little milk; sprinkle with cinnamon-sugar. Cut each circle into 6 wedges. Arrange wedges from each circle on paper towel-covered glass plate, pulling apart slightly to leave ½ inch between wedges.

3. MICROWAVE (high), one plate at a time, uncovered, 2½ to 3 minutes or until scones are no longer doughy, rotating plate once. Serve warm with butter and raspberry or other favorite jam.

12 Scones

This spicy coffee cake serves double duty as a breakfast bread or a dessert. The moist pumpkin flavor makes it a favorite for both family and guests.

PUMPKIN COFFEE CAKE

¾ cup butter or margarine
1 cup packed brown sugar
¾ cup sugar
2½ cups unsifted all-purpose flour
1 teaspoon nutmeg
¼ teaspoon ginger
½ teaspoon salt
½ cup chopped nuts, if desired
½ teaspoon cinnamon
1 cup buttermilk or sour milk
2 eggs
½ teaspoon baking powder
½ teaspoon soda
¾ cup cooked or canned pumpkin

1. MICROWAVE (high) butter in glass mixing bowl about 1 minute (3 to 4) or until melted. Blend in sugars. Mix in flour, nutmeg, ginger and salt until crumbly. Remove ½ cup of mixture; mix in nuts and cinnamon. Set aside.

2. To remaining mixture, add buttermilk, eggs, baking powder, soda and pumpkin. Beat until smooth.

3. Grease 12 x 8-inch glass baking dish on bottom only. Pour batter into dish, spreading evenly. Sprinkle with reserved mixture.

4. MICROWAVE (medium — 50%), uncovered, 10 minutes, rotating dish once. Then, MICROWAVE (high) 8 to 10 minutes or until toothpick inserted near center comes out clean, rotating dish once. Serve warm or cold.

15 to 18 Servings

TIPS • To help assure complete cooking of the bottom of the cake, microwave 1 cup of water in baking dish while mixing up cake. Then, discard water and grease hot dish before adding batter.

• With Full Power, microwave in step 4 for 11 to 13 minutes, rotating dish about 3 times.

• With Combination Oven, microwave in step 4 for 25 minutes, rotating dish once. Or, bake at 350° for 15 minutes and then microwave-bake for 5 to 6 minutes.

Mrs. Nancy Hogg of Chambersburg, Pennsylvania, asked for help in adapting her favorite coffee cake to microwave preparation. It is important, with this type cake, that the crumb mixture is very fine in order for it to remain atop the cake during cooking.

COWBOY COFFEE CAKE

2⅓ cups unsifted all-purpose flour
2 cups packed brown sugar
2 teaspoons cinnamon
½ teaspoon nutmeg
¾ teaspoon salt
¾ cup shortening
1¼ teaspoons baking powder
½ teaspoon soda
1 cup sour milk
2 eggs
½ cup chopped nuts

1. Combine flour, brown sugar, cinnamon, nutmeg and salt in large mixing bowl. Cut in shortening until mixture resembles fine crumbs. Set aside ½ cup of crumb mixture. To remaining crumb mixture, add baking powder and soda; mix well. Stir in sour milk and eggs; mix just until combined. Pour into 12 x 8-inch glass baking dish, greased on bottom only. Sprinkle with nuts and then crumbs.

2. MICROWAVE (medium — 50%), uncovered, 9 minutes, rotating dish once or twice. Then, MICROWAVE (high) 6 to 7 minutes or until cake springs back when touched lightly, rotating dish once or twice.

12 to 15 Servings

TIPS • For sour milk, place 1 tablespoon vinegar in measuring cup. Add milk to 1 cup level. Let stand a few minutes.

• With Full Power, microwave 10 to 12 minutes, rotating dish once or twice.

• With Combination Oven, bake in preheated 350° oven for 15 minutes. Then, microwave-bake 3 to 5 minutes.

Favorite Recipes from

The Microwave Times

Chapter 8

Desserts & Pies

Fruit Bavarian, page 101, Brownie Mint Pie, page 118, and Pecan-Praline Cheesecake, page 111.

Although we've dressed up this recipe with gelatin, extra flavoring and whipped cream, this is the basic cooking method for pudding mixes.

PUDDING SUPREME

- **2 cups milk**
- **1 package (4-serving size) favorite flavor pudding and pie filling mix**
- **1 teaspoon unflavored gelatin**
- **1 teaspoon rum flavoring**
- **½ cup whipping cream, whipped, or 1 cup whipped topping**

1. Measure milk into 4-cup glass measure. Add pudding mix and gelatin; mix well.

2. MICROWAVE (high), uncovered, 5 to 6 minutes or until mixture boils, stirring once or twice during last half of cooking time. Stir in rum flavoring; cool until thickened.

3. Fold in whipped cream. Spoon into serving dishes.

5 to 6 Servings

Homemade tapioca pudding is delicious. This recipe is extra light from the beaten egg whites. It is also fairly low in calories, if you don't eat too much.

LEMON CREME TAPIOCA

- **2 cups milk**
- **⅓ cup sugar**
- **¼ cup quick-cooking tapioca**
- **¼ teaspoon salt**
- **2 eggs, separated**
- **2 tablespoons sugar**
- **1 tablespoon grated lemon peel**
- **2 tablespoons lemon juice**

1. Measure milk into 2-quart mix 'n pour bowl. Add ⅓ cup sugar, the tapioca, salt and egg yolks; beat until yolks are combined.

2. MICROWAVE (high), uncovered, 5 to 6 minutes or until mixture just begins to boil, stirring once or twice during last half of cooking time.

3. Beat egg whites until frothy. Gradually beat in 2 tablespoons sugar until soft peaks form. Fold in lemon peel and juice. Add mixture to cooked pudding; fold just until combined. Serve warm or cold.

About 5 Servings

For special occasions, top this pudding with whipped cream or layer it with whipped cream in parfait glasses.

PINEAPPLE-LEMON CREME

- **½ cup sugar**
- **3 tablespoons cornstarch**
- **1 can (8 oz.) crushed pineapple, undrained**
- **⅔ cup water**
- **1 teaspoon grated lemon peel**
- **2 tablespoons lemon juice**
- **2 eggs, separated**
- **1 package (3 oz.) cream cheese**
- **¼ cup sugar**

1. Combine sugar, cornstarch, pineapple and water in medium glass bowl.

2. MICROWAVE (high), uncovered, 4 to 5 minutes or until mixture boils, stirring once or twice during last half of cooking time. Stir in lemon peel and juice and beaten egg yolks. Add cream cheese.

3. MICROWAVE (high), uncovered, 1 minute or until bubbly around edges. Beat to blend in cream cheese. Cool.

4. Beat egg whites until frothy. Gradually beat in ¼ cup sugar until soft peaks form. Add to cooked pudding; fold just until combined. Spoon into dessert dishes; refrigerate until served.

5 to 6 Servings

Pudding Supreme, Lemon Creme Tapioca, and Pineapple-Lemon Creme, this page.

Mounds of delicate meringue float atop this honey-orange sauce. It looks elegant served plain or over fresh fruits or angel food cake slices. And, both calories and cholesterol are minimal.

ORANGE CLOUDS

2 cups orange juice
2 tablespoons cornstarch
2 tablespoons honey
1 cinnamon stick
2 egg whites
¼ teaspoon cream of tartar
3 tablespoons sugar
1 teaspoon grated orange peel

1. Combine orange juice, cornstarch, honey and cinnamon in 4-cup glass measure.

2. MICROWAVE (high), uncovered, 4½ to 5½ minutes (9 to 11) or until mixture boils, stirring once. Pour into 8-inch round glass serving dish; remove cinnamon stick.

3. Beat egg whites and cream of tartar until frothy. Gradually beat in sugar until soft peaks form. Spoon mounds of meringue onto orange sauce; sprinkle with orange peel.

4. MICROWAVE (high), uncovered, 1½ to 2 minutes (2 to 3) or until meringue is set. Serve warm or cool, plain or over fruit.

5 Servings, about 105 calories each

Meringue does not brown, but it will poach nicely in the microwave.

PEACHY CLOUDS

1 can (29 oz.) peach halves
2 egg whites
3 tablespoons sugar
½ teaspoon almond extract
Nutmeg

1. Arrange peach halves cut-side-up in glass pie plate. Add syrup from peaches.

2. MICROWAVE (high), uncovered, about 4 minutes or until heated; set aside.

3. Beat egg whites in small bowl until frothy. Gradually beat in sugar until mixture forms soft peaks. Beat in almond extract. Place a rounded spoonful of mixture on top of each peach half.

4. MICROWAVE (high), uncovered, about 1½ minutes or until egg whites are set. Sprinkle with nutmeg. Serve warm or cold.

6 Servings, about 85 calories each

TIP • When placing the peaches in the pie plate, place them in a circle around the edge, leaving only one peach in the center.

This lower calorie dessert has a luscious Bavarian Creme flavor. It is a perfect base for favorite fresh fruits.

FRUIT BAVARIAN

1½ cups milk
¼ cup sugar
1 envelope unflavored gelatin
2 eggs, separated
1 teaspoon vanilla
¼ teaspoon cream of tartar
1 tablespoon sugar
1½ cups sliced or chopped fresh fruit (strawberries, peaches, raspberries or blueberries)

1. Combine milk, ¼ cup sugar and the gelatin in 4-cup glass measure.

2. MICROWAVE (high), uncovered, 3 to 4 minutes or until mixture boils. Beat egg yolks slightly; slowly stir small amount of hot mixture into egg yolks. Return all of mixture to 4-cup measure, mixing well.

3. MICROWAVE (medium — 50%), uncovered, 1¼ to 1½ minutes or until mixture just begins to bubble, stirring once. Stir in vanilla. Refrigerate until mixture begins to thicken.

4. Beat egg whites and cream of tartar in medium-sized bowl until frothy. Gradually add 1 tablespoon sugar, beating until mixture forms soft peaks. Fold in cooled mixture and fruit. Pour into 6 serving dishes. Refrigerate until set, about 1 hour.

6 Servings, about 110 calories each

TIPS • With Full Power in step 3, microwave ¾ to 1½ minutes, stirring twice.
• With Combination Oven, microwave in step 2 for 7 to 8 minutes and in step 3 for 2 to 3 minutes.

Rich, creamy custard topped with mounds of meringue makes a lovely dessert. The meringue poaches beautifully in the microwave.

FLOATING ISLANDS

⅔ cup sugar
1 tablespoon cornstarch
¼ teaspoon salt
2 cups milk
3 eggs, separated
1 teaspoon vanilla
¼ teaspoon cream of tartar
⅓ cup sugar
½ teaspoon vanilla

1. Combine ⅔ cup sugar, the cornstarch, salt and milk in 4-cup glass measure.

2. MICROWAVE (high), uncovered, 4½ to 5½ minutes or until mixture boils, stirring occasionally during last half of cooking time. Beat egg yolks; beat in some of hot milk mixture. Return all of mixture to 4-cup measure.

3. MICROWAVE (high), uncovered, 1½ to 2 minutes or until mixture thickens slightly, stirring every ½ minute. Stir in 1 teaspoon vanilla. Cool 15 minutes.

4. Pour into shallow glass serving dish or 8-inch round glass baking dish. Beat egg whites and cream of tartar until frothy. Gradually add ⅓ cup sugar, beating until soft peaks form. Beat in ½ teaspoon vanilla. Spoon egg white mixture in mounds on custard sauce.

5. MICROWAVE (high), uncovered, 2 to 2½ minutes or until egg whites are set. Serve warm or cold.

About 6 Servings

TIPS • To reduce stirring in step 3, microwave with medium — 50% power 2½ to 3 minutes.

• An orange-flavored liqueur, like Grand Marnier or Curacao can be used for vanilla in custard sauce. Use 1 to 2 tablespoons.

Floating Islands.

Chilled squares of pumpkin and cream to serve with coffee or after a meal.

PUMPKIN CHIFFON SQUARES

- **¼ cup butter or margarine**
- **1¼ cups graham cracker crumbs**
- **3 tablespoons sugar**
- **¾ cup packed brown sugar**
- **1 teaspoon cinnamon**
- **½ teaspoon salt**
- **½ teaspoon nutmeg**
- **½ teaspoon ginger**
- **1 envelope unflavored gelatin**
- **1 can (13 fl. oz.) evaporated milk (1⅔ cups)**
- **3 eggs, separated**
- **2 cups cooked or canned pumpkin**
- **¼ teaspoon cream of tartar**
- **1 cup (½ pt.) whipping cream**
- **¼ cup powdered sugar**

1. MICROWAVE (high) butter in 12 x 8-inch glass baking dish about 1 minute or until melted. Mix in crumbs and sugar. Set aside ¼ cup. Press remainder into bottom of dish; set aside.

2. Combine brown sugar, cinnamon, salt, nutmeg, ginger and gelatin in glass mixing bowl; mix well. Stir in milk.

3. MICROWAVE (high), uncovered, 3 to 3½ minutes or until mixture boils, stirring once. Beat egg yolks slightly. Beat in a small amount of hot milk mixture. Return all of mixture to hot milk, blending thoroughly.

4. MICROWAVE (medium — 50%), uncovered, 2½ to 3 minutes or until slightly thickened, stirring twice. Blend in pumpkin. Cool until mixture mounds slightly, about 1 hour.

5. Beat egg whites with cream of tartar until soft peaks form. Fold into pumpkin mixture. Pour over crust; spread evenly. Refrigerate until set, about 4 hours. Beat cream and powdered sugar until thickened; spoon evenly over pumpkin. Sprinkle with reserved crumbs. Refrigerate until served.

12 to 15 Servings

TIPS • With Full Power in step 4, microwave 1½ to 2 minutes, stirring 2 or 3 times.

• With Combination Oven, microwave in step 1 for 2 to 3 minutes, in step 3 for 5 to 6 minutes and in step 4 for 3 to 4 minutes.

You can serve this refreshing lower calorie dessert year around . . . just select a fresh fruit that is in season. Try orange sections in January, bananas in March, strawberries in June, pears in October and of course, peaches in August and September.

PEACHY YO-GO DESSERT

- **2 tablespoons butter or margarine**
- **¾ cup graham cracker crumbs**
- **½ cup milk**
- **1 envelope unflavored gelatin**
- **2 tablespoons sugar**
- **1 egg**
- **2 cups vanilla-flavored yogurt (two 8-oz. cartons)**
- **¾ teaspoon almond extract**
- **1½ cups sliced, peeled fresh peaches**

1. MICROWAVE (high) butter in 8 or 9-inch round glass baking dish about 1 minute or until melted. Stir in cracker crumbs. Press into bottom of dish.

2. MICROWAVE (high), uncovered, 1½ to 2 minutes or until heated through, rotating dish once. Set aside.

3. Combine milk, gelatin and sugar in 4-cup glass measure.

4. MICROWAVE (high), uncovered, 1 to 1½ minutes or until mixture boils. Beat egg; slowly blend in small amount of hot mixture. Return all of mixture to 4-cup measure, mixing well.

5. MICROWAVE (medium — 50%), uncovered, ½ to 1 minute or until mixture just begins to bubble around edge. Stir in yogurt and almond extract.

6. Arrange peaches on crust. Pour yogurt mixture evenly over peaches. Refrigerate until set, about 2 hours. Store in refrigerator.

8 Servings, about 150 calories each

TIPS • With Full Power in step 5, microwave ½ to 1 minute, stirring twice.

• With Combination Oven, microwave in step 2 for 2 to 3 minutes, step 4 for 3 to 4 minutes and in step 5 for 1½ to 2 minutes.

This is one of the best bread puddings we've found for microwaving. It is also good even without the blueberries.

BLUEBERRY-LEMON BREAD PUDDING

¼ cup butter or margarine
4 slices bread, cubed
½ cup sugar
2 tablespoons lemon juice
1 cup blueberries, rinsed
1 cup milk
3 eggs
Cinnamon

1. MICROWAVE (high) butter in 1-quart glass casserole about 1 minute or until melted.

2. Add bread, sugar, lemon juice and blueberries. Toss to lightly mix. Combine milk and eggs; beat until smooth. Pour over bread mixture. Sprinkle with cinnamon.

3. Place casserole in 8-inch square glass baking dish. Add 1 cup warm water to baking dish.

4. MICROWAVE (high), uncovered, 11 to 13 minutes or until center is just about set. Serve warm or cold.

5 to 6 Servings

TIP • With Variable Power, omit baking dish with water and microwave with medium-high — 70% power 11 to 13 minutes.

When fresh fruits are abundant and flavorful, make some of your gelatin salads with natural fruit flavors. It's easy to do and is an excellent way to control additions of sugar and food colorings.

FROTHY FRUIT CUPS

1 cup orange juice
2 envelopes unflavored gelatin
¼ cup sugar
1 cup orange juice
2 medium-sized ripe bananas
2 cups (1 pint) strawberries
2 cups whipped topping or 1 cup whipping cream, whipped

1. Add gelatin to 1 cup orange juice in 4-cup glass measure. Let stand 5 minutes to soften. Blend in sugar.

2. MICROWAVE (high), uncovered, 2 to 3 minutes (5 to 6) or until mixture boils and gelatin is dissolved. Cool 10 minutes. Stir in remaining 1 cup orange juice. Place mixture in blender container or bowl of food processor. Add bananas. Process until smooth. Gradually add strawberries, processing until smooth. Set aside 1 cup of mixture at room temperature.

3. Pour remaining mixture into 6 clear glass goblets or parfait dishes. Place in refrigerator in tilted position by resting top of glass against side of refrigerator. Refrigerate until set.

4. Fold reserved gelatin into whipped topping or cream. Place glasses upright and spoon topping into each. Refrigerate until set, about 1½ hours. If desired, garnish with whole strawberries.

6 Servings, about 204 calories each

TIP • Frozen strawberries or other types of berries can be substituted for fresh strawberries.

Frothy Fruit Cups.

Apple crisp is always a favorite and is super easy in the microwave. This recipe was from a feature on energy consumption; noticeable savings are possible when prepared with microwaves rather than in a conventional oven.

APPLE CRISP

6 cups (6 med.) peeled, sliced cooking apples
1 tablespoon lemon juice
1 tablespoon water
¾ cup packed brown sugar
½ cup unsifted all-purpose flour
½ cup rolled oats
1 teaspoon cinnamon
½ cup butter or margarine

1. Place apples in 8-inch square glass baking dish. Sprinkle with lemon juice and water.

2. Combine brown sugar, flour, rolled oats and cinnamon; cut in butter until mixture is crumbly. Sprinkle over apples.

3. MICROWAVE (high), uncovered, 12 to 14 minutes or until apples are tender, rotating dish once.

About 6 Servings

Cook this dessert right in the dish from which it will be served. It cooks up quickly for a dessert or between-meal snack. You can make extra quantities of the topping and store in the refrigerator. Then, just sprinkle over the apple or other fruit and cook as needed.

INDIVIDUAL APPLE CRISP

2 tablespoons butter or margarine
¼ cup packed brown sugar
3 tablespoons flour
2 tablespoons rolled oats
2 tablespoons shredded coconut, if desired
⅛ teaspoon cinnamon
1 medium apple, peeled and sliced
1 tablespoon raisins

1. MICROWAVE (high) butter in glass bowl ¼ to ½ minute or until softened. Mix in brown sugar, flour, oats, coconut and cinnamon.

2. Combine apple and raisins in glass serving dish. Spoon topping over apple.

3. MICROWAVE (high), uncovered, 2½ to 3½ minutes (5 to 6) or until apple is tender.

1 Serving

Pineapple halves make decorative servers for colorful fruit combinations.

FESTIVE PINEAPPLE BOATS

¼ cup sugar
2 tablespoons cornstarch
¼ cup maraschino cherry liquid
¼ cup orange or cranberry juice
6 maraschino cherries, chopped
2 to 3 drops red food coloring, if desired
1 fresh pineapple
1 can (16 oz.) sliced peaches, drained
1 can (11 oz.) mandarin oranges, drained

1. Combine sugar, cornstarch and juices in 2-cup glass measure. Stir well.

2. MICROWAVE (high), uncovered, 2½ to 3 minutes (4 to 4½) or until mixture boils and is slightly thickened, stirring once. Stir in cherries and food coloring. Cool.

3. Cut pineapple in half lengthwise through leafy top. Cut around pineapple to remove fruit pulp, using grapefruit knife and leaving about ¼-inch rim. Cut pineapple pulp into chunks, discarding core.

4. Mix other fruits with pineapple.

5. Spoon fruits into pineapple shells. Drizzle with sauce. Refrigerate until served.

About 8 Servings

TIPS • Other combinations of fruits can be added to fresh pineapple. Just keep the quantity about the same (3 cups).

• To Make Ahead, prepare through step 4 and refrigerate. Complete step 5 shortly before serving time.

Thickened fresh fruits cook easily in the microwave. Here the cooled fruit mixture is layered with wafer crumbs, almond-flavored buttercream and whipped cream. Not a low calorie idea, but one that is very good eating.

REFRIGERATOR PEACH DELIGHT

6 medium fresh peaches, peeled and thinly sliced
¾ cup sugar
¼ cup cornstarch
¼ cup water
½ cup butter or margarine
¾ cup unsifted powdered sugar
1 egg
½ teaspoon almond extract or vanilla
1 package (about 10 ozs.) vanilla ice cream wafers, crushed
1 carton (8 oz.) frozen whipped topping, thawed

1. Combine peaches, sugar, cornstarch and water in 2-quart glass casserole. Cover with casserole lid.

2. MICROWAVE (high) 10 to 12 minutes (20 to 22) or until mixture boils and thickens, stirring 2 or 3 times. Refrigerate.

3. MICROWAVE (high) butter in glass mixing bowl ¼ to ½ minute (1 to 1½) or until softened. Beat at high speed until creamy. Gradually beat in powdered sugar. Add egg; beat until light and fluffy. Beat in almond extract.

4. Spread about ⅔ of wafer crumbs over bottom of 12 x 8-inch baking dish. Spoon butter mixture evenly over crumbs; spread carefully to cover. Top with chilled peach mixture, spreading evenly. Spoon on whipped topping; spread evenly. Sprinkle with remaining wafer crumbs.

5. Cover and refrigerate until chilled, at least 2 hours.

About 15 Servings

TIPS • Other fruits can be substituted for peaches. Blueberries, strawberries or apricots would be good.

• If desired, 1 cup chopped nuts can be added with crumb topping.

• One pint (2 cups) whipping cream, whipped and sweetened with ¼ cup sugar, can be substituted for whipped topping.

This dessert is a favorite of Mrs. Donald Rockley's family and friends in Waukesha, Wisconsin. We found the recipe required a few more changes than normal to adapt it to microwave cooking. However, we were successful and pleased with the results.

PEACHEE PIE SUPREME

3 tablespoons butter or margarine
1 egg
1 package (3⅛ oz.) vanilla pudding mix (not instant)
¾ cup unsifted all-purpose flour
1 teaspoon baking powder
½ cup milk
1 can (15 oz.) sliced peaches
1 package (8 oz.) cream cheese
¾ cup powdered sugar
1 tablespoon sugar
½ teaspoon cinnamon

1. MICROWAVE (high) butter in glass mixing bowl ½ to ¾ minute or until melted. Add egg, pudding mix, flour, baking powder and milk. Blend on low speed; then beat 2 minutes at medium speed. Pour into greased 8-inch round glass cake dish, spreading evenly.

2. MICROWAVE (high), uncovered, 4½ to 5½ minutes or until center is almost done, rotating dish once or twice.

3. Drain peaches, reserving 3½ tablespoons syrup. Arrange drained peaches on cake; set aside.

4. MICROWAVE (high) cream cheese in glass bowl ¾ to 1 minute or until softened. Blend in powdered sugar and reserved peach syrup. Beat 2 minutes at medium speed. Pour over peaches. Combine sugar and cinnamon; sprinkle on cream cheese.

5. MICROWAVE (high), uncovered, 4 to 5 minutes or until mixture is bubbly near edge, rotating dish twice. Serve warm or cold.

6 to 8 Servings

TIP • With Combination Oven, assemble batter, peaches and toppings in 8-inch round glass dish. Defrost-bake at 350° for 12 to 15 minutes or until center is set.

Here is another favorite from our Bicentennial issue. Called "pie plant" by our forefathers, rhubarb was as welcome as the first robin as a sign of Spring. Often, thrifty homemakers combined the pale pink stalks with pieces of leftover bread for this tart, homespun treat. It is as delicious warm from the oven as it is simple to prepare. Fruit sauce recipes, such as this, are ideal for microwave cooking.

RHUBARB BETTY

4 cups sliced rhubarb (about 1 lb.)
4 slices bread, cubed
1 cup sugar
½ teaspoon cinnamon
¼ cup butter or margarine

1. Combine rhubarb, bread cubes, sugar and cinnamon in large bowl; mix well. Spoon into 1-quart casserole, mounding mixture in casserole.

2. MICROWAVE (high) butter in glass dish ½ to 1 minute or until melted. Drizzle over rhubarb mixture. Sprinkle lightly with additional cinnamon.

3. MICROWAVE (high), uncovered, 10 to 11 minutes or until rhubarb is tender. Serve warm with plenty of light cream.

5 to 6 Servings

Peachee Pie Supreme, page 106.

Here is a quick snack or dessert for 1 or 2.

CARAMEL BAKED APPLES

1 medium cooking apple
2 caramels

1. Halve apple lengthwise; remove core. Unwrap caramels; place one in each of two glass custard cups or dessert dishes. Place apple cut-side-down over caramel.

2. MICROWAVE (high), uncovered, 2½ to 3½ minutes or until apples are tender. Place apples right-side-up on serving plate. Stir melted caramel into juices in dish. Spoon over apple halves.

2 Servings, about 70 calories each

TIP • For 2 apples, microwave 3½ to 4 minutes.

When guests drop in, prepare this elegant dessert in just minutes. Delightful topped with whipped cream.

BAKED PEARS IN CINNAMON SAUCE

3 pears, halved and cored
¼ cup water
⅓ cup packed brown sugar
½ tablespoon flour
¼ teaspoon cinnamon
2 tablespoons butter or margarine

1. Arrange pears, cut-side-up, in 9-inch glass pie plate. Combine water, brown sugar, flour and cinnamon; spoon onto pears. Dot with butter. Cover with waxed paper.

2. MICROWAVE (high) 5 to 6 minutes or until pears are tender. Serve warm or cold. If desired, top with whipped cream or cream cheese.

About 6 Servings

TIPS • Canned pears can be used for fresh. Drain a 28-oz. can, using ⅓ cup of syrup in place of water. Reduce brown sugar to 2 tablespoons.

• If desired, add 1 tablespoon brandy or rum along with cinnamon.

This quick and easy peach cobbler uses prepared pie filling and a packaged yellow cake mix for double convenience.

PEACHY COBBLER

⅓ cup butter or margarine
1 can (21 oz.) prepared peach pie filling
1 can (8 oz.) fruit cocktail, drained
1 package (9 oz.) yellow cake mix (one-layer size)
⅓ cup chopped nuts
Nutmeg

1. MICROWAVE (high) butter in glass cup about 1 minute or until melted.

2. Combine pie filling and fruit cocktail in 8-inch round glass cake dish. Sprinkle dry cake mix and nuts onto fruit; drizzle with melted butter. Sprinkle with nutmeg.

3. MICROWAVE (high), uncovered, 10 to 12 minutes or until bubbly throughout, rotating dish once. Serve warm or cold.

About 6 Servings

Peachy Pudding Cobbler.

This recipe was originally from our freezer-to-microwave issue. It makes a tasty dessert that can be assembled ahead and frozen (see Tip) or cooked immediately.

PEACHY PUDDING COBBLER

1 can (29 oz.) peach slices
1 package (4-serving size) butterscotch pudding and pie filling mix (not instant)
¼ cup butter or margarine
⅔ cup rolled oats
½ cup unsifted all-purpose flour
⅓ cup packed brown sugar
½ cup chopped nuts
1 teaspoon cinnamon

1. Drain peach slices, reserving ½ cup liquid. Place peach slices and reserved liquid in 8 or 9-inch round glass cake dish. Sprinkle with 2 tablespoons dry pudding mix.

2. MICROWAVE (high) butter in glass bowl ¼ to ½ minute or until softened. Mix in remaining ingredients including remaining pudding mix until crumbly. Spoon onto peach mixture.

3. MICROWAVE (high), uncovered, 10 to 11 minutes or until bubbly near center, rotating dish once or twice. Serve warm with cream or ice cream.

5 to 6 Servings

TIPS • When peaches, pears or apples are in season, substitute 5 cups sliced fresh fruit for canned fruit. Omit fruit liquid.

• With Combination Oven, microwave-bake at 375°, uncovered, 15 to 20 minutes in step 3.

• The cobbler can be assembled through step 2 and frozen up to 3 months. (If desired, line dish with foil so mixture can be removed from dish after frozen.) To cook, cover with paper towel and microwave 13 to 15 minutes.

As British and elegant as the Crown Jewels, this dessert was concocted not only to impress guests, but to use up smidgens of jam, pieces of leftover cake and whatever fruit was in season. It is a tasty lesson in using leftovers to full advantage, passed down to us by the prudent, resourceful cooks of yesteryear.

ENGLISH TRIFFLE

- **½ cup sliced almonds**
- **1 tablespoon butter or margarine**
- **12 sponge-type shortcake bases**
- **1 cup raspberry jam**
- **1 tablespoon grated lemon peel**
- **½ cup medium-dry sherry**
- **1½ tablespoons cornstarch**
- **¼ cup sugar**
- **3 cups milk**
- **3 eggs, beaten**
- **1 teaspoon vanilla**
- **1 to 2 cups whipping cream**
- **2 to 4 tablespoons sugar**

1. MICROWAVE (high) almonds and butter in small glass dish, uncovered, 4 to 5 minutes or until toasted, stirring once. Set aside.

2. Slice shortcakes horizontally and layer ⅓ of cake in 3-quart serving bowl.

3. MICROWAVE (high) jam in jar (remove lid) 1 to 1¼ minutes or until heated. Drizzle about ⅓ of jam over cake. Sprinkle with ⅓ of lemon peel and ⅓ of sherry. Top with 2 more layers of cake, jam, lemon peel and sherry; set aside. Combine cornstarch, sugar and milk in 4-cup glass measure.

4. MICROWAVE (high), uncovered, 6 to 7 minutes or until mixture boils, stirring 2 or 3 times during last half of cooking. Beat in eggs.

5. MICROWAVE (medium — 50%), uncovered, 3 to 3½ minutes or until mixture thickens to sauce-like consistency, stirring every minute. Stir in vanilla. Cool 15 minutes. Pour over cake layers. Cover and refrigerate. Just before serving, beat cream and sugar until thickened. Spoon cream over top of cake. Sprinkle with toasted almonds.

12 to 15 Servings

TIPS • A yellow cake mix (cook in microwave oven if desired) can be substituted for sponge cakes. Cut into slices and layer as described.

• Lady fingers (about 24) can also be substituted for sponge cakes.

• With Full Power in step 5, microwave 1½ to 2 minutes, stirring every ½ minute.

Fragrant, spicy gingerbread tops apple slices for a winning combination in this cobbler recipe.

GINGERBREAD APPLE COBBLER

- **4 medium apples, peeled and sliced (4 cups)**
- **½ cup packed brown sugar**
- **1 teaspoon cornstarch**
- **2 tablespoons water**
- **1 tablespoon lemon juice**
- **½ teaspoon cinnamon**

Gingerbread Topping:

- **1 egg**
- **½ cup buttermilk or sour milk**
- **¼ cup molasses**
- **2 tablespoons cooking oil**
- **1 cup unsifted all-purpose flour**
- **¼ cup sugar**
- **½ teaspoon soda**
- **½ teaspoon ginger**
- **¼ teaspoon salt**
- **¼ teaspoon baking powder**
- **¼ teaspoon nutmeg**

1. Combine apples, brown sugar, cornstarch, water, lemon juice and cinnamon in 8-inch round glass cake dish. Cover with waxed paper.

2. MICROWAVE (high) 4 to 5 minutes or until apples are tender-crisp, stirring once.

3. Beat together egg, buttermilk, molasses and oil in mixing bowl. Add remaining ingredients; beat until smooth. Pour over apples.

4. MICROWAVE (high), uncovered, 6 to 7 minutes or until toothpick inserted near center comes out clean, rotating dish once or twice. Serve warm or cold, plain or with whipped cream.

6 to 8 Servings

TIP • With Combination Oven, microwave in step 2 for 7 to 8 minutes. In step 4, bake at 350° for 10 minutes and then microwave-bake 3 to 4 minutes.

Chocolate-Almond Cheesecake.

This cheesecake is one of our favorites. The food processor can be used to crush and mix the graham cracker crust and chop the nuts. (See Tip if you don't have a food processor.)

CHOCOLATE-ALMOND CHEESECAKE

12 graham cracker squares, broken in half
1/3 cup slivered almonds
2 tablespoons sugar
1/4 cup butter or margarine
2 packages (8 ozs. each) cream cheese
2 eggs
2/3 cup sugar
1 teaspoon almond extract
1/3 cup semi-sweet chocolate pieces
1 cup sour cream
2 tablespoons sugar
1/2 teaspoon vanilla

1. Insert metal blade into food processor bowl. Add crackers; process with short on-off motion until mixture is fine. Add almonds; continue processing until finely chopped. Add 2 tablespoons sugar and the butter; process until thoroughly mixed. Press mixture into bottom and up sides of 8 or 9-inch round glass baking dish.

2. MICROWAVE (high), uncovered, 2 to 3 minutes or until heated through.

3. Cut cream cheese into 1-inch pieces. Reinsert metal blade into food processor bowl. Add 1/2 package of cream cheese and 1 egg; process until creamy. Slowly add remaining cheese and egg, processing until smooth. Add 2/3 cup sugar and the extract; process until thoroughly mixed. Pour about 2/3 of mixture into crust.

4. MICROWAVE (high) chocolate pieces in glass dish 1 1/2 to 2 minutes or until glossy. Add chocolate to mixture in processor bowl. Process until thoroughly mixed. Pour chocolate mixture over mixture in crust. Swirl lightly with knife.

5. MICROWAVE (medium — 50%), uncovered, 14 to 16 minutes or until center is almost set, rotating dish twice.

6. Combine sour cream, 2 tablespoons sugar and the vanilla. Spoon over cheesecake; spread carefully to cover.

7. MICROWAVE (high) 1 1/2 to 2 minutes or until heated. Cool. Refrigerate at least 6 hours before serving.

8 to 10 Servings

TIPS • With Full Power, microwave 8 to 9 minutes in step 5, rotating dish 2 or 3 times.

• If you don't have a food processor, crush the crackers in a blender or with a rolling pin and finely chop the almonds. Soften the cream cheese in the microwave for about 1 minute, and then blend the mixture with a mixer.

• With Combination Oven, microwave in step 2 for 3 to 4 minutes, in step 4 for 7 to 8 minutes, step 5 for 9 to 10 minutes and in step 7 for 4 to 5 minutes.

Here is a luscious cheesecake with a pecan-praline topping that is sure to become a favorite. For a creamy, evenly cooked filling, the mixture is partially cooked in the mixing bowl before being added to the crust. This is best made at least a day ahead so it can thoroughly chill.

PECAN-PRALINE CHEESECAKE

Crust:
- **3 tablespoons butter or margarine**
- **¾ cup graham cracker crumbs**
- **3 tablespoons sugar**

Filling:
- **2 packages (8 ozs. each) cream cheese**
- **⅔ cup packed brown sugar**
- **2 eggs**
- **½ cup evaporated milk**
- **1 tablespoon flour**
- **1 teaspoon vanilla**

Topping:
- **½ cup dark corn syrup**
- **¼ cup packed brown sugar**
- **1 teaspoon vanilla**
- **½ cup chopped pecans**

1. MICROWAVE (high) butter in 8 or 9-inch round glass cake dish ½ to 1 minute (2 to 2½) or until melted. Mix in graham cracker crumbs and sugar. Press evenly in bottom of dish.

2. MICROWAVE (high), uncovered, 1¼ to 1¾ minutes (2 to 2½) or until heated through, rotating once. Set aside.

3. MICROWAVE (high) cream cheese in large glass mixing bowl 1 to 1½ minutes (2½ to 3) or until softened. Beat until smooth. Blend in brown sugar and eggs. Mix in milk, flour and vanilla.

4. MICROWAVE (high), uncovered, 3½ to 4½ minutes (6½ to 7½) or until slightly thickened, stirring 3 or 4 times. Beat until smooth. Pour into crust.

5. MICROWAVE (high), uncovered, 2½ to 3 minutes (5 to 5½) or until center is just about set. Cool and refrigerate until set, 4 to 6 hours.

6. Combine corn syrup and brown sugar in 4-cup measure; mix well.

7. MICROWAVE (high), uncovered, 1 to 1½ minutes (3 to 4) or until mixture boils, stirring once. Stir in vanilla and pecans. Cool.

8. Spoon cooled topping onto each cheesecake serving.

8 to 10 Servings

These delectable desserts are pictured on our cover. They taste as great as they look.

GRASSHOPPER TARTS

- **4 ozs. milk chocolate candy**
- **2 tablespoons butter or margarine**
- **20 large marshmallows**
- **⅓ cup milk**
- **2 tablespoons white crème de cacao**
- **2 tablespoons green crème de menthe**
- **½ cup whipping cream, whipped, or 1 cup whipped topping**

1. Make a few chocolate curls for garnish by peeling thin layers of chocolate with a vegetable peeler. Set aside.

2. MICROWAVE (high) remaining chocolate and butter in 2-cup glass measure 1 to 1½ minutes or until softened. Stir until smooth.

3. Divide chocolate among 6 paper-lined custard cups. Spread chocolate evenly over bottom and up side of paper lining, using back of spoon. Refrigerate to set.

4. Combine marshmallows and milk in glass mixing bowl.

5. MICROWAVE (high), uncovered, 1¼ to 1½ minutes or until marshmallows are puffed. Stir until smooth. Blend in crème de cacao and crème de menthe. Refrigerate until partially set, about 45 minutes. Fold in whipped cream. Spoon into chocolate cups. Refrigerate until set, 2 to 3 hours.

6. Remove tarts from cups; peel off paper. If desired, top with additional whipped cream and chocolate curls.

6 Servings

TIP • The chocolate becomes quite brittle when refrigerated. For ease in serving, allow the tarts to stand at room temperature 20 to 30 minutes before serving.

This easy-to-make chilled cheesecake from Mrs. Marna Winn of Burnsville, Minnesota, was easily adapted to microwave cooking. Serve this lower calorie cheesecake with your favorite fresh fruits.

LIGHT AND CREAMY CHEESECAKE

1 cup milk
2 envelopes unflavored gelatin
4 eggs
1 cup sugar
1 carton (32 oz.) small curd creamed cottage cheese
1 teaspoon vanilla

1. Combine milk and gelatin in 4-cup glass measure. Beat in eggs and sugar.

2. MICROWAVE (high), uncovered, 4 to 5 minutes (5 to 7) or until mixture is thickened and creamy, stirring every minute. Beat until smooth.

3. Combine cottage cheese and vanilla in blender container. Process at medium speed until smooth. Blend in as much of custard mixture as blender will hold. Pour mixture into 12 x 8-inch or 13 x 9-inch pan. Stir in any remaining custard mixture. Refrigerate until set, about 2 hours. Serve cut into squares and topped with favorite sweetened fresh or frozen fruit—peaches, strawberries, blueberries, raspberries, or a colorful combination.

12 to 15 Servings

TIP • To eliminate some of the stirring in step 2, microwave with medium — 50% power for 8 to 9 minutes.

Gingerbread Apple Cobbler, page 109, and Butterscotch-Walnut Pie, page 113.

This recipe illustrates the versatility of the microwave oven. The crust, filling and topping are all prepared separately and then combined to create the luscious pie.

BUTTERSCOTCH-WALNUT PIE

¼ cup butter or margarine
1¼ cups graham cracker crumbs (15 squares)
2 tablespoons sugar

Filling:
1 cup packed brown sugar
¼ cup cornstarch
½ teaspoon salt
3 cups milk
4 egg yolks or 2 whole eggs, slightly beaten
1 tablespoon butter or margarine
1 teaspoon vanilla

Topping:
½ cup chopped walnuts or other nuts
1 tablespoon brown sugar
1 tablespoon butter or margarine

1. MICROWAVE (high) butter in glass mixing bowl ½ to 1 minute or until melted. Stir in crumbs and sugar until combined. Press mixture into bottom and up sides of 9-inch glass pie plate.

2. MICROWAVE (high), uncovered, 1½ to 2½ minutes or until heated through, rotating plate once. Cool.

3. Combine brown sugar, cornstarch and salt in 2-quart glass mixing bowl. Stir in milk.

4. MICROWAVE (high), uncovered, 9 to 10 minutes or until mixture boils and thickens, stirring 2 or 3 times during last half of cooking time. Pour small amount of milk mixture into egg yolks, stirring constantly; return egg mixture to remaining milk mixture, blending well.

5. MICROWAVE (high), uncovered, 2 to 3 minutes or until mixture bubbles around edges, stirring once. Stir in butter and vanilla. Pour into cooled pie shell. Combine ingredients for Topping in small glass dish.

6. MICROWAVE (high), uncovered, 2½ to 3½ minutes or until nuts are toasted, stirring 2 or 3 times. Spoon over top of pie. Refrigerate pie at least 4 hours or until set.

9-inch Pie

Simplify pastry making by using your microwave oven to cook the pie shell. You'll have a tender, flaky crust without the danger of scorching or overcooking.

BAKED PASTRY SHELL

1. Prepare pastry for 1-crust pie using pie crust mix or favorite recipe. Roll out on floured cloth-covered surface to circle 1 inch larger than 9 or 10-inch glass pie plate. Fit into pie plate. Fold under edge, forming standing rim; flute. Prick bottom and sides 4 or 5 times with fork.

2. MICROWAVE (high), uncovered, 4 to 5 minutes (7 to 8) or until crust has a dry flaky appearance, rotating plate once or twice.

1 Pastry Shell

This apple pie can be cooked totally with microwaves since the crust is precooked and the apples are topped with a crunchy streusel topping.

FRENCH APPLE PIE

10-inch baked pastry shell
5 cups sliced apples (about 5 medium)
⅔ cup sugar
1 tablespoon flour
½ teaspoon cinnamon
1 tablespoon lemon juice

Streusel Topping:
1 cup unsifted all-purpose flour
½ cup packed brown sugar
½ teaspoon cinnamon
⅓ cup butter or margarine

1. Prepare and cook pastry shell in glass pie plate as directed above. Set aside.

2. Combine apples, sugar, flour, cinnamon and lemon juice. Arrange in pie shell.

3. Combine flour, brown sugar and cinnamon for topping; cut in butter until crumbly. Spoon evenly over apples.

4. MICROWAVE (high), uncovered, 8 to 10 minutes (11 to 12) or until apples are tender. Serve warm or cool, plain or with ice cream.

10-inch Pie

Fresh pears and sour cream create an unusual but delightful combination for this pie.

FRESH PEAR-SOUR CREAM PIE

10-inch baked pastry shell
4 cups sliced, peeled fresh pears
½ cup sugar
¼ cup all-purpose flour
¼ teaspoon nutmeg
½ cup raisins
1 tablespoon lemon juice
2 tablespoons butter or margarine

Sour Cream Topping:

1 cup sour cream
¼ cup sugar
½ teaspoon vanilla

1. Prepare pastry shell in glass pie plate as directed on page 113. Set aside.

2. Combine pears, sugar, flour, nutmeg, raisins, lemon juice and butter in 1½-quart glass casserole. Cover with casserole lid.

3. MICROWAVE (high) 5 to 6 minutes (9 to 10) or until mixture boils and thickens, stirring once. Pour into pastry shell. Combine sour cream, sugar and vanilla for topping. Spoon over filling, spreading to cover. Sprinkle with additional nutmeg.

4. MICROWAVE (high), uncovered, 1½ to 2½ minutes (3 to 4) or until topping is heated. Cool.

10-inch Pie

TIP • Peaches can be substituted for pears.

Light and creamy custard teams with fresh peaches for this refreshing dessert. The custard is partially cooked in the mixing bowl before pouring into the precooked pastry shell.

PEACH CUSTARD PIE

10-inch baked pastry shell
4 cups sliced, peeled fresh peaches
1 cup sugar
3 tablespoons flour
¼ teaspoon nutmeg
1 tablespoon butter or margarine
2 eggs, beaten

1. Prepare pastry shell in glass pie plate as directed on page 00. Set aside.

2. Combine peaches, sugar, flour, nutmeg and butter in 1½-quart glass casserole. Cover with casserole lid.

3. MICROWAVE (high) 5½ to 6½ minutes (9 to 10) or until mixture boils and thickens, stirring once. Stir in eggs. Pour into pastry shell. If desired, top with a baked top crust.

4. MICROWAVE (high), uncovered, 1½ to 2 minutes (4 to 5) or until filling is bubbly around edge. Serve warm or cool.

10-inch Pie

This recipe illustrates cooking pastry shells and fruit fillings in the microwave. The topping is a combination of yogurt and whipped topping and is an ideal garnish for many fruit desserts.

SNOW-TOPPED BLUEBERRY PIE

9-inch baked pastry shell
4 cups fresh or thawed, frozen blueberries
⅔ cup sugar
3 tablespoons cornstarch
¼ teaspoon cinnamon
2 tablespoons butter or margarine
1 cup (half a 4-oz. carton) frozen whipped topping, thawed
½ cup plain yogurt

1. Prepare pastry shell as directed on page 113. Set aside.

2. Combine blueberries, sugar, cornstarch and cinnamon in 2-quart glass casserole. Cover with casserole lid.

3. MICROWAVE (high) 11 to 13 minutes (13 to 15) or until mixture boils and thickens, stirring 2 or 3 times. Stir in butter; cool.

4. Spoon cooled filling into pastry shell. Combine whipped topping and yogurt; spoon onto blueberries. Refrigerate until served.

9-inch Pie

TIP • Other fruits such as boysenberries, peaches or cherries can be substituted for blueberries.

Classic sour cream-raisin pie, easily prepared in the microwave oven.

SOUR CREAM-RAISIN PIE

10-inch baked pastry shell
½ cup milk
¾ cup sugar
2 tablespoons cornstarch
3 eggs
1 cup sour cream
½ teaspoon salt
½ teaspoon cinnamon
1½ cups raisins

Topping:
1 cup whipping cream
2 tablespoons sugar
½ teaspoon rum or vanilla extract
Nutmeg

1. Prepare pastry shell as directed on page 113. Set aside.

2. Combine milk, sugar and cornstarch in 4-cup glass measure.

3. MICROWAVE (high) 2½ to 3 minutes or until mixture boils, stirring once or twice. Beat together eggs, sour cream, salt and cinnamon. Beat into cornstarch mixture. Stir in raisins.

4. MICROWAVE (medium — 50%), uncovered, 5 to 6 minutes or until mixture is thickened, stirring occasionally. Spread evenly in pastry shell. Refrigerate.

5. Beat whipping cream, sugar and extract for Topping until thickened. Spoon over filling, spreading to cover. Sprinkle with nutmeg. Refrigerate until served.

10-inch Pie

TIPS • When using a 9-inch pastry shell, reduce raisins to 1 cup.

• With Full Power in step 4, microwave 3 to 4 minutes, stirring every ½ minute.

Fresh Pear-Sour Cream Pie, page 114, French Apple Pie, page 113, and Peach Custard Pie, page 114.

Raspberry Cheesecake Pie and Coco-Nut Chocolate Pie, page 117.

For a creamy, evenly cooked filling, partially cook the filling in a mixing bowl before adding to the precooked crust.

RASPBERRY CHEESECAKE PIE

9-inch baked pastry shell
1 package (8 oz.) cream cheese
½ cup sugar
2 eggs
1 cup sour cream
½ teaspoon almond extract
1 package (10 oz.) frozen sweetened raspberries
1 tablespoon cornstarch

1. Prepare pastry shell in glass pie plate as directed on page 113. Set aside.

2. MICROWAVE (high) cream cheese in glass mixing bowl 1 to 1½ minutes (2 to 2½) or until softened. Beat in sugar and eggs.

3. MICROWAVE (high), uncovered, 2 to 2½ minutes (5 to 6) or until mixture is thickened, stirring every 30 seconds. Stir in sour cream and almond extract. Pour into pastry shell.

4. MICROWAVE (high), uncovered, 1½ to 2 minutes (3 to 4) or until mixture begins to bubble around edge, rotating plate once. Cool.

5. Remove metal cover from one end of raspberries. MICROWAVE (high) in package about 2 to 2½ minutes (3 to 4) or until just about thawed. Combine cornstarch and juice from berries in 2-cup glass measure.

6. MICROWAVE (high), uncovered, 1¼ to 1¾ minutes (3 to 4) or until mixture boils, stirring once or twice. Stir in raspberries. Spoon evenly onto cooled cheesecake layer. Refrigerate until set, about 2 hours.

9-inch Pie

Here's a creamy chocolate custard pie with the added attractions of coconut and nuts. Minimal cooking is required in the pie crust since the filling is precooked in the mixing bowl.

COCO-NUT CHOCOLATE PIE

9-inch baked pastry shell
¼ cup butter or margarine
2 ozs. (half a bar) German-sweet chocolate
1 can (13 fl. oz.) evaporated milk
½ cup packed brown sugar
3 eggs
1 cup flaked coconut
⅓ cup chopped nuts
1 teaspoon vanilla
Whipped cream

1. Prepare pastry shell in glass pie plate as directed on page 113. Set aside.

2. Combine butter and chocolate in 1-quart glass mixing bowl.

3. MICROWAVE (high), uncovered, 2½ to 3 minutes (3 to 4) or until melted, stirring once. Stir in milk and brown sugar.

4. MICROWAVE (high), uncovered, 3½ to 4 minutes (6 to 7) or until mixture just about boils (chocolate may not be completely melted).

5. Beat eggs; beat in small amount of hot mixture. Return all of mixture to mixing bowl, blending well. Stir in coconut, nuts and vanilla.

6. MICROWAVE (high), uncovered, 1½ to 2½ minutes (3 to 4) or until mixture boils around edge and is slightly thickened, stirring every 30 seconds. Pour into pastry shell, spreading evenly.

7. MICROWAVE (high), uncovered, 1 to 2 minutes (3 to 4) or until edges just start to bubble, rotating pie once. Cool and refrigerate until served. Serve with whipped cream.

9-inch Pie

TIP • Two squares (2 ozs.) semi-sweet chocolate can be substituted for the German-sweet chocolate.

Imagine topping off a meal with a moist, yummy brownie pie crowned with a cool, green mint topping. This is truly a grand finale!

BROWNIE MINT PIE

9-inch baked pastry shell
¼ cup butter or margarine
1 cup (6 ozs.) semi-sweet chocolate pieces
½ cup packed brown sugar
2 eggs
1½ teaspoons vanilla
⅓ cup all-purpose flour
1 cup chopped pecans

Topping:
6 marshmallows
2 tablespoons milk
3 tablespoons green créme de menthe
1 cup whipping cream

1. Prepare pastry shell as directed on page 113. Set aside.

2. Combine butter and chocolate pieces in 2-quart glass mixing bowl.

3. MICROWAVE (high), uncovered, 1 to 1½ minutes (2 to 2½) or until softened. Stir until smooth. Beat in brown sugar and eggs. Stir in vanilla, flour and pecans. Pour into pastry shell, spreading evenly.

4. MICROWAVE (high), uncovered, 4½ to 5 minutes (6½ to 7½) or until filling is puffed (don't overcook or it will become hard), rotating once or twice. Cool.

5. Combine marshmallows and milk in glass mixing bowl.

6. MICROWAVE (high), uncovered, ¾ to 1 minute (1 to 1½) or until puffed. Stir until smooth. Stir in créme de menthe. Cool.

7. Add whipping cream to cooled marshmallow mixture; beat until thickened. Spoon onto cooled pie, spreading to cover. Refrigerate several hours or until served.

9-inch Pie

This simple chilled pumpkin pie makes a light, delicately spiced finale for a Fall dinner.

PUMPKIN-YOGURT PIE

¼ cup butter or margarine
1 cup graham cracker crumbs
2 tablespoons sugar
1 cup cooked or canned pumpkin
¼ cup packed brown sugar
1 teaspoon cinnamon
½ teaspoon nutmeg
¼ teaspoon ginger
¼ teaspoon salt
1 carton (9 oz.) frozen whipped topping
1 carton (8 oz.) vanilla or orange-flavored yogurt

1. MICROWAVE (high) butter in 9-inch glass pie plate ½ to 1 minute or until melted. Mix in cracker crumbs and sugar. Press mixture into bottom and up sides of pie plate.

2. MICROWAVE (high), uncovered, 1½ to 2½ minutes or until heated through, rotating plate once or twice.

3. Combine pumpkin, brown sugar, cinnamon, nutmeg, ginger and salt in large glass bowl.

4. MICROWAVE (high), uncovered, 1½ to 2 minutes or until mixture starts to boil. Cool 10 minutes.

5. MICROWAVE (low — 30%) frozen whipped topping, uncovered, 1 minute to begin to thaw. Stir gently.

6. MICROWAVE (low — 30%) ½ to 1 minute or until just about thawed.

7. Fold yogurt and thawed whipped topping into pumpkin mixture. Spoon into crust. Refrigerate or freeze about 4 hours or until served. If frozen, remove from freezer about 15 minutes before serving.

9-inch Pie

TIPS • If whipped topping is already thawed, omit microwaving in steps 5 and 6.

• With plain yogurt (homemade or purchased), add ¼ cup additional sugar in step 7.

• With Combination Oven, microwave 2 to 2½ minutes in step 1, 2 to 3 minutes in step 2, 2½ to 3½ minutes in step 4 and about 1 minute in step 5; omit step 6.

A refreshing dessert after a hearty meal.

FROSTY PUMPKIN PRALINE PIE

Crust:
- **¼ cup butter or margarine**
- **1¼ cups graham cracker crumbs (about 15 squares)**
- **2 tablespoons sugar**

Praline Pieces:
- **¼ cup firmly packed brown sugar**
- **¼ cup sliced or slivered almonds**
- **1 tablespoon butter or margarine**
- **1 teaspoon water**

Filling:
- **1 cup canned pumpkin**
- **½ cup firmly packed brown sugar**
- **¼ cup milk**
- **1 teaspoon cinnamon**
- **½ teaspoon nutmeg**
- **¼ teaspoon ginger**
- **¼ teaspoon salt**
- **1 pint (2 cups) vanilla ice cream**

Topping:
- **1 cup (½ pt.) whipping cream**
- **2 tablespoons sugar**
- **1 teaspoon vanilla or 2 tablespoons brandy**

1. MICROWAVE (high) butter for crust in glass bowl ½ to 1 minute or until melted. Stir in crumbs and sugar until combined. Press mixture into bottom and up sides of 9-inch glass pie plate.

2. MICROWAVE (medium-high — 70%), uncovered, 2½ to 3 minutes or until heated through, rotating plate once. Cool.

3. Combine all ingredients for Praline Pieces in 8-inch round glass baking dish.

4. MICROWAVE (medium-high — 70%), uncovered, 2 to 3 minutes or until bubbly and nuts are lightly toasted, stirring once or twice. Cool, stirring once to break into pieces.

5. Combine all ingredients for Filling except ice cream in glass mixing bowl.

6. MICROWAVE (high), uncovered, 3 to 4 minutes or until sugar is dissolved, stirring once. Stir in ice cream. Let stand until ice cream can be easily mixed in. Pour into crust. Freeze until firm.

7. Beat cream until thickened; beat in sugar and vanilla. Spread over pie; sprinkle with praline pieces. Freeze until served.

About 6 Servings

TIPS • With Full Power, microwave 1½ to 2½ minutes in step 2, rotating plate twice and in step 4, microwave 2 to 3 minutes, stirring 2 or 3 times.

• Crushed gingersnaps can be substituted for graham crackers.

Pumpkin-Yogurt Pie, page 118.

Frosty Pumpkin Praline Pie.

Here we have used the basics of a baked pastry shell, changed to individual tart shells. They are not difficult to prepare, yet make a very special looking dessert. You may wish to make extras and keep in the freezer for quick, last minute desserts. If you lack the time to make a filling, just fill with a scoop of ice cream and sweetened fresh fruit.

SUMMERTIME TART SHELLS

1. Prepare favorite mix or home recipe pastry for 1-crust pie; divide dough into six equal portions.
2. Roll out each on floured cloth-covered surface to a 5-inch circle or square. Cut pieces of paper towel about the same size as pastry.
3. Turn six 5 or 6-oz. glass custard cups upside down. Place a piece of paper towel and then a pastry circle over each, allowing pastry to drape into 4 or 5 pleats.
4. MICROWAVE (high) 4 to 5 minutes or until crust has a dry, flaky appearance (it should no longer have a moist greasy look).
5. Within 5 minutes, remove each pastry shell from cup; carefully peel off paper. Place on serving plates or in serving dishes. Fill with desired filling.

6 Tart Shells

TIP • If tart shells become too cool, the paper will be difficult to remove.

Summertime Tart Shells.

A summer spectacular. The tart shells make serving simple and attractive.

FRESH STRAWBERRY FILLING

1 quart fresh strawberries, washed and hulled
About 1/4 cup water
2/3 cup sugar
2 tablespoons cornstarch
2 teaspoons lemon juice
Sweetened whipped cream

1. Place about 3/4 cup of berries in blender container. Process at medium speed until smooth. Add water to make 1 cup. Combine in glass mixing bowl with sugar and cornstarch.
2. MICROWAVE (high), uncovered, 3 to 4 minutes or until mixture boils, stirring once or twice. Cool about 30 minutes. Stir in lemon juice. Slice remaining berries; add to cooked mixture. Mix lightly to coat evenly. Spoon into six tart shells. Refrigerate until served. Serve with whipped cream.

6 Servings

Fresh Strawberry Filling.

Favorite Recipes from

The Microwave Times

Chapter 9

Cakes, Cookies & Candies

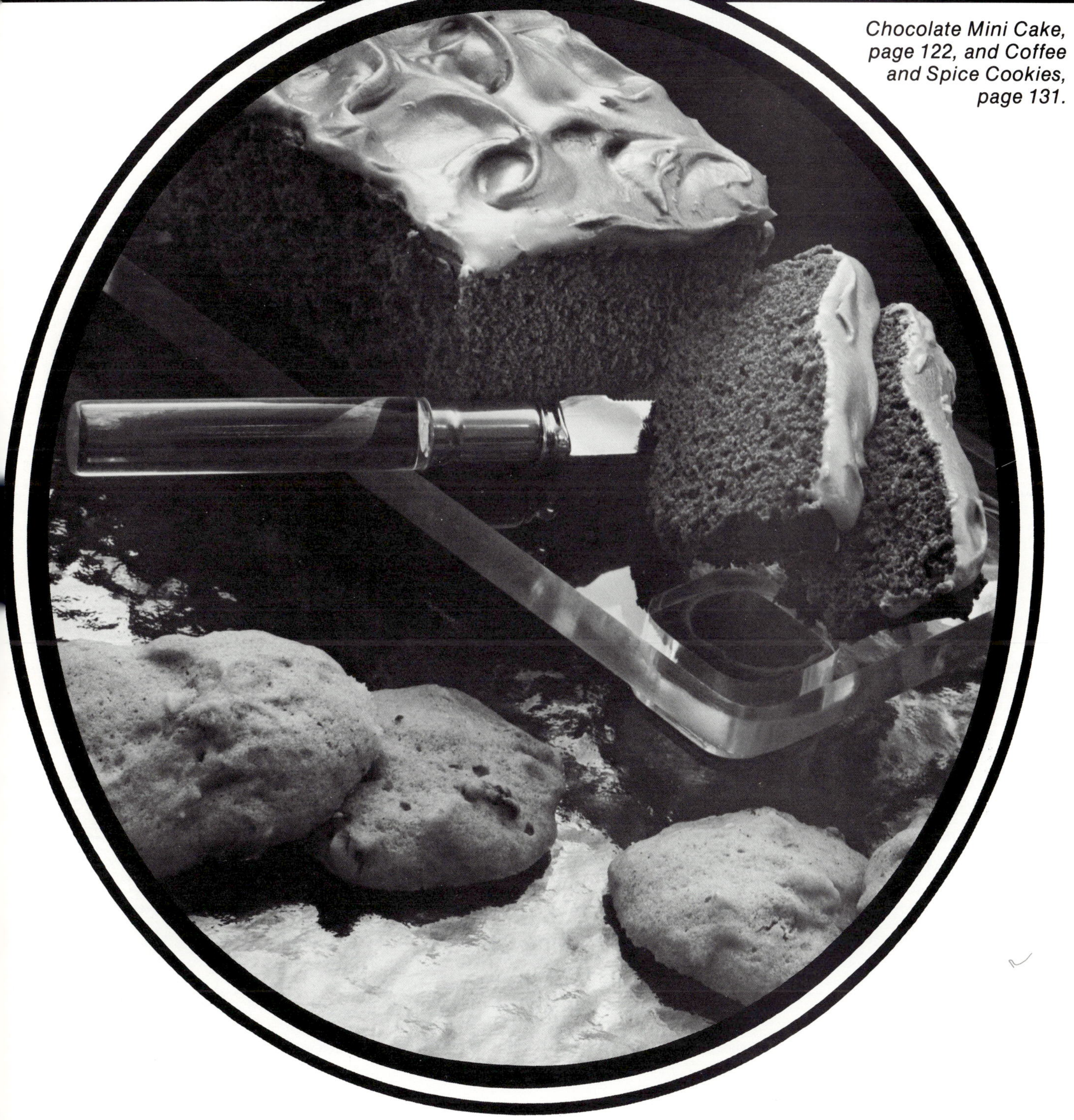

Chocolate Mini Cake, page 122, and Coffee and Spice Cookies, page 131.

When you have a cake like this with a unique characteristic only achievable with conventional heat, this combination method is good to use. The cake looks and tastes like conventionally prepared, but is quicker to cook. You have your choice with this cake . . . an outstanding cake if you use your conventional oven for part of the preparation, or a good cake, if you follow the directions in the Tips and prepare it totally in the microwave.

CHOCOLATE CHIP CAKE

1 cup water
1 cup chopped dates
1 teaspoon soda
1 cup butter or margarine
1 cup sugar
2 eggs
1 teaspoon vanilla
1½ cups unsifted all-purpose flour
1 tablespoon unsweetened cocoa
1 to 2 cups (6 to 12-oz. pkg.) semi-sweet chocolate pieces
½ cup sugar

1. Preheat oven to 350°.

2. MICROWAVE (high) water in 1-cup glass measure 2 to 3 minutes or until hot. Combine dates and soda in shallow dish; add water. Set aside to cool.

3. MICROWAVE (high) butter in glass mixing bowl about ½ minute or until softened. Blend in 1 cup sugar; beat in eggs, one at a time. Mix in vanilla. Add flour and cocoa; stir just until moistened. Add cooled date mixture; mix until blended. Pour into 12 x 8-inch glass baking dish, greased on bottom only. Sprinkle with chocolate pieces, then with ½ cup sugar.

4. Bake in preheated oven 15 minutes; then transfer to microwave oven.

5. MICROWAVE (high) 2 to 3 minutes or until toothpick inserted in center comes out clean.

12 x 8-inch Cake

TIPS • If you prefer an entirely microwave method, omit the topping of chocolate pieces and sugar in step 3. Microwave (high) 8 minutes, rotating dish once. Sprinkle chocolate pieces onto cake. Microwave (high) 6 to 8 minutes or until toothpick inserted near center comes out clean, rotating dish once.

• With Combination Oven, bake as directed in step 4. Then, microwave-bake 5 to 7 minutes or until done.

Since this cake has no egg, it is easily reduced to a small size. The loaf dish is just the right size for this quantity.

CHOCOLATE MINI CAKE

1 cup unsifted all-purpose flour
½ cup sugar
2 tablespoons unsweetened cocoa
½ teaspoon baking powder
¼ teaspoon soda
¼ teaspoon salt
¼ cup mayonnaise
½ cup cold water
½ teaspoon vanilla

1. Combine flour, sugar, cocoa, baking powder, soda and salt in mixing bowl. Stir in mayonnaise, water and vanilla; beat until smooth.

2. Pour into 8 x 4 or 9 x 5-inch loaf dish, greased on bottom only.

3. MICROWAVE (high), uncovered, 4 to 4½ minutes or until top springs back when touched lightly, rotating dish once. Cool; frost as desired.

6 to 8 Servings

TIP • With Combination Oven, pour batter into greased and floured loaf dish. Bake in preheated 350° oven for 10 minutes. Microwave-bake 3 to 5 minutes or until cake tests done.

German Chocolate Cake is always popular. This moist cake utilizes the microwave for several steps.

GERMAN CHOCOLATE OATMEAL CAKE

1 cup quick-cooking rolled oats
1¾ cups water
1 bar (4 oz.) German sweet chocolate
½ cup butter or margarine
1 cup sugar
1 cup packed brown sugar
3 eggs
1 teaspoon vanilla
1½ cups unsifted all-purpose flour
1 teaspoon soda
1 teaspoon salt

Coconut-Nut Topping:
1 cup flaked coconut
⅔ cup packed brown sugar
⅓ cup chopped nuts
⅓ cup butter or margarine
2 tablespoons light cream or milk

1. Combine rolled oats and water in large glass mixing bowl.

2. MICROWAVE (high), uncovered, 2 to 3 minutes or until mixture boils and thickens, stirring once or twice. Break chocolate into pieces; add to hot mixture along with butter. Stir occasionally until melted.

3. Mix sugars into oatmeal mixture. Beat in eggs, one at a time. Stir in vanilla, flour, soda and salt until smooth.

4. Grease bottom only of 12 x 8-inch glass baking dish. Pour in cake batter.

5. MICROWAVE (high), uncovered, 11 to 13 minutes or until no longer doughy in center, rotating dish 3 or 4 times. Cool slightly.

6. Combine all Topping ingredients in 4-cup glass measure.

7. MICROWAVE (high), uncovered, 3 to 4 minutes or until mixture boils and thickens, stirring every minute. Spread on cake.

12 x 8-inch Cake

TIPS • To assure the cooking of the bottom of the cake, first microwave 2 cups water in the baking dish about 10 minutes (do this after step 2 while preparing cake batter). Discard the water, dry the dish and grease the bottom of the dish. Pour in cake batter and microwave as directed.

• With Combination Oven, microwave in step 2 for 8 to 10 minutes. For step 5, bake in preheated 350° oven for 20 minutes; then, microwave-bake 5 to 7 minutes. Cool oven and microwave in step 7 for 5 to 6 minutes.

German Chocolate Oatmeal Cake.

Who said microwaved cakes couldn't be scrumptious or beautiful? This simplified version of Schwartzwalder Kirsch Torte will be a favorite any season.

BLACK FOREST CHERRY CAKE

- **1 package (2-layer size) chocolate cake mix**
- **½ cup water**
- **½ cup sugar**
- **3 tablespoons Kirsch or cherry-flavored liqueur**
- **1 pint (2 cups) whipping cream**
- **⅓ cup powdered sugar**
- **2 tablespoons Kirsch or cherry-flavored liqueur**
- **1 can (16 oz.) pitted dark sweet (Bing) cherries, drained**
- **Semi-sweet chocolate, if desired**

1. Prepare cake mix as directed on package. Cut waxed paper rounds to fit bottoms of three 8 or 9-inch round glass cake dishes. Divide batter evenly among paper-lined dishes.

2. MICROWAVE (medium — 50%) one cake at a time, uncovered, 5 minutes, rotating dish once.

3. MICROWAVE (high) 2 to 2½ minutes or until cake springs back when touched lightly. Cool 5 minutes; invert layers and place top-side-up on waxed paper-lined tray.

4. Combine water and sugar in 1-cup glass measure.

5. MICROWAVE (high), uncovered, 1½ to 2 minutes or until mixture boils and sugar is dissolved, stirring once. Cool to lukewarm. Stir in 3 tablespoons Kirsch. Prick holes, using toothpick, over entire surface of cake layers. Spoon Kirsch mixture evenly over each layer, allowing liquid to soak into cake. Refrigerate layers until cold.

6. Beat cream until thickened. Gradually beat in powdered sugar; blend in 2 tablespoons Kirsch. Cut cherries in half, reserving about 12 cherries for garnish.

7. Arrange one cake layer top-side-down on serving plate. Spread with layer of whipped cream. Top with half of sliced cherries. Place second cake layer, top-side-up atop first. Spread with cream and top with remaining cherry halves. Add last cake layer, top-side-up. Frost top and sides of cake with remaining cream. Sprinkle cake with shaved or grated semi-sweet chocolate. Garnish with whole cherries. Refrigerate several hours or overnight before serving.

12 to 15 Servings

TIPS • With Full Power, microwave 4½ to 5½ minutes in step 2; omit step 3.

• With Combination Oven, microwave in step 2 for 6 to 8 minutes and omit step 3. In step 5, microwave 2 to 3 minutes.

POWDERED SUGAR GLAZE

- **1 cup unsifted powdered sugar**
- **½ teaspoon vanilla**
- **Dash salt**
- **1½ to 2 tablespoons milk**

1. Mix together all ingredients, adding milk until mixture reaches glaze consistency.

2. Spoon over cooled cake.

Glaze for 1 Cake

Black Forest Cherry Cake.

A unique chocolate bundt-type cake with special moistness from the addition of mashed potatoes and sour cream. The cherries add a holiday touch, but it would be good served any time of year.

HOLIDAY CHOCOLATE CAKE

1 cup water
1 bar (4 oz.) German sweet chocolate, broken into pieces
1 cup instant mashed potato granules
1½ cups unsifted all-purpose flour
1½ cups sugar
1½ teaspoons soda
1 teaspoon cinnamon
½ teaspoon nutmeg
½ teaspoon cloves
½ teaspoon salt
½ cup shortening
½ cup sour cream
4 eggs
½ cup chopped maraschino cherries
Powdered Sugar Glaze, page 124.

1. MICROWAVE (high) water in 1-cup glass measure 1½ to 2 minutes or until boiling. Pour over chocolate and instant potatoes in large mixing bowl. Let stand until chocolate has softened. Beat until smooth. Add remaining ingredients, except cherries.

2. Blend at low speed until moistened; beat 3 minutes at medium speed, scraping bowl occasionally. Fold in cherries.

3. Generously grease 10 to 12-cup fluted cake dish. Spoon batter into dish.

4. MICROWAVE (high), uncovered, 12 to 14 minutes or until toothpick inserted near center comes out clean, rotating dish 2 or 3 times. Cool 30 minutes; invert onto serving plate. Cool completely.

5. Prepare Powdered Sugar Glaze; spoon over cake, allowing mixture to drizzle down sides of cake. If desired, garnish with additional cherries.

12 to 15 Servings

TIPS • With Combination Oven, spoon batter into greased and floured glass or metal fluted pan. Bake in preheated 350° oven for 15 minutes. Then, microwave-bake 8 to 10 minutes or until toothpick inserted near center comes out clean. Cool 10 minutes; invert onto serving plate.

• If you don't have the fluted cake dish, spoon batter into 12 x 8-inch glass baking dish which has been greased on bottom only. Microwave as directed.

This recipe makes an outstanding microwaved cake. Lower power helps even the cooking, although full power also works well since the bottom layer is partially cooked before the other layers are added.

CHERRY CAKE SUPREME

4 eggs
1 cup sugar
1 cup cooking oil
2 cups unsifted all-purpose flour
1½ teaspoons baking powder
¼ teaspoon salt
1 can (21 oz.) prepared cherry pie filling
2 tablespoons sugar
½ teaspoon cinnamon

Glaze:
2 tablespoons butter or margarine
¾ cup powdered sugar
⅛ teaspoon almond extract
½ to 1 tablespoon milk

1. Beat together eggs, 1 cup sugar, the oil, flour, baking powder and salt. Pour half of batter into ungreased 12 x 8-inch glass baking dish; spread evenly.

2. MICROWAVE (medium — 50%), uncovered, 4 minutes. Spoon cherries onto partially cooked cake; top with remaining batter, spreading to cover cherries. Combine 2 tablespoons sugar and the cinnamon; sprinkle on batter.

3. MICROWAVE (medium — 50%), uncovered, 15 minutes, rotating dish once. Then, MICROWAVE (high) 3 to 5 minutes or until no longer doughy. Cool.

4. MICROWAVE (high) butter in glass dish ¼ to ½ minute or until softened. Beat in powdered sugar, extract and enough milk until of drizzling consistency. Spoon onto cake.

15 to 18 Servings

Betty Lester of Veneta, Oregon, sent us this cake recipe to adapt to microwave cooking. Although we use a fluted tube pan, the 12 x 8-inch loaf pan can be used when a lower power setting is used.

ORANGE-NUT CAKE

- **½ cup butter or margarine**
- **1 cup sugar**
- **2 eggs**
- **2 cups unsifted all-purpose flour**
- **½ teaspoon soda**
- **¼ teaspoon salt**
- **¾ cup buttermilk or sour milk**
- **½ cup chopped pecans or other nuts**
- **¾ cup chopped dates**
- **½ tablespoon grated orange peel**

Orange Glaze:

- **1 cup sugar**
- **1 tablespoon grated orange peel**
- **½ cup orange juice**

1. MICROWAVE (high) butter in glass mixing bowl about ½ minute or until softened. Blend in sugar until well mixed. Beat in eggs, one at a time; continue beating until light and creamy. Add flour, soda, salt and buttermilk; mix just until combined. Stir in nuts, dates and orange peel.

2. Generously grease 10 to 12-cup fluted cake dish. Sprinkle with cinnamon-sugar, tapping out excess. Spoon cake into dish.

3. MICROWAVE (high), uncovered, 9 to 10 minutes or until top of cake is no longer doughy, rotating dish 2 or 3 times.

4. Combine ingredients for Glaze in 2-cup glass measure.

5. MICROWAVE (high), uncovered, 1½ to 2 minutes or until heated, but not boiling. Poke holes in cake using a long skewer and inserting all the way to bottom. Spoon about ⅔ of glaze over warm cake. Let cool 15 minutes. Invert cake onto serving plate. Spoon remaining glaze over cake.

12 to 15 Servings

TIPS • Cake can also be cooked in a glass 12 x 8-inch baking dish. Microwave (medium — 50%) 9 minutes, rotating dish once. Then, microwave (high) 5½ to 6½ minutes or until top is no longer doughy, rotating dish once.

• With Combination Oven, use a greased and floured glass or metal fluted pan. Bake in preheated 350° oven for 15 minutes. Then, microwave-bake 4 to 6 minutes or until toothpick inserted in center comes out clean.

This popular variation for cake mix cooks very well in the fluted cake dish. With the microwave, you'll keep the house cool and save energy besides.

POPPY SEED POUND CAKE

- **1 package (2-layer size) yellow cake mix**
- **1 package (3 oz.) instant lemon pudding mix**
- **4 eggs**
- **½ cup cooking oil**
- **1 cup water**
- **⅓ cup poppy seed**

1. Combine all ingredients in large mixing bowl. Blend on low speed until moistened. Beat at medium speed 4 minutes, occasionally scraping sides of bowl.

2. Generously grease 12-cup fluted cake dish; sprinkle with sugar, removing any excess. Spoon batter into cake dish.

3. MICROWAVE (medium — 50%), uncovered, 10 minutes, rotating dish once. Then, MICROWAVE (high) 6 to 8 minutes or until top is no longer doughy, rotating dish once. Cool 10 minutes. Invert onto serving plate. Cool. If desired, sprinkle with powdered sugar.

12 to 15 Servings

TIPS • With Full Power, microwave cake 11 to 13 minutes, rotating dish 3 or 4 times.

• If you don't have the fluted cake dish, reserve 1½ cups batter. Spoon remaining batter into 12 x 8-inch glass baking dish which has been greased on bottom only. Microwave as directed. Make cupcakes with remaining batter.

• With Combination Oven, spoon batter into greased and floured glass or metal fluted pan. Bake in preheated 350° oven for 15 minutes. Then, microwave-bake 3 to 5 minutes or until toothpick inserted in center comes out clean. Cool 10 minutes; invert onto serving plate.

This moist cake stores well and is ideal for snacks. It's chock full of dried fruits rather than the more traditional candied fruit. A cooking dish without a center or a lower power setting for the traditional loaf shape are essential for even cooking.

BANANA FRUITCAKE

2 eggs
⅔ cup packed brown sugar
½ cup cooking oil
1 teaspoon grated orange peel
½ cup orange juice
¾ cup mashed ripe banana (about 2 medium)
1 cup (4 ozs.) chopped pitted dates
1 cup chopped nuts
½ cup raisins
2 cups (11-oz. pkg.) chopped mixed dried fruits
1½ cups unsifted all-purpose flour
1 teaspoon cinnamon
½ teaspoon baking powder
½ teaspoon soda
½ teaspoon salt
½ teaspoon nutmeg
¼ teaspoon allspice

1. Beat eggs until frothy in large mixing bowl. Beat in brown sugar and oil. Blend in orange peel and juice and banana. Stir in remaining ingredients until just moistened.

2. Pour into greased 10 to 12-cup fluted cake dish.

3. MICROWAVE (high), uncovered, 12 to 13 minutes or until no longer doughy, rotating dish 2 or 3 times. Cool 10 minutes. Invert onto serving plate.

16 to 20 Servings

TIPS • Cake can be cooked in two 8 x 4-inch loaf dishes by using a lower power setting. Line bottom of dishes with waxed paper. Spread batter evenly in dishes. Microwave (medium-high — 70%), uncovered, 20 minutes and then microwave (high) 3 to 5 minutes, rotating dishes 3 times.

• With Combination Oven, grease and flour baking dish, bake in preheated 350° oven for 20 minutes and then microwave-bake 5 to 7 minutes.

Pumpkin Spice Cake, page 129, Daisy Butter Cake, page 128 and Banana Fruitcake, this page.

The light texture of this cake allows it to cook quickly and evenly in a round cake dish. Since the cake lacks color, a golden-brown coconut and nut topping is used. This moist topping keeps the cake fresh for several days.

DAISY BUTTER CAKE

¼ cup butter or margarine
¼ cup milk
1 teaspoon vanilla
2 eggs
¾ cup sugar
¾ cup unsifted all-purpose flour
1 teaspoon baking powder
½ teaspoon salt
Caramel Topping

1. MICROWAVE (high) butter ¾ to 1 minute or until melted. Add milk and vanilla; set aside.

2. Beat eggs in small mixer bowl at high speed until frothy. Gradually add sugar, beating until thickened and ivory colored. Add flour, baking powder, salt and milk mixture. Mix at lowest speed just until combined. Pour into 8-inch round glass cake dish, greased on bottom only.

3. MICROWAVE (high), uncovered, 4½ to 5 minutes or until almost done, rotating dish once (cake will appear very moist on surface, but is set beneath this moist area). Cool 5 minutes. Prepare Topping; spoon Topping onto cake, carefully spreading to cover.

4. MICROWAVE (high) 1 minute to complete the cooking of the cake.

8-inch Cake

TIP • With Combination Oven, bake in preheated 350° oven for 10 minutes and then microwave-bake 3 to 5 minutes.

Use this topping on the Daisy Butter Cake or other favorite cakes of similar size.

CARAMEL TOPPING

½ cup packed brown sugar
¼ cup butter or margarine
1 tablespoon milk
½ cup flaked or shredded coconut
¼ cup chopped nuts

1. Combine all ingredients in 4-cup glass measure.

2. MICROWAVE (high), uncovered, 2½ to 3 minutes or until thickened and bubbly, stirring 2 or 3 times. Spread on warm or cooled cake.

Topping for 8-inch Cake

A smooth, creamy frosting for microwaved cakes.

CREAM CHEESE FROSTING

1 package (3 oz.) cream cheese
2 tablespoons butter or margarine
2 cups powdered sugar
1 to 2 teaspoons milk
½ teaspoon vanilla

1. MICROWAVE (high) cream cheese and butter in small glass dish ¼ to ½ minute or until softened.

2. Beat in sugar and enough milk for spreading consistency. Blend in vanilla.

Frosts 12 x 8-inch Cake

A moist family-sized spice cake that cooks nicely in the oblong baking dish.

PUMPKIN SPICE CAKE

2 eggs
1 cup packed brown sugar
½ cup sugar
¾ cup cooking oil
1 cup cooked or canned pumpkin
1 teaspoon vanilla
2 cups unsifted all-purpose flour
1 teaspoon salt
½ teaspoon baking powder
½ teaspoon soda
½ teaspoon cinnamon
¼ teaspoon nutmeg
¼ teaspoon ginger
¼ cup milk
Cream Cheese Frosting, page 128.

1. Beat eggs until frothy in large mixing bowl. Beat in sugars and oil. Blend in pumpkin and vanilla. Stir in remaining ingredients just until smooth.

2. Pour into 12 x 8-inch glass baking dish, greased on bottom only.

3. MICROWAVE (high), uncovered, 9½ to 10½ minutes or until top springs back when touched lightly, rotating dish once or twice. Cool. Frost with Cream Cheese Frosting.

12 x 8-inch Cake

TIPS • To use fresh pumpkin, cube and peel 2 cups of pumpkin. Cover 2-cup glass measure with plastic wrap. Microwave (high) 9 to 10 minutes or until tender, stirring twice. Cool and mash to make 1 cup.

• With Combination Oven, bake in preheated 350° oven for 20 minutes and then microwave-bake 3 to 5 minutes.

A rich cake that "frosts itself" while cooking. The chocolate and nut topping is placed in the baking dish first and batter poured on top. When the cake is inverted—a delicious frosting.

NUT AND CHIP OATMEAL CAKE

Topping:
2 tablespoons butter or margarine
¼ cup packed brown sugar
⅓ cup semi-sweet chocolate pieces
⅓ cup chopped nuts

Cake:
¾ cup water
½ cup quick-cooking rolled oats
¼ cup butter or margarine, cut into pieces
½ cup sugar
½ cup packed brown sugar
1 egg
¾ cup unsifted all-purpose flour
½ teaspoon soda
½ teaspoon salt
½ teaspoon cinnamon
¼ teaspoon nutmeg

1. MICROWAVE (high) 2 tablespoons butter in 8-inch square glass baking dish ½ to 1 minute or until melted. Mix in brown sugar, chocolate pieces and nuts. Spread evenly in bottom of dish.

2. MICROWAVE (high) water in glass mixing bowl 1½ to 2 minutes or until water boils. Stir in oats. Add butter pieces and allow to stand until butter is softened. Beat in sugars and egg. Stir in remaining ingredients just until blended. Pour over nut mixture in baking dish.

3. MICROWAVE (medium-high — 70%), uncovered, 10 to 11 minutes or until cake springs back when touched lightly, rotating dish once. Cool 5 minutes. Invert onto serving plate. Serve warm or cold.

8-inch Square Cake

TIP • With Full Power, microwave 5½ to 6½ minutes, rotating dish twice.

This deliciously moist cake makes good use of zucchini from the garden. The whipped creamy-type frosting adds a nice finishing touch without the added calories of real whipped cream.

ZUCCHINI CAKE

Frosting:

- **1/3 cup sugar**
- **2 tablespoons flour**
- **1/3 cup milk**
- **1/4 cup butter or margarine**
- **1/2 teaspoon vanilla**

Cake:

- **1 1/4 cups sugar**
- **2/3 cup cooking oil**
- **1/2 teaspoon vanilla**
- **2 eggs**
- **1 1/3 cups unsifted all-purpose flour**
- **3/4 teaspoon salt**
- **1 1/4 teaspoons soda**
- **1 1/2 teaspoons cinnamon**
- **1 1/2 cups shredded, unpeeled zucchini**
- **1/3 cup chopped nuts**

1. Combine sugar, flour and milk in 2-cup glass measure.

2. MICROWAVE (high), uncovered, 2 to 2 1/2 minutes or until mixture boils and thickens. Refrigerate while preparing cake (at least 1 hour).

3. For cake, blend together sugar, oil and vanilla. Beat in eggs, one at a time. Mix in remaining ingredients until thoroughly combined.

4. Pour into 8-inch square glass baking dish, greased on bottom only; spread evenly in pan.

5. MICROWAVE (medium — 50%), uncovered, 10 minutes, rotating dish once. Then, MICROWAVE (high) 7 to 8 minutes or until no longer doughy, rotating dish twice. Cool.

6. Complete frosting by microwaving butter 10 to 15 seconds or until slightly softened (don't allow to melt). Beat with mixer until creamy. Slowly beat in cooled milk mixture. Beat until fluffy. Blend in vanilla. Spread on cooled cake. If desired, sprinkle with nutmeg.

8-inch Square Cake

TIPS • With Full Power, microwave in step 5 for 5 minutes; let stand 5 minutes. Then, microwave 7 to 8 minutes.

• With Combination Oven, microwave in step 2 for 5 to 6 minutes and in step 5 for a total of 14 to 15 minutes.

Zucchini Cake.

Some ovens cook small items like cookies more evenly than others. If you have problems with scorching or undercooking, you may have better results with a lower power setting.

PEANUT BUTTER-BRAN COOKIES

½ cup shortening
½ cup peanut butter
¾ cup packed brown sugar
¼ cup sugar
1 egg
½ teaspoon vanilla
1¼ cups unsifted all-purpose flour
1 cup bran flakes
¾ teaspoon soda
¼ teaspoon salt

1. Blend together shortening, peanut butter and sugars in mixing bowl. Beat in egg and vanilla. Stir in remaining ingredients.

2. Form dough into 1-inch balls. Arrange 16 balls on layer of paper toweling. Flatten balls with a fork in criss-cross fashion.

3. MICROWAVE (medium-high — 70%), uncovered, 3 to 4 minutes or until set, rotating paper once. Cool slightly; remove from paper toweling. Repeat with remaining dough.

40 to 48 Cookies

TIPS • For ease in moving cookies to and from oven, make a tray of cardboard slightly smaller than the inside of oven and cover it with paper toweling.

• With Full Power, microwave 2 to 3 minutes, rotating paper 2 or 3 times.

• With Combination Oven, microwave-bake cookies on metal cookie sheet in preheated 350° oven 3½ to 4½ minutes.

Bake these cookies all at once or refrigerate the dough and cook as needed.

COFFEE AND SPICE COOKIES

½ cup butter or margarine
1 cup packed brown sugar
1 egg
¼ cup cold coffee or milk
2¼ cups unsifted all-purpose flour
½ teaspoon soda
½ teaspoon salt
½ teaspoon cinnamon
½ teaspoon nutmeg
½ cup raisins or chopped dates
½ cup chopped nuts

1. MICROWAVE (high) butter in glass mixing bowl ½ to ¾ minute or until softened. Blend in brown sugar. Beat in egg and coffee. Stir in remaining ingredients until combined.

2. Drop about 16 rounded teaspoonsful dough onto waxed paper covered cardboard.

3. MICROWAVE (medium — 50%), uncovered, 5 to 6 minutes or until no longer doughy, rotating cardboard once. Repeat with remaining dough.

4 to 5 Dozen Cookies

TIPS • With Full Power, microwave 2½ to 3 minutes.

• With Combination Oven, microwave-bake in preheated 400° oven on metal cookie sheet 2 to 3 minutes.

• Dough can be covered and refrigerated for up to 1 week. Drop dough by teaspoonsful and microwave as directed.

Individual cookies can be difficult to prepare in the microwave because some cook faster than others. This recipe eliminates the problem because the mixture is cooked in a casserole and then formed into individual cookies when cooled.

DATE-NUT COOKIE BALLS

2 eggs
1 cup sugar
1 cup chopped walnuts or pecans
1 cup shredded or flaked coconut
1 cup chopped dates
1 teaspoon vanilla
Powdered or granulated sugar

1. Beat eggs slightly in 1½-quart glass casserole. Mix in sugar, nuts, coconut and dates.

2. MICROWAVE (high), uncovered, 5 to 6 minutes or until bubbly and thickened, stirring once or twice. Stir in vanilla. Cool completely.

3. Form mixture into balls by dropping rounded teaspoonful of mixture into sugar and coating with sugar while pressing into a ball. Let stand uncovered.

About 36 Cookies

TIP • For surprise centers, roll the mixture around candied cherries.

Individual cookies are possible, but difficult to make in the microwave because they each cook at different rates. This recipe eliminates the potential problem of uneven cooking by precooking the mixture in a bowl. The hot mixture is then quickly spooned onto waxed paper to form cookies.

MICROWAVED MACAROONS

2⅔ cups flaked coconut
⅔ cup (half a 14-oz. can) sweetened condensed milk
1 teaspoon vanilla or almond extract
Food coloring, if desired

1. Combine all ingredients in 2-quart glass mixing bowl. Tint mixture with favorite food coloring if desired.

2. MICROWAVE (high), uncovered, 6 to 7 minutes (7 to 8) or until mixture loses its gloss, stirring 3 or 4 times. Immediately spoon by teaspoonful onto waxed paper, pressing together with fingers to form cookies. Cool completely. Remove from paper to airtight storage container.

About 36 Macaroons

TIP • For other variations, add 1 cup chopped nuts or use colored coconut.

In this nutritious bar recipe, chances of overcooking are eliminated by precooking the mixture in a bowl prior to pressing it into the baking dish.

"OH HENRY" BARS

2 cups quick-cooking rolled oats
½ cup butter or margarine
½ cup packed brown sugar
¼ cup light corn syrup

Frosting:
⅓ cup semi-sweet chocolate pieces
2 tablespoons peanut butter

1. Combine oats and butter in glass mixing bowl.

2. MICROWAVE (high), uncovered, 3 to 4 minutes (6 to 7) or until heated through. Stir in brown sugar and corn syrup.

3. MICROWAVE (high), uncovered, 1½ to 2½ minutes (4 to 5) or until heated and sugar is dissolved. Turn into greased 10 x 6-inch glass baking dish. Press evenly in dish. Place chocolate pieces in 1-cup glass measure.

4. MICROWAVE (high), uncovered, 1½ to 2½ minutes (4 to 5) or until chocolate is glossy; stir until smooth. Blend in peanut butter; spread over warm bars. Refrigerate until chocolate is set. Cut into squares.

24 Bars

Applesauce adds a moist texture to these spicy raisin bars. They are sure to become a favorite.

APPLESAUCE-RAISIN BARS

- **¼ cup butter or margarine**
- **⅔ cup packed brown sugar**
- **1 egg**
- **1 cup sweetened applesauce**
- **1 cup unsifted all-purpose flour**
- **½ teaspoon soda**
- **½ teaspoon salt**
- **½ teaspoon cinnamon**
- **¼ teaspoon nutmeg**
- **⅛ teaspoon ground cloves**
- **½ cup raisins**

Frosting:

- **2 tablespoons butter or margarine**
- **2 cups powdered sugar**
- **2 to 3 tablespoons milk**
- **½ teaspoon vanilla**

1. MICROWAVE (high) butter in glass mixing bowl ¼ to ½ minute (1 to 1½) or until softened. Blend in brown sugar; beat in egg and applesauce. Stir in remaining ingredients, except raisins and frosting; beat until smooth. Stir in raisins.

2. Pour into 12 x 8-inch glass baking dish, greased on bottom only.

3. MICROWAVE (high), uncovered, 9 to 10 minutes (14 to 15) or until no longer doughy, rotating dish twice. Cool.

4. MICROWAVE (high) butter for Frosting in small glass mixing bowl covered with paper towel 2 to 3 minutes (12 to 14) or until lightly browned. Blend in powdered sugar and enough milk for spreading consistency. Beat until smooth. Blend in vanilla. Spread on cooled bars. Cut into bars.

About 32 Bars

Lemon Light Bars, page 136, Applesauce-Raisin Bars, this page, "Oh Henry" Bars, page 132 and Microwaved Macaroons, page 132.

The spicy flavor of these cake-like bars is crowned with a cream cheese frosting.

PUMPKIN BARS

¼ cup butter or margarine
¾ cup packed brown sugar
2 eggs
1 teaspoon vanilla
1 cup cooked pumpkin (half of 16-oz. can)
1 cup unsifted all-purpose flour
½ teaspoon baking powder
½ teaspoon salt
¼ teaspoon soda
½ teaspoon cinnamon
½ teaspoon nutmeg
¼ teaspoon ginger

Cream Cheese Frosting:
1 package (3 oz.) cream cheese
1 tablespoon butter or margarine
2 cups powdered sugar
1 to 1½ tablespoons milk
⅓ cup chopped nuts, if desired

1. MICROWAVE (high) butter in glass mixing bowl about ¼ minute or until softened. Blend in brown sugar. Beat in eggs, one at a time. Blend in remaining ingredients except Frosting, mixing until smooth. Spread evenly in 12 x 8-inch glass baking dish, greased on bottom only.

2. MICROWAVE (medium — 50%), uncovered, 8 minutes. Rotate dish. Then, MICROWAVE (high) 3½ to 4½ minutes or until toothpick inserted near center comes out clean, rotating dish once. Cool.

3. MICROWAVE (high) cream cheese and butter for Frosting in glass mixing bowl about ½ minute or until softened. Blend in powdered sugar. Beat in enough milk for proper spreading consistency. Spread over bars. If desired, sprinkle with chopped nuts. Cut into squares.

32 to 40 Bars

TIP • With Full Power, microwave 8 to 9½ minutes, rotating dish once.

With 10 minutes notice, you can have warm, freshly baked cookies to serve with a glass of iced tea or a bowl of fresh fruit. One of our favorite microwave cookies!

SHORTBREAD COOKIE WEDGES

½ cup butter or margarine
¼ cup sugar
½ teaspoon almond extract
1⅓ cups unsifted all-purpose flour
1 tablespoon sugar
⅛ teaspoon nutmeg

1. MICROWAVE (high) butter in glass mixing bowl ¼ to ½ minute or until softened. Blend in ¼ cup sugar and the extract. Mix in flour until crumbly and evenly mixed. Place a paper towel in 8-inch round glass baking dish, pressing into bottom and allowing edges to extend. Place crumb mixture in pan; press firmly and evenly in pan. Press edges with tines of fork.

2. MICROWAVE (high), uncovered, 3 to 4 minutes or until shortbread has a dry, flaky appearance, rotating dish 2 or 3 times. Cut into 12 wedges. Combine 1 tablespoon sugar and the nutmeg; sprinkle over shortbread. Lift from the pan using edges of paper towel. Cool slightly; remove from paper.

12 Cookies

TIP • Make a double or triple recipe, but always microwave one dish at a time.

Shortbread Cookie Wedges.

A candy-like topping completes this basic cookie base.

PRALINE SQUARES

- **⅓ cup butter or margarine**
- **½ cup packed brown sugar**
- **1 cup unsifted all-purpose flour**
- **¼ teaspoon salt**

Praline Topping:

- **¾ cup packed brown sugar**
- **¼ cup butter or margarine**
- **2 tablespoons milk**
- **½ teaspoon vanilla**
- **½ cup pecan or walnut pieces**

1. MICROWAVE (high) butter in glass mixing bowl about ½ minute or until softened. Blend in brown sugar. Mix in flour and salt until mixture is crumbly.
2. Press mixture firmly and evenly into 8-inch square glass baking dish.
3. MICROWAVE (high), uncovered, 3 to 3½ minutes or until mixture has a dry appearance, rotating dish once or twice. Set aside.
4. Combine brown sugar, butter and milk for Topping in glass mixing bowl.
5. MICROWAVE (high), uncovered, 3 minutes, stirring once or twice. Stir in vanilla. Pour over crust. Sprinkle with pecans.
6. MICROWAVE (high), uncovered, 2 to 2½ minutes or until mixture is bubbly. Cool. Cut into squares while slightly warm.

About 20 Squares

A round dish is better than a square shape for brownies because there are no corners that can overcook.

BROWNIES SUPREME

- **¼ cup butter or margarine**
- **½ cup sugar**
- **2 eggs**
- **½ cup unsifted all-purpose flour**
- **½ cup chopped nuts**
- **½ cup chocolate-flavored ice cream syrup**
- **¼ teaspoon salt**
- **½ teaspoon vanilla**

1. MICROWAVE (high) butter in mixing bowl ¼ to ½ minute or until softened. Blend in sugar. Beat in eggs, one at a time. Stir in remaining ingredients. Spread in lightly greased 8-inch round glass baking dish.
2. MICROWAVE (high), uncovered, 5 to 6 minutes or until no longer doughy, rotating dish once. Cool. Cut into wedges. Serve topped with ice cream and additional chocolate syrup or cut into squares and serve as bars.

6 to 8 Servings

Praline Squares.

These refreshing lemon bars are just right for entertaining. Both the base and filling are partially cooked before going into the baking dish. The broiler or browning unit is used to cover the moist filling with a delicate brown crust.

LEMON LIGHT BARS

½ cup butter or margarine
¼ cup sugar
1¼ cups unsifted all-purpose flour
2 eggs
¾ cup sugar
2 tablespoons flour
¼ teaspoon baking powder
1 teaspoon grated lemon peel
3 tablespoons lemon juice
Powdered sugar

1. MICROWAVE (high) butter in 8-inch square glass baking dish ½ to 1 minute (2 to 3) or until melted. Mix in ¼ cup sugar and the flour until evenly mixed.

2. MICROWAVE (high), uncovered, 3 to 3½ minutes (6 to 6½) or until crumbly, stirring 2 or 3 times. Press firmly and evenly into bottom of baking dish.

3. MICROWAVE (high), uncovered, 2½ to 3½ minutes (4 to 4½) or until mixture starts to brown.

4. Beat eggs in glass mixing bowl; blend in remaining ingredients except powdered sugar.

5. MICROWAVE (high), uncovered, 2 to 2½ minutes (5 to 6) or until mixture begins to thicken, stirring once or twice. Pour over crust.

6. Preheat broiler or browning unit. Place bars 3 inches from heat and broil until lightly browned, 3 to 4 minutes. Sprinkle with powdered sugar. Refrigerate several hours before cutting into bars with knife dipped in water. Store in refrigerator.

About 24 Bars

Josephine Real of Chula Vista, California, enjoys candy making with the microwave. She requested help in adapting the fudge recipe given on the jar of marshmallow creme. Here are our suggestions.

FANTASY FUDGE

3 cups sugar
¾ cup butter or margarine
1 can (5⅓ oz.) evaporated milk (⅔ cup)
2 cups (12 ozs.) semi-sweet chocolate pieces
1 jar (7 oz.) marshmallow creme
1 teaspoon vanilla
1 cup chopped nuts

1. Combine sugar, butter and milk in 2-quart glass mix 'n pour bowl.

2. MICROWAVE (high), uncovered, 4½ to 5 minutes (7 to 8) or until mixture starts to boil, stirring once.

3. MICROWAVE (high), uncovered, 5 minutes (5). Stir in chocolate pieces until smooth. Blend in marshmallow creme and vanilla. Stir in nuts. Pour into buttered 12 x 8-inch baking dish. Cool until set; cut into squares.

About 3 Pounds

This candy is a delightfully quick fudge variation that uses powdered sugar. It is so easy you'll want to make it again and again.

QUICK FUDGE

1 lb. powdered sugar (about 3½ cups)
½ cup unsweetened cocoa
½ cup butter or margarine
¼ cup milk
1 tablespoon vanilla
½ cup chopped nuts

1. Combine powdered sugar and cocoa in glass mixing bowl. Add butter and milk; do not mix.

2. MICROWAVE (high) 2½ to 3 minutes or until butter is melted. Beat until smooth; stir in vanilla and nuts. Spread in buttered dish. Freeze for 20 minutes or refrigerate 1 hour. Cut into squares.

About 24 Pieces

A reader, Marcia Bernick, from St. Paul, Minnesota, shares her husband's favorite candy recipe. It's as easy to prepare as it is good to eat.

ROCKY ROAD CANDY

2 cups (12 ozs.) semi-sweet chocolate pieces
2 cups (12 ozs.) butterscotch pieces
1 cup peanut butter
1 package (10½ oz.) miniature marshmallows
1 cup salted peanuts

1. Combine chocolate and butterscotch pieces and peanut butter in large glass mixing bowl.

2. MICROWAVE (medium-high — 70%), uncovered, about 5 minutes. Stir until melted. Fold in marshmallows and peanuts. Spread in buttered 13 x 9-inch pan. Refrigerate 2 hours or until set. Cut into squares.

About 36 Squares

TIPS • With Full Power, microwave about 3 minutes, stirring once.

• This makes a large recipe. For half a recipe, reduce microwave time by half and use 8-inch square pan.

• For individual candies, spoon mixture into small paper candy cups. Refrigerate until set.

These yummy bars taste very much like a popular candy bar by a similar name and are a favorite of Mrs. Marilyn Erickson of Bloomington, Minnesota. They were easily adapted to microwave preparation since the mixture only required heating.

YUMMY MOUND BARS

½ cup butter or margarine
2 cups graham cracker crumbs
¼ cup sugar
2⅔ cups (8 ozs.) flaked coconut
1 can (14 oz.) sweetened condensed milk
2 cups (12 ozs.) milk chocolate pieces

1. MICROWAVE (high) butter in 12 x 8-inch glass baking dish about 1 minute (1½ to 2) or until melted. Stir in crumbs and sugar until combined. Press mixture firmly and evenly into bottom of dish.

2. Stir together coconut and condensed milk. Spoon over crust; spread evenly.

3. MICROWAVE (medium — 50%), uncovered, 9 to 11 minutes or until heated through, rotating dish once.

4. MICROWAVE (high) chocolate pieces in uncovered glass bowl 2 to 3 minutes or until softened. Stir until smooth. Spoon onto coconut mixture; spread to cover. Refrigerate to set chocolate, about 1 hour. Cut into bars.

About 48 Bars

TIPS • Add ½ cup chopped, toasted almonds to coconut mixture for a delicious variation.

• With Full Power, microwave in step 3 for 4½ to 5 minutes, rotating dish twice.

• With Combination Oven, microwave in step 1 for 1½ to 2 minutes, step 3 for 8 to 9 minutes and in step 4 for 4 to 5 minutes.

This recipe relies on purchased candy which is melted and formed into a new shape.

CARAMEL SNAPPERS

Pecan halves (about 4 ozs.)
1 package (14 oz.) caramels, unwrapped
1 tablespoon butter or margarine
1 tablespoon milk
½ cup semi-sweet chocolate pieces

1. Arrange pecan halves in clusters of 3 each on buttered cookie sheet or buttered waxed paper. Form about 36 clusters.

2. Combine caramels, butter and milk in glass bowl.

3. MICROWAVE (high), uncovered, 2 to 3 minutes (6 to 7) or until melted, stirring once or twice. Stir until smooth. Cool until slightly thickened. Spoon a rounded spoonful onto center of each pecan cluster. Cool until set, about 30 minutes.

4. MICROWAVE (high) chocolate pieces in glass dish 1½ to 2 minutes (2 to 2½) or until softened. Stir until smooth. Spoon a little chocolate onto each candy and spread to cover caramel. Refrigerate until set. Allow to warm to room temperature for serving.

About 36 Snappers

TIP • If caramel mixture becomes too set before all is spooned, just return bowl to oven for a few seconds to warm mixture.

English Toffee, page 140, Peanut Brittle, page 139, Caramel Snappers, this page, Divintiy, page 139 and Apri-Nut Clusters, page 139.

Everybody's favorite, peanut brittle, is a snap to make using the microwave. Be sure to use raw peanuts as toasted ones will overcook.

PEANUT BRITTLE

1½ cups sugar
½ cup light corn syrup
½ cup water
Dash salt
2 cups raw peanuts
1 tablespoon butter or margarine
1 teaspoon soda
1 teaspoon vanilla

1. Combine sugar, corn syrup, water, salt and peanuts in 2-quart glass mix 'n pour bowl.

2. MICROWAVE (high), uncovered, 5 minutes. Stir. Then, MICROWAVE (high), uncovered, 13 to 15 minutes or until about 300° is reached, checking temperature during last few minutes.

3. Stir in butter, soda and vanilla just until light and bubbly. Pour onto buttered cookie sheet and spread to desired thickness. Cool. Break into pieces. Store in covered container.

About 1¼ Pounds

Apricots give these super simple candies a delicious sweet-tart flavor.

APRI-NUT CLUSTERS

16 ozs. candy coating for almond bark, broken into pieces
1 cup (about 6 ozs.) chopped dried apricots
1 cup granola cereal
½ cup salted peanuts
½ cup raisins

1. MICROWAVE (high) candy coating in uncovered 1½-quart glass bowl 3 to 4 minutes or until melted, stirring once. Stir until smooth.

2. Stir in remaining ingredients until coated. Drop by teaspoonful onto waxed paper. Refrigerate until set, about 20 minutes.

About 40 Candies

Watch the temperature carefully for this candy and be sure to beat it long enough to avoid stickiness.

DIVINITY

2 cups sugar
½ cup water
⅓ cup light corn syrup
¼ teaspoon salt
2 egg whites
1 teaspoon vanilla
Food coloring, if desired
½ cup chopped nuts

1. Combine sugar, water, corn syrup and salt in 4-cup glass measure.

2. MICROWAVE (high), uncovered, 3 minutes. Stir. Then, MICROWAVE (high), uncovered, 6 to 8 minutes or until 250° is reached, checking temperature during last few minutes.

3. Meanwhile, beat egg whites in large bowl until they form stiff peaks. Pour hot syrup in thin stream over egg whites while beating at high speed. Continue beating until mixture holds its shape and starts to lose gloss. Beat in vanilla and tint with coloring if desired. Fold in nuts. Spoon onto waxed paper. When set, remove from paper and store in tightly covered container.

About 36 Pieces

These crunchy snacks quickly became favorites when they were published in our "Kids Cooking" issue.

CRUNCHY MUNCHERS

1 cup (6 ozs.) semi-sweet chocolate pieces
1 cup (6 ozs.) butterscotch pieces
⅓ cup peanut butter
2 cups miniature marshmallows
3 cups crisp rice cereal

1. Combine chocolate pieces, butterscotch pieces and peanut butter in 2-quart glass bowl.

2. MICROWAVE (high), uncovered, 3 to 4 minutes or until pieces are melted, stirring once. Stir until smooth; stir in marshmallows. Mix in cereal until evenly coated with chocolate. Pour into buttered 8-inch square pan; press evenly into pan with spoon. Refrigerate about 1 hour or until set. Cut into squares.

24 to 30 Snacks

Buttery rich toffee coated with chocolate and nuts. Absolutely delicious.

ENGLISH TOFFEE

1 cup butter or margarine
1⅓ cups sugar
1 tablespoon light corn syrup
2 tablespoons water
1 teaspoon vanilla
½ cup semi-sweet chocolate pieces
⅓ cup finely chopped nuts

1. Combine butter, sugar, corn syrup and water in 2-quart glass mix 'n pour bowl.

2. MICROWAVE (high), uncovered, 4 minutes. Stir. Then, MICROWAVE (high), uncovered, 6 to 8 minutes or until about 300° is reached, stirring and checking temperature during last few minutes. Stir in vanilla.

3. Pour into ungreased 13 x 9-inch pan. Sprinkle with chocolate pieces. Let stand until chocolate is softened; spread evenly over toffee. Sprinkle with nuts, pressing them into chocolate. Refrigerate to set chocolate. When cool, turn out of pan and break into pieces.

About 1¼ Pounds

A lower power setting reduces the stirring required in this type of recipe.

SUNNY CARAMEL CORN

4 quarts unsalted popped corn (16 cups)
1 cup packed brown sugar
½ cup butter or margarine
¼ cup light corn syrup
½ teaspoon salt
½ teaspoon soda
⅔ cup raw or toasted sunflower seeds

1. Divide popped corn between two 4-quart glass bowls or casseroles; set aside.

2. Combine brown sugar, butter, corn syrup and salt in 2-quart glass casserole.

3. MICROWAVE (high), uncovered, 3 to 3½ minutes or until mixture boils, stirring once.

4. MICROWAVE (low — 30%) 4 minutes. Stir in soda.

5. Pour half of syrup evenly over each bowl of popped corn; sprinkle with sunflower seeds. Stir to lightly coat.

6. MICROWAVE (medium — 50%), one bowl at a time, uncovered, 6 to 7 minutes or until lightly toasted, stirring twice.

16 Cups Caramel Corn

TIPS • About 2 cups peanuts can be substituted for sunflower seeds.

• With Full Power, microwave in step 4 for 3 minutes, stirring every minute, and in step 6 for 3½ to 4½ minutes, stirring every minute.

• With Combination Oven, microwave in step 3 for 3½ to 4½ minutes, in step 4 for 4 to 5 minutes, stirring every 2 minutes and in step 6 for 6 to 7 minutes, stirring every 2 minutes.

Mrs. James Dumond of Mulliken, Michigan, describes this recipe as "a popular treat that disappears instantly". She used to spend an hour preparing it conventionally and can now make it in 20 minutes. To prevent separation, be sure to stir condensed milk into hot mixture gradually.

CARAMEL TEMPTATIONS

2 cups sugar
1 cup butter or margarine
1 cup light corn syrup
1 can (13 oz.) sweetened condensed milk
1 teaspoon vanilla
1 cup chopped nuts

1. Combine sugar, butter and corn syrup in 3-quart glass bowl.

2. MICROWAVE (high) 5 minutes or until butter is melted. Stir mixture to dissolve sugar. Gradually blend in condensed milk.

3. MICROWAVE (high), uncovered, 15 to 17 minutes or until 240° is reached, stirring 4 or 5 times and checking temperature during last few minutes.

4. Stir in vanilla and nuts. Pour onto buttered cookie sheet or 13 x 9-inch pan. Cool; cut into squares as needed.

About 2 Pounds

TIP • Caramels should be cut as served since the cutting marks will disappear as they stand in pan.

Creamy Choco-Mint Melts.

Homemade dinner mints are extra special. Serve them after dinner or use them for delightful hostess gifts. The microwave eases the preparation considerably.

CREAMY CHOCO-MINT MELTS

1½ lbs. candy coating for almond bark
1 cup (6 ozs.) semi-sweet chocolate pieces
1 teaspoon peppermint extract
4 drops green food coloring
3 tablespoons whipping cream

1. Line bottom and sides of 12 x 8-inch glass dish with sheet of waxed paper.

2. Combine ⅔ of candy coating and the chocolate pieces in 4-cup glass measure.

3. MICROWAVE (high), uncovered, 2½ to 3 minutes (8 to 8½) or until mixture is softened. Stir until smooth.

4. Spread half of chocolate in bottom of baking dish; refrigerate to set, about 20 minutes. (Allow remaining chocolate to stand at room temperature.)

5. Place remaining almond bark in 2-cup glass measure.

6. MICROWAVE (high), uncovered, 1½ to 2 minutes (7 to 7½) or until softened. Stir in extract and coloring (mixture will become very stiff). Mix in cream until of spreading consistency. Spread over chilled chocolate mixture. Refrigerate until set, about 20 minutes.

7. Spread remaining chocolate mixture over mint layer. Chill until set. Before serving, allow to warm to room temperature. Then, holding onto waxed paper edges, lift mints from pan. Cut into serving pieces.

About 2 Pounds

TIP • Mints need to be at room temperature to cut without the chocolate cracking.

The nuts toast while the candy-like coating is cooking. An easy-to-do favorite for all nut-lovers.

SUGAR AND SPICE NUTS

2 tablespoons butter or margarine
¼ cup packed brown sugar
½ teaspoon cinnamon
¼ teaspoon salt
¼ teaspoon nutmeg
¼ teaspoon grated orange peel, if desired
1 tablespoon water
2 cups (about 8 ozs.) shelled walnut or pecan halves or whole almonds

1. MICROWAVE (high) butter in 1-quart glass bowl or casserole ½ to 1 minute (2 to 2½) or until melted. Add remaining ingredients; stir until nuts are coated evenly.

2. MICROWAVE (high), uncovered, 4 to 5 minutes (9 to 10) or until nuts are toasted and glazed, stirring 2 or 3 times.

3. Spoon nuts in single layer onto waxed paper. Cool.

About 2½ Cups

This candy favorite is popular any time.

BUTTERMILK PRALINES

1 cup sugar
1 cup packed brown sugar
1 cup buttermilk
1 teaspoon soda
¼ teaspoon salt
1 tablespoon butter or margarine
2 cups chopped pecans
1 teaspoon vanilla

1. Combine sugars, buttermilk, soda, salt and butter in 2-quart glass mix 'n pour bowl.

2. MICROWAVE (high), uncovered, 7 minutes, stirring twice. Stir in pecans.

3. MICROWAVE (high), uncovered, 11 to 12 minutes or until 230° is reached, stirring every 4 minutes. (Use the soft ball test if a thermometer is not available.) Stir in vanilla.

4. Stir until mixture begins to thicken. Drop by teaspoons onto waxed paper. Cool until set.

50 to 60 Candies

Use the microwave to toast the almonds and melt the candy mixture—all in just minutes.

ALMOND BARK

1 cup whole blanched or unblanched almonds
1 teaspoon butter or cooking oil
16 ounces candy coating for almond bark

1. Combine almonds and butter in 9-inch glass pie plate.

2. MICROWAVE (high), uncovered, 4½ to 5½ minutes or until toasted, stirring 2 or 3 times; set aside.

3. MICROWAVE (high) candy coating in glass mixing bowl 2½ to 3 minutes or until softened. Stir in almonds. Pour onto waxed paper-lined baking sheet; spread to desired thickness. Refrigerate until set, about 1 hour. Break into pieces.

About 1¼ Pounds

TIPS • For Sunflower Bark, substitute 1 cup raw sunflower seeds for almonds. Increase microwave time in step 2 to 6 to 7 minutes.

• For less stirring in step 2, use (medium-high — 70%) and increase time to 5½ to 6½ minutes. Use Full Power for step 3.

Buttermilk Pralines.

Favorite Recipes from

The Microwave Times

Chapter 10

Potpourri

Strawberry Leather, page 148 and Fresh Berry-Banana Jam, page 144.

Combine fruits for a new, interesting fruit jam. Since this jam relies on the natural sweetness and pectin of the fruit, there are less calories (16/tablespoon) than in most commercially prepared jams (about 50/tablespoon). Note, though, that refrigerator or freezer storage is required.

FRESH BERRY-BANANA JAM

- **1 pint fresh strawberries**
- **1 medium-sized ripe banana**
- **2 teaspoons lemon juice**
- **1 cup sugar**

1. Wash and hull strawberries. Process in blender on medium speed until smooth to make 1½ cups. Add banana and lemon juice. Process on medium speed until smooth. Pour into 2-quart glass casserole. Stir in sugar.

2. MICROWAVE (high), uncovered, 10 to 11 minutes (14 to 15) or until sugar is dissolved, stirring twice. Cool. Pour into storage containers; cover and refrigerate or freeze until used.

1¾ Cups

TIP • Peaches can be substituted for the strawberries. Combined with the banana, the flavor is equally delicious.

This uncooked jam requires freezer storage.

FRESH PINEAPPLE-PAPAYA FREEZER JAM

- **½ fresh pineapple**
- **1 papaya, peeled**
- **1 tablespoon lemon juice**
- **4 cups sugar**
- **¾ cup water**
- **1 package (1¾ oz.) powdered fruit pectin**

1. Cut off outer portion of pineapple with sharp knife. Remove eyes with pointed end of knife or vegetable peeler. Cut pineapple into wedges and remove core. Cut into smaller pieces and place in blender container. Halve papaya and remove seeds. Gradually add pieces of papaya to blender container. Process at medium speed until fruit is finely chopped. Measure 2½ cups fruit into large glass dish. Stir in lemon juice and sugar; let stand 10 minutes.

2. Combine water and pectin in 4-cup glass measure, stirring until well mixed.

3. MICROWAVE (high), uncovered, 2 to 3 minutes or until mixture boils about 1 minute, stirring once.

4. Stir into fruit mixture until well mixed and sugar is dissolved. Pour into jars; cover. Let stand at room temperature about 24 hours or until set. Label and store in freezer.

6 Cups

When citrus peel is called for, avoid using the white portion which imparts a bitter flavor.

GOLDEN PEAR MARMALADE

- **2 medium oranges**
- **1 medium lemon**
- **1 can (8¼ oz.) crushed pineapple, undrained**
- **5 to 6 medium-sized pears**
- **1 package (1¾ oz.) powdered fruit pectin**
- **4½ cups sugar**

1. With vegetable peeler remove thin outer layer from 1 orange and the lemon, taking as little of the white part as possible. Cut peel into thin strips. Finish peeling both oranges and lemon. Slice fruit thinly and quarter; remove seeds. Place in 2½-quart glass casserole. Add pineapple. Peel, core and finely chop pears; mix with other fruits. Stir in fruit pectin.

2. MICROWAVE (high), uncovered, 15 to 20 minutes or until mixture boils hard for at least 1 minute, stirring 2 or 3 times. Stir in sugar.

3. MICROWAVE (high), uncovered, 10 to 12 minutes or until mixture boils throughout for 1 minute, stirring twice. Cool 5 minutes. Skim off any foam. Pour marmalade into hot sterilized jars; seal.

8 Cups

Use this recipe as a guide for jam cooking times when powdered pectin is added.

STRAWBERRY-RHUBARB JAM

1½ pints fresh strawberries
2 cups sliced rhubarb
1 package (1¾ oz.) powdered fruit pectin
4 cups sugar

1. Wash and hull strawberries. Crush strawberries to make 2½ cups; combine with rhubarb in 2-quart glass bowl. Cover with plastic wrap.

2. MICROWAVE (high) 5 to 5½ minutes or until fruit is softened. Stir in pectin.

3. MICROWAVE (high), uncovered, 3½ to 4½ minutes or until mixture boils, stirring once. Stir in sugar.

4. MICROWAVE (high), uncovered, 3 to 4 minutes or until mixture boils hard for at least 1 minute. Pour into hot sterilized jars; seal.

5 Cups

TIP • If desired, 3 cups frozen unsweetened strawberries, thawed, can be substituted for fresh berries.

Strawberry-Rhubarb Jam, this page, Golden Pear Marmalade, page 144, Cranberry-Apple Jelly, page 146, and Fresh Pineapple-Papaya Freezer Jam, page 144.

This particular conserve is delicious tasting and uses fruits common most of the year. The orange gelatin enhances the golden color of the fruits, but cherry gelatin can be substituted for a pretty red color.

FESTIVE FRUIT CONSERVE

5 cups chopped apples or pears
1 cup (6 ozs.) chopped, dried apricots
1 lemon
1 orange
1 can (20 oz.) crushed pineapple, undrained
7 cups sugar
1 package (6 oz.) orange-flavored gelatin

1. Prepare apples and apricots; place in 3 or 4-quart glass casserole.

2. Slice off ends of lemon and orange; discard. Slice remaining lemon and orange into very thin slices (an electric knife or very sharp knife is helpful). Cut the slices into quarters and remove any seeds. Add slices to casserole along with pineapple and sugar. Stir to combine. Cover with casserole lid.

3. MICROWAVE (high) 22 to 25 minutes or until fruit is tender and translucent, stirring once or twice. Stir in gelatin.

4. MICROWAVE (high), uncovered, 5 minutes. Ladle into sterilized glasses or other containers, filling to within ½ inch of top. Wipe rim of glasses to remove any fruit mixture and push fruit pieces into syrup so surface is smooth. Seal with hot paraffin. Cool. Cover and store in cool place.

About 10 Half Pints

TIP • Conserve can be spooned into jars that can be sealed and then topped with lids and bands for sealing, thus omitting the paraffin. Or, conserve can be stored in the freezer.

Jellies using powdered pectin are easily adapted to microwave cooking.

CRANBERRY-APPLE JELLY

2½ cups cranberry juice
1½ cups apple juice
1 package (1¾ oz.) powdered fruit pectin
4 cups sugar

1. Combine juices and pectin in 2-quart glass bowl. Cover with plastic wrap.

2. MICROWAVE (high) 11 to 13 minutes or until mixture boils, stirring once. Stir in sugar.

3. MICROWAVE (high), uncovered, 10 to 12 minutes or until mixture boils hard for at least 1 minute. Skim off any foam with metal spoon. Pour into hot sterilized glasses; seal.

6 Cups

TIP • For a hint of orange flavor, remove several thin strips of peel from a fresh orange with a vegetable peeler. Add in step 1. Remove strips of peel before pouring jelly into glasses.

The food processor aids in making Fresh Tomato Sauce, page 147.

Make up several recipes of this sauce when tomatoes are abundant and at their peak. Use the sauce as you would a commercially prepared product. Each packet is the equivalent of an 8-oz. can.

FRESH TOMATO SAUCE

4 to 5 large fresh unpeeled tomatoes, quartered (8 cups)
6 sprigs parsley
3 sprigs basil (1 teaspoon dried)
3 sprigs oregano (1 teaspoon dried)
1 medium onion, quartered
1 stalk celery, cut into pieces
1 tablespoon sugar
2 tablespoons olive oil, if desired
1 bay leaf
1 teaspoon salt
¼ teaspoon pepper

1. Combine tomatoes, parsley, basil, oregano, onion and celery in bowl of food processor with metal blade. Process with on-off motion until mixture is smooth. Pour into 2-quart glass casserole.

2. Stir in sugar, oil, bay leaf, salt and pepper.

3. MICROWAVE (high), uncovered, 25 to 35 minutes (50 to 55) or until bubbly and thickened, stirring 2 or 3 times. Cool. Remove bay leaf and spoon into 1-cup containers. Seal, label and freeze up to 6 months.

About 4 Cups

TIP • A blender can be used in place of food processor.

Elaine Parker of Bloomington, Minnesota, reported a way of making your own sweetened condensed milk. The microwave is not essential for the preparation, but it is a timesaver.

MAKE-YOUR-OWN SWEETENED CONDENSED MILK

½ cup cold water
1¼ cups nonfat dry milk powder
¾ cup sugar

1. Measure water into 2-cup glass measure. Gradually stir in dry milk powder until smooth.

2. MICROWAVE (high), uncovered, ¾ to 1 minute or until milk is steaming hot.

3. Stir in sugar until dissolved. Allow to cool before using. Use as a substitute in recipes for 1 can (14 oz.) sweetened condensed milk.

1⅓ Cups

We've published several variations on granola. This one came from Joan Barker of Mankato, Minnesota, and is a popular use of the microwave.

GRANOLA

8 cups rolled oats (quick or old-fashioned)
1⅓ cups shredded or flaked coconut
½ cup wheat germ
½ cup sunflower seeds or chopped nuts
½ cup packed brown sugar
½ cup honey
½ cup cooking oil
½ teaspoon salt, if desired
1 teaspoon vanilla

1. Combine all ingredients in 4-quart glass mixing bowl; mix well.

2. MICROWAVE (high), uncovered, 14 to 16 minutes or until toasted, stirring every 4 or 5 minutes. Cool. Serve as a cereal with milk or use as a topping for ice cream, yogurt or pudding.

About 10 Cups

Use this same method for toasting squash and sunflower seeds, too.

TOASTED PUMPKIN SEEDS

1 cup fresh pumpkin seeds
2 tablespoons butter or margarine
Salt

1. Wash seeds, removing any membrane; pat dry. Place butter in 12 x 8-inch glass baking dish.

2. MICROWAVE (high), uncovered, about 1 minute (2 to 3) or until melted. Stir in seeds, coating evenly with butter; sprinkle lightly with salt. Spread evenly in dish.

3. MICROWAVE (high), uncovered, 10 to 12 minutes (15 to 17) or until lightly toasted, stirring occasionally during last half of cooking time. Sprinkle with additional salt if desired.

1 Cup Seeds

We had a request for Beef Jerky, and one of our readers, Mrs. Mary Stackley of El Dorado, Kansas, responded with her recipe. Beef Jerky is a nutritious snack anytime, but especially suited for outdoor activities like ski touring and back packing.

BEEF JERKY

1½-lb. flank steak
1½ teaspoons salt
½ teaspoon garlic salt
¼ teaspoon pepper

1. Trim any excess fat from steak. Partially freeze steak for easy slicing. Cut steak lengthwise with grain into ⅛-inch slices.

2. Combine salt, garlic salt and pepper; sprinkle over sliced meat. Arrange 4 to 6 slices at a time on microwave roasting rack in 12 x 8-inch glass baking dish or on bacon-meat rack. Cover with paper towel.

3. MICROWAVE (high) 2½ to 3 minutes or until slices are browned and slightly dried. Turn slices over. Cover with paper towel.

4. MICROWAVE (high) 1 to 1½ minutes or until meat has a dry appearance. Allow to dry on paper toweling until crisp-dry.

About 32 Strips

TIP • For extra-thin strips of jerky, flatten strips with flat side of meat mallet.

Turn puréed fruit mixtures into dried fruit snacks using a lower power setting on your microwave. We've received many favorable comments on this recipe.

STRAWBERRY LEATHER

1 quart strawberries
¼ cup honey

1. Wash and hull strawberries. Process in blender at medium speed until smooth. Blend in honey. Pour into 12 x 8-inch glass baking dish.

2. MICROWAVE (low — 30%), uncovered, 1 hour, stirring after 30 minutes. Stir.

3. MICROWAVE (low — 30%), uncovered, 45 to 55 minutes or until mixture is very thick, stirring every 15 minutes. Cool until warm.

4. Place a piece of plastic wrap on counter surface. Top with fruit mixture, spreading evenly to a 15 x 12-inch rectangle. Let stand, uncovered, 12 to 24 hours or until layer is no longer sticky and can easily be lifted from plastic. Roll up sheet, starting with 15-inch side. Store, wrapped in plastic. For longer storage, refrigerate or freeze.

About 12 snacks, 40 calories each

TIPS • This recipe requires long, slow cooking and is not recommended for Full Power microwaving.

• Damp, humid weather will slow the air drying time in step 4.

• With Combination Oven, microwave-defrost-bake at 150° (or lowest possible temperature) for 1 to 1½ hours, stirring every 30 minutes. Cool and continue with step 4.

Beef Jerky.

Microwaves heat the water to dissolve the gelatin for these summer favorites.

FRUIT-SICLES

- **½ cup water**
- **1 envelope unflavored gelatin**
- **⅓ cup honey**
- **4 cups (1 quart) fruit juice (grape, apple or orange)**
- **½ cup crushed berries or mashed banana**

1. Mix together water and gelatin in 2-quart glass bowl. Stir in honey.

2. MICROWAVE (high), uncovered, 1 to 1½ minutes or until mixture boils. Stir in juice and fruit.

3. Place about ten 5-oz. paper drinking cups in shallow baking pan or tray. Pour fruit mixture into cups, filling just about full. Cover with foil. Find position of cups under foil by pressing foil. Make a small hole through foil in center of each cup. Insert a wooden stick or plastic spoon. Freeze until firm.

4. Remove paper cups by running warm water over outside of cups to easily loosen fruit-sicles inside.

About 10 Servings

TIP • Once fruit-sicles are solidly frozen, store them in a tightly closed plastic bag in freezer.

Fruit-Sicles.

This is one of the best methods we've found for microwaved sauces. It's also convenient for crumbling into vegetables or meats for an easy sauce. Here's the recipe for the sauce stick mix.

SAUCE-IN-A-STICK MIX

½ cup butter or margarine
1¼ cups nonfat dry milk powder
½ cup all-purpose flour
1¼ teaspoons salt
⅛ teaspoon pepper
3 tablespoons water

1. MICROWAVE (high) butter in glass bowl ½ to 1 minute (1 to 2) or until softened. Mix in dry milk powder, flour, salt pepper. Stir in water until mixture is moistened and can be formed into a ball.

2. Shape dough into 8-inch roll on waxed paper or plastic wrap. Make indentations at 1-inch intervals, dividing roll into eighths. Wrap tightly and store in refrigerator.

8 Recipes (4 Cups)

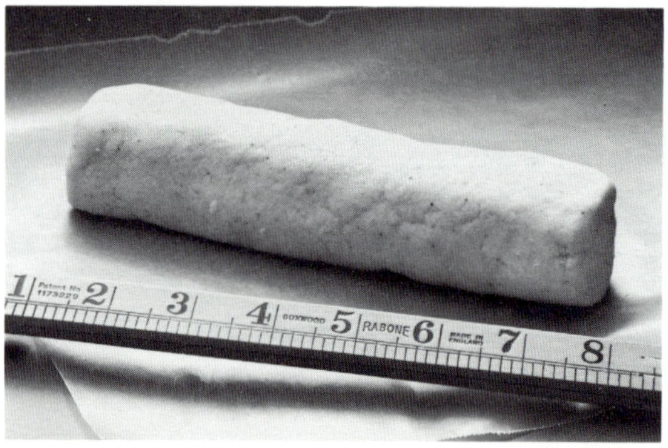

For Sauce-in-a-Stick Mix, shape dough into 8-inch roll.

Crumble desired amount of Sauce-in-a-Stick Mix into boiling water.

To turn the sauce stick mix into sauce, just crumble it into boiling water.

EASY SAUCE PREPARATION

½ cup water
1 section Sauce-in-a-Stick Mix

1. MICROWAVE (high) water in uncovered 2-cup glass measure 1½ to 2 minutes (3 to 4) or until boiling. Crumble sauce mix into hot water. Stir with fork until smooth.

2. MICROWAVE (high), uncovered, ¾ to 1½ minutes (1 to 2) or until mixture boils.

½ Cup Sauce

TIP • Try these Variations: Cheese—stir in ½ cup shredded cheese before microwaving in step 2.

Tangy Mustard—stir in ½ teaspoon sugar and 1 to 2 teaspoons prepared mustard before microwaving in step 2.

Easy Hollandaise—stir in ¼ cup mayonnaise and 1 tablespoon lemon juice after cooking in step 2.

These directions are for larger frozen vegetables that do not allow stirring such as broccoli spears or whole asparagus spears.

FROZEN VEGETABLES IN EASY SAUCE

½ cup water
1 section Sauce-in-a-Stick Mix
1 package (10 oz.) favorite frozen vegetable
¼ teaspoon salt

1. Place water in 1-quart glass casserole. Cover with casserole lid.

2. MICROWAVE (high) 1 to 2 minutes (2 to 3) or until water boils. Crumble in sauce mix; stir to combine. Add vegetable. Cover.

3. MICROWAVE (high) 7 to 9 minutes (10 to 12) or until vegetable is desired doneness, rearranging once. Sprinkle with salt.

3 to 4 Servings

Use these directions for small vegetables that are easily stirred such as peas, corn and chopped broccoli or spinach.

SAUCY FROZEN VEGETABLES

1 package (10 oz.) favorite frozen vegetable
½ cup water
1 section Sauce-in-a-Stick Mix
¼ teaspoon salt

1. Combine vegetable and water in 1-quart glass casserole. Cover with casserole lid.

2. MICROWAVE (high) 6 to 8 minutes (10 to 12) or until almost done. Crumble in sauce mix; stir in salt. Stir until combined. Cover.

3. MICROWAVE (high) 1 to 2 minutes (2 to 3) or until mixture boils.

3 to 4 Servings

Add sauce stick mix directly to partially cooked vegetables.

Top cooked vegetables with creamy sauce.

This interesting recipe for Play Dough came from Ann Finlayson of Portland, Oregon. Since it was a mixture that was just cooked in a saucepan until thickened, it was easily adapted to microwave methods. It's a delightful recipe and one that children may even enjoy helping prepare. If not, we are certain they will enjoy playing with the end results.

PLAY DOUGH

2 cups unsifted all-purpose flour
1 cup salt
½ cup cornstarch
1 tablespoon powdered alum
2 cups water
1 tablespoon cooking oil
Food coloring, if desired

1. Combine flour, salt, cornstarch and alum in 2-quart glass bowl; gradually stir in water and oil until just about smooth.

2. MICROWAVE (high), uncovered, 4½ to 5 minutes (6 to 8) or until mixture is very thick, stirring every minute (mixture will be very lumpy).

3. Cool enough to handle. Turn onto countertop and knead until smooth, about 2 minutes. Divide dough into sections and knead in food coloring as desired. Store each color separately in air-tight containers in refrigerator. It keeps for months and is a perfect rainy day diversion to have on hand.

Index

D

E

F

G

H

I

J

K

L

M

Q

R

S

T

V

W

Y

Z

Handy Order Form

Use the form below for ordering additional copies of this book or other offerings published by Recipes Unlimited. The books are printed on excellent quality stock and contain exciting photography and recipes created and tested for perfection in our kitchens.

Favorite Recipes from The Microwave Times, Volume I.

Our popular cookbook, filled with favorite recipes from the first 5 years of "The Microwave Times." Organized in easy-to-use chapters. 160 pages, large 8x10-inch format, spiral bound so the book always lies flat. Black and white photography throughout. Handy to use, filled with delicious, interesting recipes.

Volume II.

The sequel to our popular Volume I. Same easy-to-use format but with all new recipes from volumes 6, 7, 8 and 9 of "The Times." 160 pages. Attractive spiral binding. Black and white photography throughout.

Enjoying Microwave Cooking.

This all-time best seller includes easy to understand basics on microwave cooking and special "Tips" throughout the book. Full color photography. Over 200 recipes. 96 pages. Great reference for the beginner and experienced microwave cook, alike.

Microwave Meals Made Easy.

37 complete meal plans arranged for top efficiency. All recipes for each menu are printed on the same pages. A step-by-step Time Guide is given for each menu so you'll know at a glance how much time is needed and the sequence for preparing each recipe resulting in perfectly coordinated meals.

The Microwave Times.

Six valuable issues of this informative publication will keep you up-to-date over the coming year with new recipes, time and moneysaving tips, new developments in the use and manufacture of microwave ovens, creative ideas and projects, plus questions and answers from fellow readers.

Favorite Recipes from The Microwave Times, Vol. I
______Spiral bound, $8.95 ea.
Favorite Recipes from The Microwave Times, Vol. II
______Spiral bound, $8.95 ea.
Enjoying Microwave Cooking
______Hardbound, $6.45 ea.
______Softbound, $5.25 ea.
Microwave Meals Made Easy
______Hardbound, $6.45 ea.
______Softbound, $5.25 ea.
The Microwave Times Subscription:
______One year, 6 feature-packed issues, $8.95
______Two year, 12 feature-packed issues, $13.95

Please send the items indicated at left to:

Name ______________________________

Address ______________________________

City__________**State**__________**Zip**__________

☐ I have enclosed instructions on the back for sending gifts.
Recipes Unlimited can provide a card or include one provided by you. Remember to include ZIP CODES.

Total amount enclosed: ______________

Minnesota residents include 6% sales tax except on *Microwave Times* subscriptions.
Make check payable to Recipes Unlimited. Send to: Box 1271, Burnsville, Minnesota, 55337. Sorry, no COD's.